MITZVAHS

BOOKS BY DANNY SIEGEL

Essays
1980 - ANGELS*

1982 - GYM SHOES AND IRISES
(Personalized Tzedakah)

1987 - GYM SHOES AND IRISES - BOOK TWO

1988 - MUNBAZ II AND OTHER MITZVAH HEROES

1989 - FAMILY REUNION:
Making Peace in the Jewish Community

1990 - MITZVAHS

Poetry
1969 - SOULSTONED*

1976 - AND GOD BRAIDED EVE'S HAIR*

1978 - BETWEEN DUST AND DANCE*

1980 - NINE ENTERED PARADISE ALIVE*

1983 - UNLOCKED DOORS
(An Anthology)

1985 - THE GARDEN:
Where Wolves and Lions Do No Harm
to the Sheep and the Deer

1985 - THE LORD IS A WHISPER AT MIDNIGHT
(Psalms and Prayers)

1986 - BEFORE OUR VERY EYES
Readings for a Journey Through Israel

Midrash and Halachah

1983 - WHERE HEAVEN AND EARTH TOUCH
(Book One)*

1984 - WHERE HEAVEN AND EARTH TOUCH
(Book Two)

1985 - WHERE HEAVEN AND EARTH TOUCH
(Book Three)*

1985 - WHERE HEAVEN AND EARTH TOUCH
SOURCE BOOK
(Selected Hebrew and Aramaic Sources)

1988 - WHERE HEAVEN AND EARTH TOUCH
(Combined Volumes: Books One, Two and Three)

1989 - WHERE HEAVEN AND EARTH TOUCH
(Combined Volumes) in Hardbound Edition

Humor
1982 - THE UNORTHODOX BOOK OF JEWISH
RECORDS AND LISTS
(With Allan Gould)

*Out of print

Mitzvahs

by

DANNY SIEGEL

THE TOWN HOUSE PRESS

Pittsboro, North Carolina

I wish to thank the following people who helped me with this book:

Amy Ripps, Glenn Easton, Louise Cohen, Dr. Abraham J. Gittelson, Jules Gutin, Vikki Bravo, Dr. Jay Masserman, Malka Edelman, Melanie Berman, Robert Sunshine, Diane Schilit, Allan Gould, Rabbi Steven Glazer, Cheryl Magen, Debra Friedmann, Marci Fox, Bob Leifert, Jack Lew, Rabbi Lyle Fishman who send me articles and newsclips and share stories with me that have been integrated into the body of this work....and Mrs. Trude Holzmann who sends me the Big Packets.
Bonnie Bergin and Katheryn Horton, for their consistent help and inspiration in writing the article about the CCI dogs.
Beth Huppin, Myra Gondos, Alan and Naomi Teperow, and Edythe Siegel ("Mom") for reading the articles as they came off the Macintosh...for their comments and insights.
I wish to express particular thanks to all those people about whom I have written who allowed me to tell their story, and who helped me
To Megan Marx, for taking me around Denver on The Day of the Mitzvah Heroes.

I am especially grateful to Ina J. Hughs of Knoxville, TN, for her kind permission to reprint her piece, "A Prayer of Responsibility for Children".

Many of these articles were published in a number of Jewish magazines and newspapers: *The Baltimore Jewish Times, The Reconstructionist, Women's League Outlook, The United Synagogue Review, Keeping Posted, Pedagogic Reporter,* and CAJE publications.
Also, thanks to The Fund for Journalism on Jewish Life, a Project of the CRB Foundation of Montreal, and the National Havurah Committee, some of which material appeared in many Jewish papers around the country.

First Printing, 1990
Cover by Fran Schultzberg

Library of Congress Catalogue Card Number: 90-70362
International Standard Book Number: 0-940653-26-5

For Jules Gutin
And Gordon and Myra Gondos.
Good friends,
Kind people,
Menschen, all of them.

Table of Contents

Introduction

Bear with me.

I have finished writing the book, and all that needs to be done is to re-arrange the articles in the proper order, to number the pages, send it off to the publisher, and, a little later on, send him the text of a few endorsements for the back cover. My publisher, Alvin Schultzberg, is my good friend. We are approaching our 20th anniversary of working together, ever since he printed my first book, *Soulstoned*, in the late 1960's.

By now, the procedure is routine, though not entirely so. The routine is this: we have minimized the glitches....I already know what he needs from me, besides simply the manuscript — a "feel" for the book, a clear idea of how many copies we should print and whether or not this is finally The Big One, some sense of what the cover should look like. Nowadays it is even simpler because this is the third time we are printing off my Macintosh and laser printer, so we don't have to worry about any typesetters doing injustices to the text. I don't have to go through the drag of re-reading and re-reading and re-reading the text that extra time because someone has played with it. Any typographical errors are mine alone, and if they are still there, buried somewhere in the many pages of the manuscript, I'll let them ride until the second edition. I am at the stage where I just can't face another reading of the book.

The magic of the computer has made it easier, this routine. Most last-minute crises can be eased with the touch of a few buttons. In addition, the turn-around time will be much briefer. It will be only a matter of a couple of months before the finished edition of *Mitzvahs* is in my hands. All Alvin has to do is take pictures of each page, reduce them by nine percent, adjust some headers, do right- and left-hand pages the way he thinks best, and number everything according to his experienced sense of how a book should look when it is ready for the readers.

So my job is almost finished, and I can stop getting up at 4:00 a.m. to write and revise and format and shift emphases and flesh out what is too bare and cut back whatever is too fluffy. My shoulders are sore from sitting at the keyboard, and I need a break. This now makes over 800 pages I have written on Mitzvahs, and I would like to return to poetry writing for a while at least. I need time to plan some vacations, to loosen up, to push Springtime to come a little faster so I can do my walking in shorts and a T-shirt.

I always hated the image of the artist so obsessed with the work-at-end that it upset the normal course of life so much. It never used to happen to me. In the early days, I would write poetry as the need arose, and when enough poems were lying around in a folder, I would select and reject and gather the selected ones and organize them and make an anthology. It was more leisurely. Only recently, in the last three or four years, have I found myself unable to break away when I am in the midst of essays or text work. I would try to stop, but I would still wake up before dawn and turn on the computer, make the coffee, and begin my work.

That is the routine.

And yet, there is something going on in my head, at this very moment — as I see that this book and this moment in my work *is* somehow different — that calls for some more serious introspection.

I am commemorating another anniversary: fifteen years ago this month I took a trip to Israel. It was January, 1975. In one sense, this was not particularly unusual, as I had been there eight or nine times before...ever since 1959, when I was 14 years old and was sent by my parents (on a whim, I believe) with a group of rabbis and educators. My Rabbi, Noah Golinkin, and his wife Dvorah, were my chaperones, and Israel was only 11 years old. I think I remember the route: Washington to New York to Gander, Newfoundland, Shannon, Ireland, one other stop in Europe, then Israel. The Constellations — those old propeller-driven planes with the triple-split tails, had to do it in short hops, and it seemed like it took an entire day to get there.

After that first trip, I kept going back, usually in the summers, in 1961 (With the United Synagogue Youth Israel Pilgrimage), 1963, 1964, 1967 (only a couple of months after The War), and then every year or every other year. Indeed, I had just spent August 1973 to August 1974 in Jerusalem. Now, fifteen years later, I cannot remember exactly why I decided to go back to Israel only a few months after I had spent a year there.

It was at that time that I made a conscious effort to ask my friends for some Tzedakah money to give to appropriate recipients when I got there. For centuries, Jews journeying to Israel had taken on this practice. The traveller became a Shaliach Li'Dvar Mitzvah, a Mitzvah-Messenger. As they handed me their checks or cash, I must not have been keeping track, because I remember being surprised that I had accumulated $955. And so the journey began. When it was over, and the money had been distributed, my friend, Bill Novak, encouraged me to write an article about the trip for a new magazine called *Moment*. That article, my 1st ever, was called "Gym Shoes and Irises" and appeared in Issue #2.

That is the rather simple story of how the 1st Mitzvah journey began and ended, and also how this adventure in writing about Tzedakah and Mitzvahs and Mitzvah heroes also began, and goes on.

By now, my friends have entrusted me with more than $725,000. The procedure is still essentially the same: people send money to my Ziv Tzedakah Fund, I seek out fine, unassuming people and projects that do things that represent the Best of Judaism and Humanness, give them the money for their work, and then send out reports of their work to my contributors and anyone else interested in reading about them. We have expanded, of course, and our focus has widened to cover many communities — the United States, Canada, Europe, and other countries — as well as Israel. Obviously, this is no longer something I can do through my personal checking account and without getting receipts. A few of my lawyer friends told me I should really incorporate the Tzedakah work, which I did in 1981 in the United States, and a short while later in Canada (as Ziv Tzedakah Foundation, Inc). In the

United States the magic numbers are "501(c)(3)", as in, "I am now a '501(c)(3)'", i.e., an IRS-registered non-profit, tax-exempt corporation. (I don't remember the Magic Number for Revenue Canada.)

So I am a 501(c)(3). It has to be that way, because last year the American fund gave out $141,000, and there may be as much as $200,000 this year. Still, we try to keep it like an "Abba and Eema Operation": no one gets paid, we keep our printing and mailing costs to a minimum (we try to stay at three-percent overhead or less, if possible), and more and more people voluntarily help me keep it flowing smoothly: my sister-in-law, Bena, who is the treasurer of the American fund; Merle Gould, who handles the deposits, mailings, and correspondence for the Canadian fund; and advises on allocations, Edythe Siegel (i.e., "Mom") and Gordon Gondos, my oldest friend in the world, who are my American board members; Amy Ripps who works on the mailing list, which now numbers five thousand people; Reuven Miller who prints the reports and handles the large mailings, and kids from around Washington who help me with other important aspects of the work. I have more people volunteering to help out than I can possibly use, and that feels good.

And so we have managed to keep it rather *haymisch*, informal and friendly.

And we hope to continue to do so.

This is a time for taking stock, and the lengthy excursus is meant to lead up to a few insights that are striking me now, at this very moment:

(1) I cannot think of a single image or analogy to capture the feeling of all the accumulated good wishes I have heard from others over the years. The sum-total of those words of kindness and encouragement is impossible to calculate. Are those feelings as high and majestic as a mountain? Are they so many that they seem as numerous as the stars in the heavens or the grains of sand on a beach? Is it not true that I feel like a "Windwalker" (as Sigrid Ueblacker, one of the people mentioned later on, speaks of her eagles and falcons and hawks and owls) when I hear these words from friends, relatives, strangers? It is not surprising that I am always using words like "sublimity", "wonder", and "awesome". That is so much the realm of Mitzvah work, it seems only natural to do so.

(2) Right now is High Season, Level II, for our fund. Our greatest flow of contributions comes in the Springtime, after Ziv issues its annual reports and before I leave for Israel. Late December and early January there is a second burst of money, because of last-minute tax deductions. This year, in particular, a friend contributed money to allow us a second mailing with updates and projects for people to know about. It is still too early to calculate precisely how much money has come in, but Bena and I are flooded with envelopes.

All that money.

All that money for Mitzvahs...much of it already destined for certain people and projects, Mitzvah programs we wanted to send more to earlier on, but had to wait for the new influx of money. There is never enough money to do all the Mitzvah work we want, but it is nice to breathe a little easier and not to have to make phone calls to come up with the remaining few hundred dollars for a late-breaking need.

　　　　　And this is just what I am leading up to, after this long, long introduction: yesterday a friend called. We discussed a particular project we have already given money to, but very passionately, she told me how disastrously short they are at this stage, and she reminded me just how critical the time factor is in this situation. Easily, Ziv would put in another $180. Then I called back and told her to make it $360. And *then*, during an ever-so-brief pause after we hung up, and realizing just how much money is coming in every day, I called her back once more. Her line was busy. I tried again, and told her "$800".

　　　　　She will pick up the check today, but, by then, it may be more, as I review the accounts.

　　　　　And *this* is the *Ikkar*, the essence of the work, the moment, the feelings, right now, 6:55 a.m., January 4, 1990: how could anyone possibly describe the feeling of power, the feeling of interconnections between all those contributors, myself, and the ultimate recipient, who so desperately needs the funds? Should we not say there is something sublime, wondrous, awesome — miraculous, even — about this. And humbling, of course, to be a part of such grand moments in life.

　　　　　That is what I wanted to say in this introduction. The rest is reportage....

As for the book itself, the articles were written for a number of periodicals or for friends, or initially for myself alone. Naturally enough, there will be some repetitions: stories of certain Mitzvah heroes in different contexts, some texts reused, recurring words. I have tried to keep the repetition to a minimum.

Sometimes the same thing is said, but in different tones of voice. At times, I can be lyrical about the work, as I was a few paragraphs ago. Other times, out of frustration and anger, I am kvetchy or grumbly or nasty. I felt it was important to keep those emotions-of-the-moment for the book, rather than alter them to make everything come out nice and smooth. I would hope that my readers would be angry and frustrated and kvetchy with me, until the sources of the dismay are removed.

Finally, let me give due credit to Gary Rosenblatt, editor of *The Baltimore Jewish Times*. A few months ago, he asked me to write a monthly column for his paper. I tried two or three or four of them, liked the idea, and — seeing that I was not doing too much lecturing on the road for the next couple of months — decided to write every morning I was home. I liked the idea of trying to write short pieces, though some got a little out of hand, and I quickly discovered there were many topics I had never written on, or had made only cursory reference to in previous books. As sometimes happens with artists, it all just came gushing out, until I called a stop to it.

I thank my friend, Gary, for giving me the opening, and while I am tired now, I am so happy I had the opportunity to enjoy these weeks of creativity. To see dawn break outside my window so many times was what we call in modern Hebrew slang *tschupar*, a pleasant treat, like chocolate cake to the body....It was a nice taste of dessert. (It is 7:10 a.m., a little overcast, but the sky is brightening again, and my friend is coming in a few hours to get the check for $800 or more.)

One more "finally". I have become less and less interested in "The Theory of Mitzvahs". Not because it isn't important, but, rather, because the *doing* of Mitzvahs seems much more critical to me nowadays. It is my hope that my readers will pause at different points in the book and say, "Yes, I can do that, I *will* do that." Otherwise, *Mitzvahs* is just another book, which could just as well have been a biography of Louis XIV or a Cajun cookbook.

Enjoy, and *Yasher Koach* — all the more strength to you.

Danny Siegel
January 4, 1990

A Prayer of Responsibility
For Children

We pray for children who put chocolate fingers everywhere, who like to be tickled, who stomp in puddles and ruin their new pants, who sneak popsicles before supper, who erase holes in math workbooks, who can never find their shoes.

And we pray for those who stare at photographers from behind barbed wire, who can't bound down the street in a new pair of sneakers, who never "counted potatoes", who are born in places in which we wouldn't be caught dead, who never go to the circus, who live in an X-rated world.

We pray for children who bring us sticky kisses and fistfuls of dandelions, who sleep with the dog and bury goldfish, who hug us in a hurry and forget their lunch money, who cover themselves with Band-aids and sing off key, who squeeze toothpaste all over the sink, who slurp their soup.

And we pray for those who never get dessert, who have no safe blanket to drag behind them, who watch their parents watch them die, who can't find any bread to steal, who don't have any rooms to clean up, whose pictures aren't on anybody's dresser, whose monsters are real.

We pray for children who spend all their allowance before Tuesday, who throw tantrums in the grocery store and pick their food, who like ghost stories, who shove dirty clothes under the bed and never rinse out the tub, who love visits from the tooth fairy, who don't like to be kissed in front of the school bus, who squirm in church or temple and scream in the phone.

And we pray for those whose nightmares come in the daytime, who will eat anything, who have never seen a dentist, who aren't spoiled by anybody, who go to bed hungry and cry themselves to sleep, who live and move and have no being.

We pray for children who want to be carried and for those who must, for those we never give up on and for those who will grab the hand of anyone kind enough to offer it.

Hear our cries, Adonai, and listen to our prayers. Amen.

Reprinted with permission by the author, Ina J. Hughs

Goodhearted People

I. It's a Dirty Job

A friend of mine, Howard Cooper, serves as the Rabbi on Maui for Rosh HaShana and Yom Kippur. No, he doesn't fly back to Boston with his family to catch up on his other work as a Jewish educator in the interim days. He's just stuck out there for the entire time.

I was speaking to him on the phone recently, and he summed up the situation as best as I have ever heard it said — "It's a dirty job, but someone has to do it."

Ah, so nicely put! I felt the same way when someone from the Palm Springs Jewish Federation told me he is considering bringing me out for a speaking engagement. I kept thinking, "Well, I'll just have to see if I can shuffle my calendar around...."

And this morning I thought, jokingly, "Another day with this dirty job as a writer."

I like to start writing at 4:00 or 5:00 a.m., when the world outside and the world inside are both quiet, before the phone rings, before errands begin. Today I am a little late; I started at 6:00, it's now 7:03 and the sun is just coming up outside the window, and I have set out to write a short piece about all the goodhearted people I know. Thanksgiving is tomorrow, and even though I planned this piece long before today, it is a good time to count blessings, specific blessings in my life. So while this piece may be particularly appropriate for this time of year, it is only accidental, and I am certain it will be a relevant reference text any time I wish to look at it.

II. Areingefallen in Kup

One day I got this idea. In Yiddish you would say, it was "Areingefallen in Kup" — an idea that just plunked itself down in my head. I decided to start making a list of all the goodhearted people I knew from whatever period in my life I knew them and from wherever I might have met them.

I was somewhat staggered by the results: in the first half hour I had assembled a list of 130 people. The names just kept pouring out, and I stopped after a half hour because I had something else to do at the time.

I neither consulted mailing lists nor checked my personal phone directory. I didn't call any mutual friends to help put the list together, nor did I say to myself, "I'll spend the entire day until I reach a certain number." I just sat there belting out the names on the word processor and then pressed the "sorting" button so they would fall into some readable categories.

III. *Criteria and Preliminary Statistical Analysis*

The criteria for making the list are simple. Actually it's just one criterion: when I think of someone, does the quality of goodheartedness come to mind. Plain and simple. I did no background checks with the FBI or CIA or Social Security or local merchants to see whether or not they scream at the waiters or browbeat the shoe salespeople. I didn't call friends to see how wrong or right I might be about a particular individual. Nor did I set a time limit: some of the people I knew for many years, some have come my way much more recently.

As to breaking them down into categories, the bad news is that I first assembled the list by first name, then last name, rather than the other way around, so all I can say is that — at present — there are 10 Davids and 6 Allans, Alans, and Allens, 4 Marks and a Marc, 2 Joels, 2 Joes, and 1 each of Curt, Ora, Zenda, Emil, Misha (but 2 Moshes), Yitz, and Uri. Every other category seems to be covered: they live everywhere, are every height imaginable, body forms ranging from endo- to ectomorphs, young and old. Most are individuals, many are couples, and a few are entire families.

This enormously detailed and informative break-down is derived from a re- cently-expanded-and-growing list totalling 171 people.

They all have good hearts.

And whatever the ultimate analysis will be, that will always be the common thread.

IV. *The Jewish Text, A Definition*

In the second chapter of Pirkay Avot is a well-known passage. Rabban Yochanan ben Zakkai asks his five favorite students what is the best thing, the best human quality, the best phenomenon in life to hold to, to make it through life well, with peace of mind and meaning, with vigor and intensity and integrity. The first four students answer, "A good eye [=generosity]", "A good friend", "A good neighbor", and "Seeing the ultimate consequences of your acts". The fifth, Rabbi Elazar ben Arach, answers, *"Lev Tov — A good heart."*

The teacher responds to them all saying, "I prefer Rabbi Elazar ben Arach's answer, because it includes all the others."

Powerful stuff. Worth teaching in religious schools early on. *Very* early on. It'd be good on Wall St., in any field where getting ahead and aggressiveness is held up as an absolute or near-absolute, anywhere where the fast track sets the accepted pace. Many analogies could be made to the new trends in exercise: walk- ing is better than running a marathon, low-intensity aerobics is better than high-in- tensity aerobics, goodheartedness is better for your health (spiritual and physical) and the health of the world (physical and spiritual) than aggressiveness and fast- trackedness. I'll even bet there's a lower burnout rate among goodhearted people than among fast-track people.

As to the definition of goodheartedness....Our Jewish text in Pirkay Avot ends where I ended my translation. They must have understood what Rabbi Elazar ben Arach meant, and I am certain we, today, have a decent "feel" for what goodheartedness means.

V. Two Recent Events

Last week I was at a convention. There were about 2,000 attendees, and I know many of them from my travels. There they were, so many of them in one place, and off and on as I would see someone or schmooze with someone, I would make a quick note to add them to my list. People whose names had slipped my mind or had not come to mind in the first rush of putting the list together. It seemed that everywhere I turned, I ran into more and more of them.

I see now that conventions, community celebrations, family gatherings, synagogue events, rallies for good causes are places to go to frequently. For Mitzvah purposes, of course, but also because they are prime meeting-grounds for keeping an accurate Goodhearted People list.

More striking — much more striking — are recent events in Washington concerning bone marrow donors. Publicity has gone out to find a bone marrow match for a young Jewish woman in town. Last night at a synagogue they shut down the operation an hour early: they had already reached capacity. They could handle no more people that evening and would set up another date besides the other date already scheduled and in addition to the first time they did it a few days before (at the JCC) when they already had an overflow crowd.

Last night at Adas Israel you had to park 3 or 4 blocks away. Cars were going up and down Quebec Street looking for a place to park. Cars were tight, but no one honked. People were making U-turns and squeezing around in opposite directions, but no one screamed at anyone else about scratching the paint job. Were it a rush hour traffic jam, all hell would have broken loose every minute, at every turn. And, in addition, it was a freezing night with high, biting winds, but I heard no one complaining about having to come down on such a night, leave the warmth of home, and go out into such a bone-chilling cold. And then they stood patiently in long lines, filling out forms, giving blood for preliminary analysis, paying all or some of the cost (besides checks, $1.00 bills and $20.00 bills and everything in between were lying all over the place in big bowls).

It was all very orderly; the conversations were low-toned, but the mood was not somber. There was, I would say, an overpowering feeling of goodheartedness in the air.

I am not sure I have ever felt anything quite like it before.

No, that's not quite right.

I *am* sure I have never felt anything quite like it before

VI. *Communal Goodheartedness, Jewish and General*

I haven't been there, but the way people tell me it happened, when the Ethiopian Jews arrived in Israel, goodheartedness flowed everywhere as neighbors and strangers and people surprised by their intensity of goodheartedness got them settled into their new lives.

It happens every day with Shalom committees in Jewish communities everywhere: the fruit basket or the bread and salt and packet of information, the greetings, perhaps hugs of hello and welcome, the "Can we do anything for you?" People abandoning for a few moments humdrum days and nights for warmth and caring and kindness.

There is no real way to really *feel* it from newspapers or TV, but out in the Big World, the extent and range of goodheartedness from the recent natural disasters would fill volumes — libraries — with stories upon stories. San Francisco, Charleston and environs, Huntsville with the catastrophic tornadoes ripping through town, tearing up lives, lives being less shattered, more whole somewhat, however much possible, by the neighbors, friends, and strangers, the goodhearted neighbors, friends and strangers. For all the tragedy, the glory of the good heart emerges and rises to the occasion.

VII. *Another Jewish Text (Ta'anit 8b)*

Rabbi Yitzchak said, "True blessings are only found in things hidden from the eye."

Our Rabbis have taught, "...True blessings cannot be weighed, measured or counted."

Not the square footage of the house, nor the number of suits.

Not the sum-total of coins and bills and CD's in the bank, nor the fancy fine cars in the garage.

Not the height of the Ark, nor the number of Torahs.

It's not even the number of good-hearted people you know — one is enough — it's the fact itself that there is at least one of them. Near or far is irrelevant, as long as that one is reachable. Even deceased, as long as memory brings the goodhearted one to life again and makes that person real for you.

VIII. *The Practical 1-2-3*

1. Make a list.
2. Keep updating the list.
3. Start spending more time with the goodhearted people. If there are qualities in our own personalities we find distasteful, what better therapy could there be than to learn from goodhearted people how to surrender the *shticklach*, the *narrischkeit*, the inauthentic cruelties or sillinesses we have acquired in our lives? I did

not write this article to brag, "See how many *I* have! I must be *better* than you because I know so many goodhearted people." I just get around more, and may very well need them more than some other people need them.

4. Share them and/or their stories with others.

5. Have a storytelling night when you get some friends together and talk about these fine people, these goodhearted people.

6. Bring the goodhearted people together to meet each other.

7. Spend more time with them than with the Momzerim of the World. I can't give statistics as to which kind of person outnumbers which, but if life is better, nicer, more decent in the presence of goodhearted people and nastier, lousier, more nerve-jangling with the Momzerim, cut back on the Momzerim...in business, in social life, at the times when there is nothing in particular to do, and you just want to hang out with someone.

It's good for you.

It's good for them.

It's good for the Jews and good for the world.

We all need it, now let's do it.

The Strange Case
Of the Accountant
Whose Mind Snapped One Day

I. *Just Exactly What Might Have Happened*

Well, not exactly.

I don't really know for sure that this CPA *actually* had a bona fide revelation, but one day he just did the strangest thing....

Daniel Cumings of San Francisco sent the following note with his tax-form packet to all his clients — "If your documented charitable donation of money or securities are less than 1 percent of your adjusted gross income (not taxable income) in 1988, I will add $100 to your tax preparation fee and donate this surcharge to a qualifying organization. You still have a month in which to increase your donations to avoid the surcharge for 1988." (*San Francisco Examiner*, 1/15/89)

I am sure Mr. Cumings knew he was risking the loss of some clients, though I do not know whether or not any of them actually left for other firms. And more likely than not, the Heavens didn't open up one day and a Voice didn't speak to Daniel Cumings to dictate the text of the letter he sent. The idea must have percolated in his mind over the years as he reviewed everyone's tax statements. But *how* it happened is not what is important. What counts is that the letter *was* sent to the clients and the beneficiaries were better off in this world as a result of his bold act. Mr. Cumings feels better for having done it; of that I am sure. And people in need no longer were in such need; of that I am also certain.

My problem as a writer is that I don't know the code of ethics of CPA's, or estate planners, or insurance people, or attorneys. I don't know whether or not some written document in their schooling or some word-of-mouth tradition states, "You are *not* overstepping your professional bounds by suggesting people contribute to Tzedakah," or whether it is understood that you *are* overstepping your bounds, or whether it is understood that it is up to the discretion of the CPA, estate planner, insurance person, or attorney, or whether it is never mentioned orally or in print at all.

Mr. Cumings did it, though, and I find it a very interesting possibility, with implications for an entire range of professions and businesses. Others disagree with me, and *have* disagreed with me during my talks, but it really is a hazy area of human endeavor, and I may be wrong to find it so admirable. Still, it is worth mentioning. And I would suspect it is worth at least throwing out the idea to people in these professions or businesses and leaving the decision on what initiative to take to the professional or business person himself or herself.

I know, for example, that the owner of a certain clothing store chain gives a certain someone else a 50% discount on all the fine clothes in the store — on condition that the other 50% be given to some Tzedakah project of the buyer's choice.

Both buyer and seller are happy with the arrangement, and, again, the beneficiaries are better off. Those in need are not so much in need anymore. The buyer merely asked — fully prepared for a yes or no answer, with no pressure intended on the merchant's good will.

II. Hairdressers and Barbers

Someone used to cut my hair (and a very nice job it was), but I had to contribute what I would have normally spent on a haircut to Tzedakah, any Tzedakah I chose. When this person was in Jerusalem for a year of study, a similar rule applied: the price of the haircut — money to Life Line for the Old.

Now haircutting and hairdressing take certain skills. Some people have those skills, and others, such as myself, do not. The same for CPA's: those who lament the annual attempt to do their own taxes must envy the accountant's ability to wade through the papers and come up with the right figure for the IRS. The general rule is: using unique abilities to make variations on the theme of Tzedakah. The sub-rules are either by dint of Revelation, Heavens, and a Voice, or through slow-and-careful consideration, or some combination of the two processes.

To illustrate my point, here are three variations on hairdressing:

1. After a 28-day program, a mental health clinic provides for its women ex-patients a free facial, colors, nails, hair-do — on the house. The clinic knows that self-image (or what Judaism calls *Tzelem,* i.e., being created in God's image) is not only a "thing in your head", but also something very physical, and this gesture, which is more than a gesture, is a significant part of the therapy.

2. A certain Colleen Ann Meyers of Boston is a haircutter. She volunteers at a battered women's shelter and always takes her scissors. As Ms. Meyers puts it, "Part of the battering process is psychological. The woman's self-image is so low, it's important to help her look in the mirror and like what she sees." (*Boston Magazine,* December, 1987) And she convinced her boss at the salon to open on a Sunday afternoon, all proceeds to go to the shelter. And, as Ms. Meyers so nicely says it, "I feel I'm affecting a negative situation *in a real way"* italics mine]. That is a very telling statement: her Mitzvah work gives her a clear perspective on what's *really* real in life, and what isn't quite so real. (Perhaps she should go lecturing on campuses, so students can avoid all those late-night philosophical discussions about "What is reality?")

3. Wig Therapy by Pearl Halikman....Not everyone loses his or her hair from chemotherapy, but many do. The hair often grows back. As Dr. Craig Deligdish, an oncologist and hematologist from Melbourne, FL, says, "...in recovery and healing, state of mind is as important as state of health." Enter Ms. Halikman, who is known throughout the area and beyond for her skill in designing wigs for those who have been through the agony of cancer therapy. The right style, the right materials, the right human touch all take inordinate skill, and Ms. Halikman uses that skill not only to design and style and fit the wig, but also to

carry through on the process as hair grows back, so there is a natural transition. Weeping (from initial sadness) and tears (of happiness) are not uncommon in her work. "The pain is double if they don't feel good about themselves and their appearance — especially if they have to continue to work," Ms. Halikman says. She can't do anything about the one pain, the chemotherapy, the anguish over the fact of cancer in the person's life, but she most assuredly *can* do something about the other kind of pain.

I don't know whether or not anyone asked the people who do the Mitzvah-hairdressing and haircutting to do what they do, but following their lead, we could (a) search our own skills and pick a balcony overlooking the sea, serve up a cup of coffee, gaze out, let our minds roll free, and see how these skills could be used for Mitzvahs, and (b) ask others if they might not like to do the same. Some people (a) will say no, and they are entitled to do so, (b) some were waiting to be asked and are delighted to do so once asked, and (c) some didn't even know they were waiting to be asked until they were asked, and, once asked, are delighted to do so.

It won't hurt to ask. It's not nickel-and-diming people, asking them for One More Thing To Give. Just ask and let them decide. If they say no, there are reasons, and if they say yes, then — as we used to say in Hebrew School — we've racked up a few more Mitzvah Points. (I have the Blue Book of Mitzvah Points: you can rack up a solid 158 points in some cases, for the right questions to the right people.)

III. *Colin Maxwell, The Man Who Finds Missing Kids*

This is a classic case, and a high-stakes example.

My good friend, Allan Gould, co-authored a book called *Child Finder* (Prentice Hall Canada, 1989) with a certain Canadian man named Colin Maxwell. Maxwell is the child finder, though he used to be a skip-tracer, i.e., a finder of people who have skipped out on paying their bills. He didn't actually go pound on the deadbeats' doors demanding payment. He only located them and passed the information on to the people they owed money to.

One day (Ah, one day!) almost 8 years ago, he was in his apartment with his brother and a former girlfriend. The Brother (Was he The Divine Messenger in Disguise? Elijah the Prophet himself?) saw an article about a woman who was looking for her two sons who had been stolen by her husband. The brother said to Colin the Skip-tracer, "Call her."

At first Maxwell didn't make the connection. The Brother reminded him that he was in the business of finding people, so why not just use those talents and tricks to find the stolen children?

Maxwell was 25 years old at the time of Revelation, and since then has found an ever-growing number of kidnapped or runaway children, relieved uncountable quantities of human anguish, and perhaps saved the very lives of many other human beings.

It took the very same talent as locating deadbeats: knowing whom to call, what directories and registries and computer files to check, whom to sweet-talk, whom to bully by phone and in person, whose sister or mother or former employer to contact.

It was all there — the talent, the creative juices, the stamina — just waiting for the switchover. Cases uncracked for months or years sometimes were solved in a matter of days. Tearful reunions that might never have taken place took place, horrifying wrongs were righted, and little chunks of peace and justice were restored to the world's grand design.

You read the book and say to yourself, "My God, he was only a kid helping bill collectors."

I am convinced his Brother had to be Elijah.

How else to explain Colin Maxwell, Child Finder?

IV. The Case of the Cop Who Was As Big As a Mountain

George Hankins's beat was the South Bronx, all 240 pounds and 6'6" of him, and even though he was a former U.S. Army Boxing Champion, he still wouldn't fool himself. There are a million ways to die in that part of town — champ or no champ.

But his mind snapped, just like Mr. Cumings the CPA.

Once upon a time, he and his partner were covering their beat in the patrol car when they saw two gangs about to engage in a classic rumble, complete with chains, bats, and fists-at-the-ready. He'd seen a lot of those rumbles, but, as he says, "I don't know what got into me." Big George Hankins got out of the squad car, and walked right into the thick of it, right between the two gang leaders. And this is what he said when his mind snapped, "You think you know how to fight? You want to see fighting? I'll show you fighting!"

While his partner held the gangs apart, he ran the few blocks to the station house, brought back three pairs of gloves, and — with his right hand behind his back (just like in the movies) — he took on the 2 gang leaders one after the other.

And laid them flat.

Then he told the gangs to come down in a few days to the precinct house after his shift was over, and he'd show them the way it is done right. The rest of the story is familiar: Big George Hankins retired from the police force so he could do this full time, and his Fort Apache Youth Center now teaches the discipline of boxing and all sorts of other things: there's the after-school tutoring, there are the field trips, the art classes, the dances, and the hot meals for kids whose parents can't always manage to feed them the right meals.

He says it so well, "I'd seen so many kids hurt and beaten — suddenly I had to do *something*."

V. In Sum

Few, if any, of us are championship-quality boxers, so we're not about to break up rumbles in the South Bronx. But the principle is the same as with the CPA Cumings, the skip-tracer Maxwell, and the hairdressers Meyers and Halikman. Whatever we *can* do well, we can also apply some of the time for Mitzvahs.

It is interesting to watch Jimmy Carter nowadays, doing so many things he couldn't seem to accomplish while he was President: building houses for the poor, furthering humanitarian causes in many places. That is just one prominent example. Another is the work of Arthur Kurzweil, the pre-eminent Jewish genealogist. Among all the other Mitzvahs he accomplishes in his teaching, he — like Colin Maxwell — has helped so many people find others whom they suspected could never be found. Most moving of all is when people tell him they have discovered relatives they had thought had died in the Shoah-Holocaust, much as he, himself, found cousins in Warsaw who had been presumed dead since the War.

It is also true that few, if any, of us will experience The Great Moments of Revelation when something bends and breaks in our mind and great floods of light and sublimely orchestrated melodies fill our heads. For us, we'll do better with a balcony, a cup of coffee, the sea in the distance, and a few precious minutes to let our minds roam free over the entire range of human experience. Indeed, there ought to be a Balcony and Coffee Club By the Sea, a kind of retreat center, where people can go for a few days or a week, with nothing on their minds, no business, no errands, no answering the phone, just time, precious time to think.

To think Mitzvahs, that is.

If someone out there has a condo or resort home they would like to make available for this project, be in touch. If someone wants to fund the train and air tickets for people to get there, and some expense money to buy ice cream or non-fat frozen yogurt in the afternoon, I'll supply the people who need the time away. We won't name the project for you, but think of the little Blue Book of Mitzvah Points. The Talmud says that one who encourages others to give [also being a giver himself or herself], gets credit for others, too, if they have played a critical role in encouraging the other people to give. (Bava Batra 9a)

Think of the Blue Book.

Even more — think of all those people who will most certainly benefit from your kindness.

Food, Glorious Food
And
Just Exactly Why
Americans Cannot Be Sued
If They Donate Leftover Food
To a Shelter or Soup Kitchen
And Someone Gets Sick

I. Some "Even If's"

Here are some *even if's* to consider:

Some of the experts on poverty and hunger in this country suggest there might be as many as 20,000,000 people who go hungry some time during every month. *Even if* they are overestimating, and — by accident or inaccuracy they have doubled the figure — 10,000,000 is still an outrageous number. (Many are Jews.)

Celeste McKinley, founder of the Gleaners food bank in Las Vegas, has figures from somewhere that there's enough food thrown out in America to feed 47,000,000 hungry people. She manages 400,000 pounds of food a month (all of which would have been thrown out) for 20,000 people, so she must know something. But, *even if*, she is way off base, overestimating by more than double, or just plain lousy at statistics, then there might still be enough thrown out to feed all the hungry people. (Many who throw out are Jewish people at Jewish events.)

A recent newscast or article, or whatever, recently put it that 20% of the food in America is thrown out. *Even if* they are way off, too, the point is clear. The essential problem could be considered logistical, though it probably isn't the whole solution. Still, it could be a real chunk of the solution.

II. The Poll I Took

Since 1976 I have been a staff member on the United Synagogue Youth Israel Pilgrimage. I have had the opportunity to see about 7,000 teen-agers over that span of time, glorious *kinderlach* from Vancouver to Miami, Maine to San Diego and just about all points in between, including Chickasha, OK, (population 15,828 according to my road atlas, Jewish population=the Miller family and *maybe* a couple of others. *Maybe*.)

I enjoy the work.

We do Tzedakah projects together.

They meet Tzedakah heroes.

They act with grandeur of the soul.

In our conversations, they teach me so much. I ask a lot of questions about their background, about their experiences with elderly people while we are at Life

Line for the Old in Jerusalem. I find out about their involvement back home with the established Jewish community, the leaders, the workers, and the quiet heroes they have met.

They teach me so much, I am sometimes stunned by their answers.

No, I am *often* stunned by their answers.

In recent years I have begun asking a long question. "How many of you belong to a synagogue where — if just a portion of the food left over from Kiddushes and bar and bat mitzvahs and weddings and luncheons and annual dinners and dessert noshes and morning minyan breakfasts were taken a shelter or soup kitchen — how many of your synagogues would have been able to provide 1,000 meals for hungry people during the course of a year?"

Hands go up all over the place, more than I would have ever expected. And I ask which synagogues, which towns. I know some, many of the synagogues, and they are not all 1,500-2,000 family congregations. Some are much smaller, but the USY'ers estimate well, and — multiplying by the number of food events/year — they consider 1,000 meals a reasonable number.

Statistics:

Let's say in the last two years I've worked with 1,000 high school students during the summer.

Let's say 200 of them raised their hands.

Let's say the 200 USY'ers represent 150 congregations (some of them, obviously are from the same congregation).

Let's say 1/3 of them are wrong in their estimation, shooting too high.

That leaves about 100 congregations @ 1,000 meals per synagogue which approximately equals 100,000 meals.

That is from a small sample, only synagogues, only Conservative synagogues, with a cutoff of 1,000 meals/year. It is a very small sample, not adjusted for bell curves or other factors known to demographers, statisticians, sociologists, and other experts who know how to make adjustments. It also doesn't take into account Federation events, JCC programs, Israel Bonds dinners, Hadassah programs, and whatever other Jewish communal events involve food. And yet, with all the inaccuracies and omissions, still a significant statistic to consider.

III. *Some Jewish Statistics*

As I travel around to my talks, and as my network of contacts grows each year, I get statistics on Jewish poverty. These are usually culled from community demographic studies or specialized task forces. Some numbers are a year or two old, some may be out of proportion for other reasons, and, most of all, hunger and poverty are not synonymous. Still, here are some numbers:

15% of the San Francisco Jewish Community lives at or near the official poverty line.

37,000 Jews in Chicago live at or near the poverty line.

65,000 Jews in Los Angeles[1].

8% of the Baltimore Jewish community earns less than $10,000/year, and 12% of that community's Jewish adults were unemployed and look for work during the 3 years previous to the study.

New York: 74,000 Jews in the 5 Boroughs at or below the poverty line, 143,000 Jews at or below 150% of the Federal poverty line.[1a]

Let us allow even for the usual statistical inaccuracies, though we ought to consider that, in most cases, if anything, the numbers have gotten worse. With all adjustments and factoring taken into account, the situation is sad and outrageous...and solvable.

IV. *Proposals*

1. Food barrels in synagogues and Jewish communal buildings: A must. Many — but not quite enough — have them. It is becoming, and I believe, *should* become a standard item in all Jewish buildings, as standard as Torahs in the Ark, as the Eternal Light, as the computer that manages the business affairs of the institution or organization.

2. The Tzedakah Habit: people should be encouraged to purchase one additional item — for Tzedakah — whenever they grocery shop....to be taken to the synagogue or JCC food barrel or directly to shelters or soup kitchens.

3. MAZON-A Jewish Response to Hunger: MAZON proposes a food tax for any Jewish food event. 3% of the cost of the food goes to MAZON and they distribute it to Jewish and non-Jewish programs involved in feeding people.

A. I am a board member. They are people of integrity, honest, devoted, and capable people. The project is growing and does wonders.

B. The National Federation of Temple Youth has instituted a policy that all its programs will include this 3% surcharge for MAZON.

C. Some Jewish Federations already have that policy. Synagogues everywhere are doing it. Other groups are doing the same. Two recent examples: (1) A staff member of a large Federation recently called to say that he is proposing that their Federation institute a 3% policy, a portion of which will go to MAZON, the rest to other similar worthwhile endeavors. (2) The Jewish teachers in the

---

[1]In Toronto, the numbers run to 15% of the Jewish community living at or near the poverty line. *However*, Canadian laws on food donations differ from those in the U.S. To be sure of the legalities across Canada, consult your local Canadian shelters and the appropriate lawyers.

[1a]My friend, Andy Frank, who used to work for the Metropolitan New York Council on Jewish Poverty, explained to me that most communities estimate "at or near" the poverty line because the Federal guidelines for determining the povery line figure (a) based the dollar amount on 3 times the cost of an average food basket, (b) certainly didn't allow for the additional cost of Kosher food, and (c) only allowed deviations for Alaska and Hawaii but not the other exceptionally expensive places to live such as New York.

Toledo area voted to cancel the dinner in their honor and to donate the funds that would have been used for the dinner to MAZON.[1b]

4. Jewish food banks: Serving Jews and also non-Jews. The following cities, among others, already have them: Los Angeles, Milwaukee, Dallas, Seattle, Chicago, Philadelphia, Chicago, Baltimore, New York. And Jewish soup kitchens, if necessary. A story: I was talking about TDD's to some teen-agers and adults in New Rochelle, NY. TDD's are the typewriters with a modem that deaf people use to communicate with others over the phone wires. I was complaining that there aren't enough of them in the Jewish community, and that one synagogue in particular irked me by saying that they didn't need one because they didn't have any deaf members. The synagogue was part of a community of 500,000-600,000 Jews. Others reacted by saying that, if they had a TDD and advertised that they would have interpreters for the deaf, they might, indeed, gain a number of new members (who just don't happen to be able to hear)....The reasoning of the "no-need faction" ran something like this: since there aren't many TDD's around in Jewish communal buildings, it must mean there aren't many deaf Jews.

Then the Heavens opened up and inspiration struck. One of the participants facetiously extended the logic of it, saying, "Since we don't have many Jewish food banks, it must mean there aren't many hungry Jews."

5. Leftovers in the general community: Members of the Jewish community should be encouraged to approach grocery stores, restaurants, bakeries, food distributors — anyone involved in bringing food to the table — to donate leftover or unsellable food that would have been thrown out to local soup kitchens and shelters. (And shoe stores for shoes, dry cleaners for unclaimed articles, bed-and-bath places for linens, towels, soap....) I encouraged a few people to try bakeries, and then talked myself into trying it once, myself, in Shreveport, LA. It worked: the Lutece Bakery gave me what must have been $300-400 worth of bread and pastries that would have been thrown away. All they wanted was a tax receipt for Sister Margaret's Mitzvah project[1c] that feeds people daily (besides offering many other services). Some cities (probably many more than I know) already have pick-up programs, most notably New York, Philadelphia, Houston. In Washington, a brand-new project called Second Helping is just starting out that way, small, direct: just pick-up and deliver.

V. The Ultimate Proposal

Here is a suggested standard synagogue (or Federation, or Hadassah, or JCC, or Israel Bonds, or Kosher caterer) policy: "The agency suggests to the peo-

---

[1b]MAZON-A Jewish Response to Hunger, 2940 Westwood Ave., #7, Los Angeles, CA 90064, 213-470-7769.

[1c]Sister Margaret McCaffrey actually calls it the Christian Service Program, though she is well acquainted with our Jewish concepts of Tzedakah and Mitzvah.

ple who are sponsoring the event that at least a portion of the leftover food be donated to a local food bank, soup kitchen, or shelter."

Only that we *suggest* it. If the sponsor wishes to do it, that is up to the sponsor. If they do not wish to do it, that is the sponsor's choice, no guilt, no judgments made. It's his or her money.

For synagogues, that means (a) less USY kids will raise their hands next summer when I ask the "1,000 Meals a Year" question, and (b) many more hungry people will be less hungry.

There is some need of clarification:

1. Many already do it.

2. Many Jewish restaurants would love to do it. For example, I was having dinner at Moshe Dragon, a Kosher Chinese restaurant in Rockville, MD, when someone who works their approached me at the table and asked what they could do with lots of leftover chicken parts they weren't using. I gave them a connection or two and they followed up. Simple.

3. Many — particularly Jewish conventions — would do it and could do it if they prepare ahead of time by:

A. Making certain their contracts with the caterers read that they, the sponsors, own the leftovers.

B. Making arrangements for pick-up and delivery to the shelter or soup kitchen[1d].

4. Many — even at the last minute — still manage to do it, announcing at the event itself that the leftovers were ready to go, and they needed someone to drop it off.[1e]

5. The issue of pick-up and delivery is solvable: people of good will who have some spare time make the rounds, load the car or station wagon or van, deliver it, and the recipient agency sends a tax receipt.

Newsflash — Worcester, MA: A coalition of Jewish women recently set up Rachel's Table, a group of women dedicated to doing exactly what I am describing — picking up the leftovers at Jewish communal events and delivering the food to soup kitchens and shelters. It seems simple enough to them. They must know something others don't know. Call 508-799-7600 and ask them how they do it. We already know *why* they do it.[1f]

[1d]Unfortunately, the General Assembly of the Council of Jewish Federations in New Orleans in 1988 began the process too late. By 1989, the leftovers from the Delegates' Lounge were donated, though I do not know about the food from other events at the conference.

[1e]Unfortunately, despite the persistent efforts of Rabbi Jack Moline and some others delegates, the Washington hotel that hosted the Rabbinical Assembly of America Convention in 1989 refused to release the leftovers. Rabbi Moline was one of the chairpeople of the convention, and he pressed the hotel on a number of occasions, but they refused, and, ultimately, enormous amounts of food were thrown out. This, in a city where you can't walk 2 blocks downtown at night without seeing people sleeping on the grates or bundled up against the cold and ready to bed down for the night on sidewalks in front of the offices of many of the government agencies.

[1f]Some additional sad news: I was speaking with a stewardess on Delta Airlines after she had just served the meal. I asked what Delta did with unopened containers of food — either

VI. The All-Holy Excuse: Lawsuits

The fact is, you can't be sued if you donate leftover food to a soup kitchen or a shelter.

That's a fact.

My good friend, Michael Bohnen, a lawyer in Boston, tracked down copies of the law in every state and the District of Columbia. For example, here is one of the laws, in part (Pennsylvania):

Notwithstanding any other provision of law, any person who, in good faith, donates food to a charitable or religious organization for ultimate free distribution to needy individuals, shall not be subject to criminal or civil liability arising from the condition of such food, if the donor reasonably inspects the food at the time of donation and finds the food fit for human consumption. The immunity provided by this subsection shall not extend to donors where damages result from the negligence, recklessness or intentional misconduct of the donor, or if the donor has, or should have had actual constructive knowledge that the food is tainted, contaminated, or harmful to the health or well-being of the ultimate recipient.

Commentary:

1. That is essentially the law everywhere in the United States. In some states, the soup kitchen or shelter may be liable, but that is *their* responsibility, and *they* can determine which foods they will serve and which they will refuse.

2. People scream, "But there's The Health Code, The Health Code!" Always with a Capital "T", capital "H", capital "C". Here are some answers to that scream:

A. Any project already picking up food (try City Harvest in New York, 212-349-4004, try Rachel's Table in Worcester) knows the health code backwards and forwards and won't handle suspect food.

B. Any soup kitchen or shelter knows the health code backwards and forwards *and won't accept* food that is in any way suspect. They have been serving food for a long time to hungry people. *They* know the rules.

C. Any project involved in picking up leftover food and delivering it can tell you what kinds of forms and waivers of responsibility you might want to sign. (Try City Harvest, try Rachel's Table.)

---

complete, untouched meals, or things like the granola bars, boxes of cereal, and little jars of peanut butter that have never been opened. She answered that (a) it was all thrown out, and (b) she was distressed that — at her own daughter's wedding — the caterer would not release the leftovers for hungry people in shelters and soup kitchens, and that, in fact, according to their particular contract, he, the caterer, owned all the leftover food and could do with it what he (damn well) pleased.

D. Strange, very strange: If some of the finest hotels and restaurants in New York, Philadelphia, Houston, etc. — who most certainly do not relish the idea of being sued — are already doing it, they must know something we don't know. (It's probably something that goes like this: "It's simple. Don't complicate matters. Do it. We always hated throwing the food out anyway...and by the way, it's also, good for business.")

So — if we are not doing it because we don't have the logistical resources to get the food from Location A to Location B, let's say it straight out.

But let us not give the All-Holy Excuse about lawsuits.

Am I angry? Yes, but only because — as I deal with this question with some audiences — that is the most commonly-given excuse.

It's not valid.

It just ain't so.

VII. In Conclusion: Combining Some Statistics

If the MAZON people are right, estimating that Jewish catered affairs cost about $500,000,000/year (that's half a *billion* dollars), and, if 20% of all the food in this country is thrown out, then that would be $100,000,000 worth of Jewish-sponsored food saved annually to feed some hungry people.

Cut it in half....say studies are wrong, there are inaccuracies in the numbers, lots of the food for one reason or another is not usable.

That still leaves $50,000,000 worth of food...annually.

Let's just do it, and let's stop making the wrong excuses.

Get a copy of the law from any lawyer.

Let's just do it.[1g]

Now.[1h]

[1g]A couple of months after this article was written, one of my friends explored the issue of food banks in his local Jewish community (one of the 10 biggest in the U.S.) There *is* a food bank run by the Jewish community, but, as my friend reports, the staff member "indicated that their clientele has not requested Kosher, and therefore it is not a consideration." Sad. They should try it the other way around: announce that there is Kosher food available, and then they will see whether or not there will be people who need it. We are back at Square 1.

[1h]On Christmas Eve, 1989 (which was the 3rd night of Channukah), my friend, Kate Kinser cooked and served dinner at a soup kitchen in Chicago. Hungry Jews were there, too. (Is it appropriate or unfair to say "of course"?) There were individual Jews, and also a family with children. Kate had brought with her a Menorah and candles, since she knew there would be a Christmas tree and carols, and suspected that Jews would be at the dinner, since she had been at the soup kitchen the week before and seen Jews then. When she announced that she would be lighting the candles, the Jews present clapped, and came up to her to join in the blessings. May the day come soon when we don't even think "of course", because there will be no more need to think it. And were the Prophets here with us today, they might add, "And the day will most surely come/when there shall be no more homeless people/Loneliness and cold shall disappear/And the scourge and agony of hunger/Shall no more be known in the land"...to which we would say, "Amen, so may it be."

A Pair of Sox

I. The Ads

If you *really* want to know what's going to happen in the Jewish community in the next generation, you have to examine 2 kinds of documents: (1) Bar/Bat Mitzvah invitations, which I leave for other articles, and (2) singles ads in Jewish newspapers. Some time many years from now, some where in our own galaxy, archivists and historians will assist sociologists in analyzing trends and realities on the basis of what Signs of the Times we could or should have read but didn't.

Sometimes I read the singles ads. When I do a talk in another town, I like to read their Jewish newspaper, so I can be up on local Jewish news. I can make reference to it in the lecture or seminar. I also make a point of glancing through the ads to see what people are looking for in other people.

I admit that it is difficult to write your entire autobiography *and* record all of your cravings for a lifelong mate in the number of words your budget can manage. And I admire the people who have mastered English words and abbreviations sufficiently to do it. I am sure they devote more hours to the 4 or 5 lines than they ever did in college to their senior thesis on "Line Structure, Rhythmic Arrhythmias, and Cultural Dysplasia in the Poetry of W.H. Auden"[1]. And even though the flow of years will modify and refine what you "want, will want, and always wanted" in a life-long partner, it is absolutely critical right now for you to put down exactly what you want, to avoid uncomfortable coffee conversation and blind dates that always seem to run just a bit too long for your patience.

The results are that you get all kinds of usual-usual and usual-unusual words like "multidimensional" (I think about that one often), "aggressive" (I'd stay away from that one), "unique" (aren't we all?), "non-smoker" (one of the more frequent points I see), and a recent addition to the list, "Must be able to tolerate Republicans".

I have reviewed 2 or 3 bunches of ads recently, and I fully realize that my analysis will break all the rules about the size and randomness of large and random samples, but I think the few I have picked are somewhat representative. It's easier to write about it than to reveal my findings in a speech, because in the speech, the audience is right there, and there is this queasy atmosphere lying heavy in the air, like a heavy smog day in Los Angeles. It gets so heavy, in fact, that I have to break the tension with fictitious ads like, "SJM, 29, into hiking, theater, whips and chains" or "DJF, Mitzvah-oriented, with three cute little children and a dog named 'Spot'" or "Older male seeking young thing for small talk, jazz, sense of humor and

---

[1]The time factor makes sense: for the college paper, it was only a matter of research, organization, writing, and filling in the fluff to reach the requisite number of pages the professor wanted. With singles ads, it is another matter. The stakes are higher; this is *real* life.

rubber and leather sessions." That usually gets them loose enough for the more serious analysis.

What I found in this particular small, random sample is the "Professional/Mensch Ratio" was not too favorable. In one series of 16 ads, the word "professional" was used 5 times, and "Mensch" only twice, plus one reference to "must like learning new things and helping others". In another series of 8 ads, "professional" came up 3 times, "Mensch" and its synonyms, 0. The third, with 10 advertisements: "professional" 3 times (with "financially stable" a borderline case, same with "lawyer-journalist, aggressive"), "Mensch" and its synonyms, still 0. In all cases, there is no pattern: sometimes it is the man looking for these qualities in a woman, sometimes the woman seeking the man; sometimes the terms are used for self-description, males and females alike trying to describe just exactly who they are, "professional", "Mensch", both, neither, or something else including or not including these 2 key terms.

So, in a faraway time in the future, somewhere in our own galaxy, archivists and historians will toss away their standard documents[1a] and use their scholarly tools instead to plow through newspapers from a hundred Jewish communities over this 10-year period we call the 80's, hand the data (along with the bar and bat mitzvah invitations) over to the sociologist, and they will find what they will find, and we will possibly be in a worse pickle than we are now: 79% professionals and only 23% refining their Menschlichkeit....Which is not to imply that there isn't overlap and that some professionals aren't Menschen and vice versa. It's only a question of focus and emphasis.

But I'd be a little worried...starting now.

II. Sox

Years ago, in one of the cities I visited for a talk (I think it was Omaha or Jacksonville), my host and hostess were a pleasant, recently-married young couple. As often happens, they had been designated the unfortunate ones who were supposed to worry about everything concerning my stay: picking me up and taking me back to the airport, podium size, microphone style, and correct seating arrangement for the talk or talks...and all the little things like ketchup for the Shabbas chicken, Wintertime thermostat set at a humanly-tolerable level. All the little things. They also had to tell me their life stories, though I never promise them that they'll wind up in one of my books, and even if I promise them that anyway, I tell them not to expect movie contracts because they most certainly will not have become so famous because they appeared in my books.

[1a]The minutes of the founding meeting of Congregation Beth Israel, communal budgets, records of Jewish school populations, demographic studies, comparative income levels, etc...important, though secondary, documents.

Over the years, I have made many, many friends by being a guest in their homes. They have extended innumerable kindnesses to me in the spirit of *Hachnassat Orchim*, the Mitzvah of Hospitality, and I stay in touch with many of them. They are kind for their hospitality, and even kinder because they tell me such great stories.

"The Story of the Pair of Sox" is one of my favorites, but let me introduce it by first indicating that the tale-tellers are not weirdos or geeks or dweebs or braggarts. They seem rather normal, nice and pleasant and decent, Jewishly involved, and normal looking. Neither is 6'6" tall with Paul Newman's eyes or Jessica Lange's bearing. Neither looks like the main character from *The Hunchback of Notre Dame*. And neither of them runs a multi-billion dollar corporation or is the leading expert on Shakespeare or Castiglione. They just seemed to be (and still seem to be) pleasant, talented, decent folk.

I elicited the story, which, in their modesty, they would have just as well not told me. It just came out in conversation. And I made sure to ask their permission to tell it, simple as it is, lest I violate their sense of privacy.

How they met: A party of some sort. Briefly.

How they got together again: One of them called the other one.

The first date: Some complications, minor glitches.

The tip-off: Walking to or from wherever they were going, He sees a homeless person without sox. He takes off his sox and gives them to the man.

She likes that in a man.

They go out again.

They go out again.

They go out again.

Sooner or later one of them asks The Big Question, and sooner or later the other gives The Big Answer.

They are married, settled and settling down, and they seem happy.

She told me about the pair of sox, asking that I not tell Him that She told me. I blew it and told Him, because I needed His permission to tell the story, and I needed Him to promise He wouldn't make it in issue with Her when He got off the phone.

He didn't make it an issue.

III. Ah, The Cynics and Sages

At this stage, the cynics and sages take over.

They always tell me when I start reviewing the life-stories of some of my married friends that I probably don't have a full-enough picture. They remind me that — single as I am — I don't see all the day-by-day and night-by-night "stuff" (you know "the stuff") that goes on between these pleasant, decent, nice people, and how hard they really have to work at it and compromise and put on a nice face for me so I can go my merry unreality-related way[1b] .

They remind me I just can't possibly understand how much *angst* [1c] and tension and boredom they must experience, how tempers flare unexpectedly, how cars break down at the wrong time and Challahs burn, how one (the slob) just never seems to be neat enough for the other (the obsessively neat one) and how this irks and grinds and eats away at their love, and that "love", anyway doesn't stay pleasant, warm, respectful, etc.

This is neither the time nor the place to present a disquisition on the origins of the cynicism and sagacity of my psychologically-damaged cynical and sagacious married friends[1d] .

All I wanted to do was tell a nice story.

Take it for whatever you want to take it. If one single single person puts in an ad, "Petite SJM, 29, into movies, Oriental food, and long walks, seeking That Special Someone who will take off her sox if we meet someone in the street who has no sox..." — then the story will have served its purpose.

I'll take care of the cynics and sages on my own.

[1b]The sages extend their purview to the topic of "children". They insist that "normal children" beat the hell out of each other every 15 minutes and wallow in rage and jealousy at their siblings (that word always sounded weird to me). (1) I have met their children, and they fit perfectly into their definition of "normal children". Most modern zoological parks would not accept them as donations to their collection of wild animals. (2) I have spent many years with some families (3 such families [the Y&B G, G&M G, and S&A G families] come to mind right away) where the kids seem to love and respect each other, are gentle with each other, help each other, and wish the best for each other. Of course they fight now and again, and I have heard *some* shouts and whines, but nothing remotely like the Sages of Family Life describe.

[1c]The all-purpose Yuppie In-Word.

[1d]The syntax is difficult. I do not mean to imply that *all* of my married friends are psychologically-damaged. The preponderant majority are not, though some are. I merely state that — on this topic in particular — the ones who *are* impaired seem to lose all sense of proportion and wisdom. On the subject of marriage, they, as it were, toss their psychological and emotional cookies, to use the accepted contemporary scholarly term.

What Some Young People
Are Writing

I. I Shouldn't Complain

When I write, I get up very early so I won't be harried by the phone and mail. I have a few hours of grace time, and there is dawn to watch in the thick of the writing, and it is very quiet, the best time of day for me.

My friends know that I go downhill as the day goes on, because it is hard coming off the high of writing to take care of apparently lesser endeavors. Some days there seem to be so many phone calls and so much mail, I just have to resign myself to plowing through it all. Those same friends know that one of my great pleasures is "X-ing them off the screen": I make lists on my computer screen — mostly lists of calls to make — and when the conversation draws to an end, I say, "I am now X-ing you off the screen", and they give a low moan and say, "Oh, No!", but there's nothing they can do about it. They are swallowed up, the electrical charges somewhere on my hard disk do their job, and they become a part of The Great Oblivion of Things That Used to Be Somewhere in There...and then they are no more.[1]

But I shouldn't complain. First of all, one of my heroes and friends, Janet Marchese, is in the midst of High Season. She has helped place over 1,500 children with Down Syndrome in adoptive homes, and during December and on into January she gets hundreds of letters and many, many phone calls from parents who want to tell her all about how the children are doing. She told me she has to remember to give a particularly nice gift for the holidays to the mailman. She gets so many letters in High Season they come bunched with big rubber bands around them. It's one of those quirks of Life — you have all known it at one time or another — you call someone like Janet, who is incredibly busy, and somehow they are almost always there to pick up the phone. You wonder when they have time for their miracle work.

So I shouldn't complain. Janet handles much more, and much more heavy, emotionally loaded work. I should just settle in and do my own work quietly.

And besides, the calls and letters I get are largely exhilarating pieces of information that people keep sending me or telling me, Mitzvah stories to make the human soul feel downright good. In the last few days I've had 3 or 4 calls and letters about wedding dresses going to Israel for the Rabbanit Kapach, so she can lend them free of charge to brides unable to buy or rent their own. Someone very well connected with Sloan-Kettering called to say he might be able to help out with a bone marrow transplant project, another call reviewed details of a future meeting

---

[1] I think of the Biblical passage, "And Chanoch walked with the Lord, and then he was no more, because the Lord took him," (Genesis 5:24) but that isn't a good comparison.

with the founder of ZEST, Inc., a group of people that takes kids living in city shelters out for healthy, ego-lifting excursions and activities here in Washington. So when I see some people standing by our mailboxes downstairs tossing all their junk mail and having nothing left for themselves, I shouldn't complain.

I want to share some of the letters, specifically from young people, but understand that I am changing names and covering over some details and transcribing only the relevant passages. I know the people who wrote these items would like to have them shared, but they wouldn't want to brag or take credit. Also, you will notice spelling mistakes. I want to leave them in, without the usual "[sic]" indicating that its their own mistakes, not mine. You'll get more of the flavor that way.

II. Letters to Trevor Ferrell, The Kid in Philadelphia Who Takes Care of Homeless People, and to His Father, Frank

1. Dear Mr. Ferrell,

Last year, my Hebrew school class visited the Trevor Shelter (I go to Keneseth Israel Reform Congregation). I really enjoyed spending time with children that enjoyed spending time with us.

I feel very strongly about the homeless. It really makes me feel how lucky I am to live in a nice house with a teriffic family, food to fill three meals for one day, education and money to live on. If everyone in the world, even the homeless, had everything that I have, or even more, and everyone would be happy, it would be the kind of world that I would like to live in.

I am writing to tell you how strongly I feel about you taking in the homeless and caring for them. It makes me feel guilty that while I'm sitting around with my family on Hanukah, there are children living without food, shelter or love and caring. This is why I'm willing to give up the money that my parents put away for me this Hanukah to your charity drive. This year, I'm willing to give a gift to the homeless, instead of receiving gifts, when I already have more than enough things to fullfil my happiness.

Again, I think your program is extremely thoughtful and helpful to the homeless.

2. Dear Trevor,

It was really a pleasure to meet you at CAJE — and an even greater pleasure to know the effect you had on my son, David. On Thursday night after the conference we walked down University Place after dinner, and approached a homeless person sitting on the ground by the corner of the building. David was eager to give him some money — which we did — but what was more important — the man said, "You look like a ray of sunshine. Could I give you a hug?" David bent down and they exchanged hugs — and at that moment our fear and discomfort completely disappeared! Thank you for teaching us all by your example.

3. Dear Trever,

Hi! My name is Myra Levy....I live in California. I go to a Jewish day school....I am an eleven year old sixth grader who is very pleased with all the work you did to help the poor and homeless. My class saw a film about you in our Jewdaic Studies. We had to think of a Mizvot project that would involve helping people and learing more about the needy. As we were thinking someone brought up the idea of going to Philadelphia and visiting you and your shelter. We thought it would just be need to go to Philadelphia itself, but fortunitily our teacher even thought it was an OK idea. But unfortunility it did not appeal to some of the other teachers and princibol. One of the reasons others didn't appove is because, we would have to raise at least 1000 dollars total, and thats a lot of money for my class to raise in a limited amout of time. But my whole class (including me) all apreceated how your courage and concern, saved so many homeless, helpless, hungary people. Sometimes I wish you would move here, so you could encourage some others of us, who just think the poor will do fine on their own. I really look up to you, and I think the whole world should because you have done something some people think is impossible to do. But you have proved everyone can do anything he or she puts there hearts and minds to. I hope someday I get the wonderful experience of meeting you and your needy. Thanks for being a part of this world and helping soooooooo much!!!!!!!!

Your friend, Myra Levy. P.S. Please write back.

III. A Letter To Me From a Friend in New York, Again, Sadly, About Homeless People

Dear Danny,

Last night, Tuesday, January 17 and today is my father's fifth Yahrzeit. Sarah, Moshe, and Rachel joined Mom and me at Mincha and Ma'ariv here at the synagogue and we went for dinner. Moshe delivered a beautiful Dvar Torah on the weekly Torah reading and tied in something about my father's life and character in a most meaningful way.

After leaving the restaurant we walked to the corner of 85th and Broadway. There, on the ground of the sidewalk, sat a homeless man huddled in a torn, dirty blanket with just a little space open around his face so that he could breathe.

Moshe gazed towards him and went over.

He said to the man, "It is a cold night and it's going to get colder. I think your hands and fingers are going to get very cold."

Taking his "freaky freezy" gloves off his hands, he said, "Take these and put them on your hands. They will keep you a little bit warmer."

("Freaky freezy's are a special kind of gloves that kids his age like to wear. Moshe is 10. When the temperature outside goes below 32 degrees, a picture appears on the top of the gloves. Moshe had wanted these for a long time and we finally gave in and bought him a pair a few months ago.)

The man tried to put the gloves on and had a little difficulty. Moshe told him to push his fingers a little bit harder because the gloves really would help him a bit. He did, and he succeeded.

It was a wonderful episode because Moshe felt really good about what he had done, and, as the Rabbi said, it was a beautiful way to commemorate a grandfather's Yahrzeit.

IV. The Carnival

She[1a] walked around the room scared, nervous, and very uneasy. She didn't know what to do with herself. The carnival took many hours of preparation, but she couldn't take part. It was hard for her to deal with seeing the mentally dis- abled adults walk with balloons and lollipops, playing children's games.

Since her first Encampment four years ago, this carnival for retarded adults was held every year. And each year, she would tell her friends that she couldn't handle it...and she wouldn't go. Her friends went every year, she couldn't. But this year, she felt guilty about saying she couldn't handle it without even giving it a try first. She knew it was an incredible mitzvah. So for the first time, she went.

It rained a lot that summer, but for some reason, it rained more than usual on the day of the carnival. Regardless of the puddles, she walked in and out of the hot and stuffy one-room building to avoid having to make contact with any of the guests. She didn't know how to handle speaking to a grown person with the tone and words one would use with a child. She couldn't look at the drooling, wheelchairs, or helmets. She could have left and gone back to her bunk, but she felt a moral responsibility to stay. But she wasn't taking an active role. She had to find a guest and walk with them. After gathering as much courage as she could muster up, she walked back in and found her friend Mark. Mark was walking with a tall thin man who had the strangest smile on his face. A red helium balloon was tied to his right wrist and with his left hand, he sucked a lollipop. The man didn't talk. He just made these incomprehensible noises. It was difficult for Mark to walk with this man because he didn't know which booths the man wanted to go to, or what games he wanted to play. Mark wanted to leave, but every time he tried, the man grabbed Mark's wrist and pointed to another booth. How could he say no?

Here she was, looking at Mark and this man; the man who didn't talk. She said Hi, but the man didn't say anything. He just looked at her and pointed to a booth. Then the man reached for her hand. She never felt so scared in her whole

---

[1a]For many years, Metropolitan Region United Synagogue Youth (METNY) has had a very special carnival at their end-of-summer encampment. Residents of a nearby institution come to camp for a day of fun at a carnival that the kids organize, set up, and run for their guests. This is a brief essay by one of the METNY teen-agers that she sent to me.

life. What was there to be scared of? She didn't want him to touch her, but he grabbed her hand. With the hand that had the balloon wrapped around it, he held her hand. And now the lollipop was in his mouth. Together, the three of them walked. Hand in hand. As the minutes went on, she felt more at ease. She found this one person to be with. Walking with Mark made it easier. But to her, it felt like a burden — a responsibility. She knew that she would ditch the man as soon as she found someone else to dump him on to. The communication problem was so frustrating. The man kept letting go of their hands to point...or show them...he used his hands...huh?...was he trying to sign?...was he deaf? Yes, the man was deaf.

She suddenly became anxious. She knew sign language and figured it was worth a try. "What's your name?" His strange smile left his face. She thought, maybe he wasn't deaf, and now she confused him. But a new, different smile came on his face.

"My name is David" his frail, nervous hands signed.

"Hi David. What booth do you want to go to next?"

"I want to go there. I want to color a picture of you. Can I? You're the only one who's talked to me all day."

"Yes, David. You can color a picture of me." And he did. And I felt great.

V. Gaining Perspective: A Brief Essay By A High school Senior Entitled "A Student's View"

I lead two lives. In one, I am writing college applications, studying biology and the French Revolution, and playing tennis after school. I worry about my grades and about the next four years of my life. Day to day, all of it seems important.

My other life exists once a week on Thursday nights. I carry a bag of bologna sandwiches and a thermos of grape juice to distribute to people who are sitting on the sidewalk with everything they own within arm's length.

During the day, I am highly visible. I follow all the rules — doing well in school and participating in extra-curricular activities. People notice me.

Once a week, I do not stand out so dramatically. To many, I am just another hand that holds dinner. I often become shy and find it difficult to speak because I do not know what to say. Shakespeare and Rousseau do not teach me what to tell a man who burns himself every day by sleeping on heating grates in order to keep warm. By understanding the laws of physics I cannot console the agony of a woman whose husband has abandoned her because she has gone insane.

When I am involved in each of these worlds, I adopt the values and priorities of its unique environment. At school and among my peers, success is determined by what I learn, what I accomplish and how I feel. While working with the homeless, success is measured in terms of what others learn, what others accomplish and how others feel.

When I first became involved with the Philadelphia Committee for the Homeless, I lived each life separately. When I was involved in one of them, I was able to completely dissociate myself from the other. On Thursday nights, when I distributed food to the homeless, nothing seemed more important than providing the most basic, physical needs of the people in order to insure that they would survive that one night. My perspective was altered so much that the homework that I knew that I would have to do when I was finished seemed insignificant. Yet the next day in school, getting a research paper completed was the most urgent matter.

As I cultivated each of these worlds, the clear distinction between the two became fuzzy. Each one had grown so much within me that they began to overlap. While I write this essay, I cannot help but wonder if it will ever affect my friend Eleanor who lives in Independence Park. I want to get into Stanford, but she needs a jacket, food and a house with heating. Instead of being set in "pre-professional" goals, I feel an overriding desire to contribute to society. My academic education also influences my views of the homeless and other people who I have tried to help. I discovered that there must be a long term solution for satisfying the needs of the "underprivileged". Because of this, I can no longer see an obvious line between my personal achievement and my social responsibility.

As I continue my education, I hope to develop these two parts of my life even further, both in a formal educational setting and also less traditional modes of education. In the future, I would like to no longer lead two lives but one — one that is integrated, productive and meaningful.

A Plea
On Behalf of the Kids

I. Introduction

Please forgive the nasty tone.

II. Your Complaints — Parents and Other Interested Adult Parties

You complain to them that they don't spend enough time doing their homework. (You are sometimes right.)

You lecture them about drugs, alcohol, driving while under the influence. (You are *always* right.)

You don't like some of their friends. (You are sometimes right. I see pictures of your daughter's new boyfriend pulling up on the newly-seeded lawn on his Harley Davidson, both bike and rider unbathed for weeks, a new record for number-of-earrings/ear set [8 is the record, I think], both right and left ears [total, 16 earrings], and a distinct air of non-Torah orientation about the young man.)

You say they abuse their privileges with the car. (Yes, you are right. But (no justification intended) peer pressure — to speed a little, to load too many people into the Buick, to stay out later with the car than what your parents say — is very strong. You have a good point, a very good point.)

You don't like their clothes, their hair-do. (What are this year's styles? Pre-washed or torn jeans? Oversized shirts or tighter-than-tight shirts? Blue hair, spiked hair, hair so short you make them wear hats when they go out in public with you?)

III. Your Complaints — The Kids

You complain that they treat you like babies. (It is fair to say that you sometimes act like babies.)

You whine that they don't let you do what your friends do. (Some of your friends would be happier in state mental hospitals, federal prisons, or homes for the morally disabled.)

You drone on and on that they keep pressuring you about getting good grades. (More about that later.)

Your bar/bat mitzvah class discusses the possibility of giving away some of your soon-to-be-garnered goodies, and you see the light. You come home all worked up about it, and you get shot down. (Aha!)

You go away to a youth group retreat or convention, and they talk about Mitzvah projects, and they take you down to the shelter for battered women, and you scrub the walls, the floors, the toilets, and you come back all enthused, ready to jump in. They shoot you down, and you are sad, angry, disappointed. (Aha!)

IV. Aha! And Another Aha!

Kids, you've been cheated.

The adults have given you a rotten deal.

As you emerge into adulthood, responsibility, and power, they have left you with varying degrees of blindness, more newly-created poverty and hunger and human suffering in America than you can ever imagine, and — among some other misplaced emphases — a backlog of acquisitiveness and love of things you will be hard pressed to overcome.

98% of all Americans my age will claim they were at Woodstock when Love and Peace were supposedly going to burst Aquarius-wise upon humanity and last forever.

Well, I wasn't there.

And 99% of the 98% who say they were there also didn't make it to that marathon concert on some muddy pasture in upstate New York. And somehow the foreverness of the Peace and Love they proclaimed didn't last forever.

So you, yourselves, will have to come up with another way to do it.

Self-indulging America — from the advertising companies down to the hot-shot with the big fancy car with all the tchatchkas in it — has taught you to get as many kicks out of life as you can because, as the advertisement says, "You only go around once in life". And the advertisements tell us to avoid as much pain as possible, *not* to get down in the mud and grime of other people's broken and breaking lives. "Living well is the best revenge," they say, but they define "well" differently than one would have hoped, and they don't tell us what the revenge is for. For dying at the end of life? For raw deals life deals out sometimes? What revenge?

But getting so many kicks and avoiding so much pain just won't do for us any more, in our day.

The stakes are too high.

Engagement was the fancy-sounding French word we learned in college, from the Existentialists. *Engagement...*getting involved.

An Involved Life is the Good Life, is "living well". (And there are too many good Talmudic quotes to quote here to that effect, quotes that pre-date Sartre and Camus by many centuries.)

Many of you kids manage to resist the onslaught of superficiality, insensitivity, and triviality. I know that, because my friends in Jewish education keep calling me with feedback: kids bucking the system, pushing back hard against the dumbness and lousiness of materialism and achievement-for-achievement's-sake. When Morah Sarah and Ms. Reinstein and Mr. Schonfeld suggest raising money for a sound system for hearing-impaired members of the synagogue, you go out and do it, with gusto, shoving aside a bit of your homework and your other extra-curricular activities and a little bit of your personal life. Or you bring your personal life into the Mitzvah work.

It is important to you, and justifiably so.

I know it.

I know it because my friends tell me, and you tell me.

Somewhere along the way you have sensed the shallowness of The Recent American Dream of Fine Things, Comfort, the Cult of Comfortableness, Success as a Good in and of itself.

Just know, kids, that your teachers, your youth group advisors, your camp counsellors are with you. They thrill at the sight of your brightening eyes, they feel your adrenalin jumping to full blast when you come alive working at a carnival for residents of the local mental hospital, when you canvass the neighborhood for bone marrow testing, when you empty your closet of all the extra clothes you really don't need...and take them down to the shelter.

You are not alone.

V. To the Parents and Other Adults

Back off.

Sure, keep picking at them if they abuse their privileges with the car, if they bring home someone who acts like Godzilla for Shabbas dinner, if they give the very slightest hint that they have been using drugs.

But back off when they want to do a canned food drive, when they want to make the Bima of the synagogue wheelchair accessible, when they wash cars to provide scholarships for camp for kids who have special needs.

Back off even if it means they'll get a B+ instead of an A- on some paper.

More than back off — add your own canned food, work with the kid on the Bima project, put on your raincoat and boots and wash cars with them.

And *please* don't keep telling them that it's a good idea because it will look good on their college applications.

Tell them it's a good idea because it's making a more Menschlich world and that it's the right thing to do.

No ulterior motives.

And don't give them the phony wisdom — after they get shot down on their heartfelt, glorious projects — that it's a good lesson for them to get shot down now and again, that it'll toughen them up for Real Life where sometimes good things get wasted by the Establishment.

Don't do it to them.

Instead, make sure their projects and plans and ideas for all these good things really happen. Throw your adult weight around. Show the kids you are with them, that you believe in them, that you think Life can be decent and overflow-ing with caring, that human beings come through for others, that what makes us different from the animals is not that we can reason, but rather, that we can plan and project and make real a life and human environment where everyone has a fair crack at things.

VI. To the Kids

Keep at it.

Whenever I see you raise your hands to take on a Mitzvah project, when I see the telltale sparkling of your eyes when you tell me you needed a pick-up truck to haul away all the goods for poor people you gathered at your bar mitzvah, whenever I can almost hear the adrenalin rushing through your systems because you have just sung your heart out at the local old age home — then, you know, and I know, that you are right and upright and safe from the glittering phoniness.

A Mensch, A Guter Yid, a good Jew.

When they beat you down — they, the powers that crush, the policy makers who at a single stroke of the pen put people on the streets and deprive others of jobs — don't say, don't even *think*, "That's just the way things are."

No, No!

Make sure, instead, that when *you* have the power, you'll make sure no kid *ever* has to go through what you did to set things right.

Just make sure it never happens in your day of glory.

Never.

Juicy, Useful Quotes

I offer a few interesting quotes (in no particular order of importance) that I have gathered over the last number of years. Some of them are used in other parts of this book; others are just too good to leave unrecorded for posterity:

"Anything worth doing is worth doing poorly."

Malka Edelman, Beth Huppin,
And Some Other Unknown Original Source

"She's available to parents 24 hours a day and says she gets emotionally involved in all the searches."

The Giraffe Gazette, III:3,
Carol Watson, Missing Children Minnesota

"Charismatic leaders make us think, 'Oh, if only I could do that, be like that.'
True leaders make us think, 'If they can do that, then...I can too.'"

John Holt, educator

"Sure enough, Becky Simpson is a statistic: she is one of a kind."

Michael Ryan, Parade Magazine, 5/28/89,
about a Mitzvah Hero in Cranks Creek, KY

"Deep down I'm really a hedonist, and this work feels so good I wouldn't think of doing anything else."

Giraffe Jim Beatty,
pro bono lawyer for Atlanta's homeless people

"The only thing left to do is to do it."

Source Unknown

"I figure what good's a clean house if your county's radioactive?"

Homemaker, Barbara Howell, Wilson, NC,
As Reported in The Giraffe Gazette

"I am Ed Landy. Being a Bar Mitzvah means reaching manhood. Today I am a man. I am 65."

"After I have my Bar Mitzvah, am I going to be normal like everyone else, and people will stop making fun of me?"

Two Jewish adults with special needs
on the occasion of their becoming B'nai Mitzvah,
Temple Bnai Israel, Revere, MA, 1989

The Nobel Laureate, Francis Crick,...who won the prize for DNA research, was once quoted as saying, "No newborn infant should be declared human until it has passed certain tests regarding its genetic endowment and...if it fails these tests, it forfeits the right to live."

Playing God in the Nursery,
Jeff Lyon, p. 198-199

"It was a long and exciting weekend....To see so many adorable Down Syndrome kids was like dying and going to heaven with all God's angels surrounding you."

Janet Marchese,
Lamed Vavnikit

"When I ask myself how it happened that I in particular discovered the Relativity Theory, it seemed to lie in the following circumstance. The normal adult never bothers his head about space-time problems. Everything there is to be thought about, in his opinion, has already been done in early childhood. I, on the contrary, developed so slowly that I only began to wonder about space and time when I was already grown up. In consequence, I probed deeper into the problem than an ordinary child would have done."

Einstein

Most people see the world as it is, and ask, "Why?"
I see the world as it should be, and ask, "Why not?"

George Bernard Shaw

"My poetry never saved a child from Auschwitz."

W.H. Auden, Poet

Matisse and Jerry:
The Story of the Mitzvah Dogs

I. Graduation Day

Jerry[1] rolled his wheelchair over to the microphone and began to address the 500 people and 40 or 50 dogs. He was chosen to speak on behalf of the graduating class, and alongside him was Matisse, his more-than-a-pet Yellow Labrador Retriever. The man spoke briefly, maybe 5 minutes, telling us how he had had his whole world laid out before him, how everything was possible for someone his age in such good health. Then he broke his neck in a diving accident, then he was in a wheelchair, then he was back in a college classroom of hundreds of students, and nobody saw him anymore.

As Jerry put it, "They could have tripped on me and they still wouldn't have seen me. All they saw was this chair."

Now Jerry's life was changing radically, because of a project called Canine Companions for Independence (CCI). He would never feel that devastating loneliness again.

II. Enter Matisse

Matisse is a Canine Companion.

He was raised for about 16 months in a private family's home. The people who handle this first stage in a Canine Companion's life are called Puppy Raisers.

Then Matisse was brought to the CCI center for extensive and meticulous training by experts who know that some dogs can do more with people than anyone could ever imagine.

Finally, Jerry and Matisse are matched up and go through 2 weeks of grueling "Boot Camp". As they learn each other's personalities, they become a team, friends, co-workers, partners in a venture in independent living, both of them determined to succeed and exceed all normal expectations for such trying circumstances. I might add that they make a handsome team: they are both young, athletic looking, exuding vigor, though at this stage it appears that Matisse shows a little more confidence than Jerry. Matisse knows this will work out just fine.

Matisse and Jerry are the story of some sort of real-live everyday miracle.

---

[1] I have changed the names of people who have received CCI dogs. If you would like to meet someone who has one, you would have to contact the CCI office and they would have to ask a local person if they would be willing to meet you or to speak to one of your groups. Many are willing to do so, but they are entitled to their privacy, which is why you have to work through the CCI office as intermediaries.

However, with their permission, I have kept the real names of people who work for CCI: the instructors, people in the administration, board members, and, of course, the founder and Executive Director, Bonnie Bergin.

III. A Little Personal Background

I am a cat man.

Throughout my childhood we had cats. My brother's cats seemed to live long, normal cat lives, and mine just dropped from disease or other disasters every few years. I don't remember all their names, other than Sam the Siamese (a diseased tail took him to the great sleeping-cushion in the sky), and Shmetena, which is Yiddish for sour cream, because my brother's cat was Blueberry, who, naturally enough outlived any pet I would have, even surviving an encounter with a car, a crooked smile on his face from a re-wired jaw being the only hint that he had taken on a 1957 Oldsmobile.

The cats played with us on snowy days. We tortured them moderately now and again as little children often do, but they were good to us, sleeping beside us, entertaining us with their antics, once doing in a parakeet we had in order to teach us some lesson or other about the Nature of Life and the Persistent Memories of the Wild.

We *did* have a few dogs along the way. This *was* after all the late '40's and early '50's and we had a big house with a big yard and plenty of room to roam around. But the family legend says my first dog, Bruce, a German shepherd, bit me, and I spontaneously — and I might add, justifiably — bit him right back. (I was 3 years old and unaware that you didn't do things like that. And I still do things like that, though I am supposed to know better by now.)

But I remained a cat man. When I am on the road lecturing, I pray (1) that my hosts will have a cat, and (2) that they most definitely won't have a dog, particularly a (a) yelper, a (b) 120-pounder, a (c) 120-pound jumper, a (d) a 120-pound ugly jumper-and-slobberer-and-yelper-and-shoe-devourer.

IV. Some Jewish Background

Dogs are mentioned in the Bible 29 times. Only once is a reference nearly positive (Ecclesiastes 9:4), "A live dog is better than a dead lion" — not a great endorsement there.

Much worse, and much more recently, in times of persecution of the Jews, dogs meant only one thing: tools of the Oppressor to seek out their human prey, for capture, for torture, for murder. In many Jewish households, dogs are still not only forbidden, but altogether forbidden topics of discussion. Young children cannot understand why they can't have a dog from their Aunt Harriet from Hungary or Uncle Moish from Czechoslovakia as so many other kids have. They just don't have enough of a historical background to grasp why they can't have one.

But things will have to change, because of people like Jerry and dogs like Matisse.

V. Some Background on Canine Companions

Canine Companions for Independence (CCI) is the brainchild of one Bonita ("Bonnie") Bergin who one day 15 years ago or so recalled how she had seen donkeys and other pack animals in Asia being used to help people with certain physical limitations. She concluded that dogs could be trained beyond anything previously considered possible and could carry out a variety of tasks for and with the human companion to make for a life of greater independence and freedom.

The struggle to make it happen was the usual one: many trials, frequent disappointments, great skepticism by the "experts". This seems particularly strange to me in light of the enormous and proven success of seeing-eye dogs over the years. Still, it was a struggle. But nowadays there are 500 of these dogs (including 2 or 3 in Israel) bringing renewed energy and hope and life to an equal number of human beings whose lives were slowed or shattered, dragging or sliding downhill. The direction is reversed, the accumulated progress reports leave the student and friend of CCI amazed and overwhelmed.

V. What the CCI Dogs Can Do

To become a certified CCI dog, the animal must learn 89 commands. (I like to ask parents, "Wouldn't you like your children to be able to follow 89 commands?")

They pull wheelchairs.

They turn light switches on and off.

They press elevator buttons.

They pick up objects that the human companion might drop and which a more able-bodied person would just bend down and pick up.

They help with the shopping, taking items off the shelf, handing over the money to the cashier, taking the change back to the Master or Mistress.

And, of course, they jump, and play, and fetch, and breathe, and speak, and heel, and lie down, and roll over, and protect, and all the other things regular dogs do.

They also serve a striking social need besides the individual companionship and unquestioning love they give the human partner — inevitably for the unmarried human, along comes someone from the opposite sex and says, "Oh, what a beautiful dog! May I pet your dog?" And then the two humans begin to talk while Matisse or Yeager or Orson or Garfield wags his or her tail or takes a nap. Then the three of them go out to dinner. Then they go out for a picnic, then shopping, then to the movies, then on a two-day outing, then to the church or synagogue to get married. The Canine Companion becomes a unique and somewhat divinely-inspired Shadchan, a Matchmaker, with a much better track record than the human matchmakers we read about in Jewish literature or in singles ads.

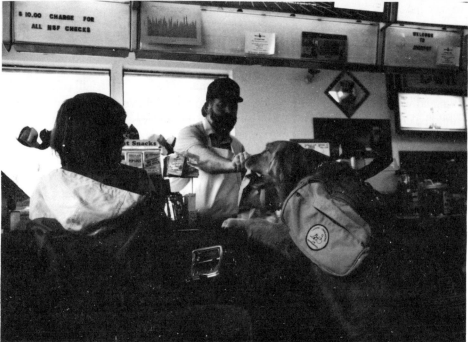

Patti Abernathy, who has multiple sclerosis, uses Inspector, a SERVICE dog trained by CCI...*above* to pull her wheelchair; *below* to purchase an item at the store.

Actually, CCI trains 4 kinds of dogs:

Service dogs, like Matisse, do the kinds of things I just described, working with people who have physical challenges brought on by accident or disease or whatever circumstances have produced the limitations.

Specialty dogs do all that and are "customized" for additional skills, if, for example, the human partner is also hearing-impaired.

Signal dogs work with deaf and hearing-impaired individuals.

And social dogs are trained for pet therapy programs in institutions such as old age homes, hospitals, and similar settings.

They are now focussing on Golden Retrievers, Yellow and Black Labradors, some mixes, Corgies and Border Collies (for signal dogs) and a few other varieties, depending on the special needs and how their continued experiences with different breeds run.

Five CCI centers around the country are now training these dogs: in Ohio (near Columbus), on Long Island (Farmingdale), in Orlando, in the San Diego area, and the main branch, along with the national office, in Santa Rosa, CA, an hour and a half north of San Francisco, in the heart of California wine country. They are hoping to turn out 100 CCI dogs a year, and are close to that goal.

The entire operation is amazing:

The devotion of the trainers,

The love and devotion of the families that raise the puppies, only to give them up so that someone else will have greater benefit,

The commitment of Charles Schulz of Snoopy fame, and his wife, Jean, who is Chairperson of the Board of CCI,

The enormous courage, physical stamina, and strength-of-will of those who own and will own CCI dogs, the people who go so far above and beyond whatever might be considered "normal" expectations, to set their lives back on course,

The sheer joy of it all, everything so upbeat, people (and dogs, I think) aware of the grandeur of the endeavor, that something sublime is happening, that it is good to be attached to such glorious and sublime endeavors.

And all this for only $10,000/dog, including breeding, training, the blue and gold backpacks the dogs wear that identify them as CCI dogs, and all other costs that go into making this everyday miracle happen. (Which isn't so bad when you do simple math: say a dog has a 10-year working life — that's $1,000/year, that's $2.74/day.)

And each person who gets a CCI dog pays only $125.

The struggles remain:

Fundraising,

Long waiting lists because there aren't sufficient facilities to train more dogs and ultimately match the dogs up with their human counterparts after Boot Camp,

Lobbying efforts to afford equal opportunities before the law for the CCI dogs, equal to seeing-eye dogs: access to public transportation,[1a] stores, theaters, restaurants.

Ah, but the devotion, the upbeat atmosphere, the magic in the air....

A visit to CCI is really the closest thing I know to a cure-all for the emotional blues.

Feeling depressed? Visit CCI. Hang out with the dogs and the trainers.

Low self-image? Raise a puppy for CCI.

Lost a little direction in your life? Ennui and melancholy got you down? Watch the CCI dogs in action in your local department store.

Afraid of physically challenged people? Try something like, "Oh, what a beautiful dog? May I pet the dog?"

VII. A Few Jewish Comments

First, there's the obvious lesson: if a dog can learn 89 commands, Jews — by dint of logical argument — ought to be able to do better with the 613 Mitzvot in the Torah.

Second — one specially-trained CCI dog, Kalob,[1b] (whose owner is one of the instructors) — is a Rottweiler. Rottweilers are normally known for their training as tough, even vicious dogs. Some think they make pit bulls look like Mickey Mouse. There are even rumors that they eat Sherman tanks for dinner and are trained to attack enemy aircraft on command. They are Big Mother Dogs, 120-plus-pounders,[1c] and none of us would want to meet up with a Rottweiler in a dark alley, unless it were Kalob. Now, if Kalob can be trained for such fine human service, such super Mitzvah work, then we, human beings, whose nature is not tough, not vicious, we certainly should be able to master whatever tendencies-to-do-bad-things we might have. I think that's a fair estimate of things.

And third, let's go back to some Mitzvah Mathematics. (A) Since Jewish law teaches[1d] that we can sell a synagogue, all holy objects, even a Torah Scroll to take care of orphans, and (B) since any person who sits in a classroom with hundreds of other students and is treated as if he or she doesn't exist — since that person is most certainly an orphan, then (C) perhaps we could divest ourselves of one or two of the extra Torahs we might have in the synagogue, sell them off, and invest in Mitzvah dogs. If (D) one used Torah is worth, say, $10,000, then (E) that's 10 years of glorious life for a person whose life may have been a dead end.

[1a]Amtrak's Fall/Winter 1989/1990 Northeast Corridor Services schedule reads as follows (Under "Pets"): Certified guide dogs accompanying blind or deaf passengers are the only animals permitted on Amtrak trains. Documentation required.

I don't know if that is actually their policy, or whether the rules have changed to allow for CCI dogs and they just haven't had a chance to change their brochure.

[1b]"Kalob" is an Anglicized form of "Kelev", Hebrew for "Dog". Clever, very clever.

[1c]Kalob looked to me like he weighed in at around 250.

[1d]Shulchan Aruch, Orach Chaim, 153:6.

VIII. A Final, Personal Note

I was invited to speak at two graduations this year.

The first was for Akiba Hebrew Academy in Philadelphia. I was thrilled and flattered to be asked to address the class, the parents, other relatives and friends. It was my first commencement exercise. My theme was, "What Do I Want To Be When I Grow Up?" That was in June.

In August, I spoke at the CCI graduation in Santa Rosa. It was then that I realized that — at least in my fantasy life — I knew I wanted to be a Canine Companion trainer when I grew up.

I won't actually do it, but thinking about it, daydreaming and nightdreaming about it, it does a lot for my soul and gives me a peace of mind and a sense of innocence I hadn't known for a long, long time. I suppose there are worse things to do than to shift occupations, take a cut in pay, make a physical move to another town and start all over. The worst that could happen is I could be eternally happy, and it would most certainly be a lot of fun, even with all the strain and pressure of preparing dogs-and-humans for a good life together.

Yes, it would be a lot of fun.

For sure.

Maybe some of the readers of this article will take it out of the fantasy realm and try it on for size.

You could certainly do a lot worse.[1e]

For information about CCI, contact Bonita Bergin at the Executive Office, 707-528-0830 (V/TDD) or Katheryn Horton in the Northwest Office, 707-579-1985 (V/TDD)

[1e]CCI has *fabulous* and also a *great* video. See "Mitzvah Videotapes" at the end of the book for information on how to order them. Great T-shirts and sweatshirts, too. But the videos — if you watch them without Kleenex nearby, you are a rock, not a human being. You will feel uplifted and moved, stirred to the bones. They are, I believe, the best anti-depressants available on the market.

The Challah Vs. The Dog

I. Four Revelations Right In A Row

1. Loneliness, that was the theme. Dan Rather's weekly show "48 Hours" was going to deal with loneliness. I expected, of course, an hour exclusively devoted to singles and singles match-ups, underestimating Big Dan. I think one unforgettable clip will remain forever unforgettable for me: A dog — it looked like a golden retriever or Labrador — goes into a hospital with its master. The dog walks down the hall and into a room where an old woman is lying in bed. She has tubes in her. (It *is* a hospital, after all.) The dog climbs into the bed, lies down, and puts its head on her lap. The old woman, hand trembling (I saw it tremble, and I *think*, but I am not sure, that it had an IV line in it), pets the dog. Wow!

2. The movie, "Dad". Well, if I were a reviewer, I would say it had its powerful moments. But it was also manipulating. I expected that. They could just as well have advertised the movie as a "2 Double-Size Tissue Box Holiday Special." Nevertheless, Jack Lemmon as the elder father and Ted Danson as the grown son share some very passionate and moving moments. One of the most unforgettable moments is when Ted Danson — the grown son who has a college-age son of his own — climbs into the hospital bed with his dying father, and, saying nothing, lies down and stretches out in the bed, putting his head on his father's shoulder. Jack Lemmon then puts his arm around Ted Danson. A few seconds later the camera fades to another scene. Wow! And a second Wow because Ted Danson has gotten a bad reputation as being capable of only playing the not-too-bright bartender in the TV series "Cheers".

3. When I prepare for my writing, I like to put together the notes, then take a few minutes' break and stare out the window, or pick up something unrelated, just to free my mind. Then I write. Getting ready for this particular piece, I picked up the November, 1989, *Smithsonian Magazine*. Thumbing through, I look at an article on truck stops around America. Having been a trucker myself (yes, Sweet Momma, a trucker — I drove the United Synagogue of America Bookmobile around the country for a year), I wanted to see what was new or different in my old haunts. Bam! Sue Hubbell, the author, writes about pulling into the Triple T, the Exxon Tucson Truck Terminal, Exit 268, off I-10 east of Tucson. Get this — there's even a Jewish element! Ira Morris built it in the mid-1960's, and there was a special twist to this Ira Morris's vision of what a truck stop ought to be. At the Triple T he had a rocking chair and a cat. Knowing how lonely the truckers could get on the long haul, Mr. Morris would let the drivers come in, plunk themselves down in the rocking chair, and just pet the cat for a while. The cat was a good purrer and very friendly. Just so the truckers could have a few moments of affection before heading down the highway. This cat (whose name is unfortunately not recorded in the article) was trained to scratch and fight if anyone was tempted to

take it out on the road. It was a communal cat and had its God-and-Ira-Morris-given purpose on this earth, kind of a Mitzvah cat. Wow!

4. I am role-playing with a group of Jewish teen-agers. The issue is: Getting Pets into Jewish Old Age Homes. One kid plays a kid going in to the home to ask if the residence allows pets, and, if not, would they consider allowing resident or visiting pets. The other kids plays the administrator. They run through a lot of questions and responses. (The kid who plays the kid is expected to get background material from a veterinarian.) Finally they hit upon the response, "Who will change the cat's box?" Or, "Who will clean the bird cage?" No "Wow" here. Instead, a giant "Feh!" and a tip-off....If they have people who change filthy sheets and pyjamas, ought they not be able to find someone to change the bird cage or litter box? (But we're only role playing.)

II. Talmudic Logic and Objections and Answers

The last paragraph's logic, i.e., if they clean bed sheets, they can more easily clean the cage or litter box, is called *Kal V'Chomer* in the Talmud and *a fortiori* in fancy scholarly English (which is Latin). The term means that, if one thing is true, simple logic would dictate that another thing is most certainly also true.

Here's another *Kal V'Chomer*: if rabbis and concerned fellow Jews try their best to get Challah, Shabbat Candles, Lulavim, Etrogim, Matzah, Maror, Charoset, Hamentaschen, Shalach Manot and other holiday needs, Tallis, T'fillin, Siddurim, Chumashim, and all kinds of other Jewish books to people in hospitals and old age homes, should they not — even before the inanimates — worry about getting pets into those same places? Resident pets (yes, Mrs. Greenberg, there *are* resident pets in some hospitals) into those same hospitals and old age homes — and into other communal situations where people would really need them: group homes, shelters for homeless people, institutions for those recovering from mental illness, etc.? (And this might also include Jewish Community Centers, Federation buildings, Jewish Family Service offices, and synagogues. It wouldn't hurt.) Is that not, *Kal V'Chomer*, the more Jewish thing to do than giving precedence to the inanimate objects, important though they may be? Forgive my harsh tone, but the text in Pirkay Avot, Chapter 5, reminds us that among the things wise people say is "Rishon Rishon-First things first." In this case, animals perhaps ought to be considered Rishon, the first priority.

Objection #1: We're talking Jewish...Jewish books, Jewish ritual objects, Jewish things needed for everyday Jewish life.

Answer to Objection #1: Jewish is restoring life, dignity, vigor to the outcasted, to the weak, to the ones whose spirits may be faltering.

Objection #2: The contact with familiar Jewish things helps restore the spirit and re-instills vigor into the minds and souls of the weak, the weakening, the despairing.

Answer to Objection #2: Purely statistically speaking *more* Jews in *more* hospitals and old age homes and other such places are *more* familiar with and more responsive to a live, breathing, affectionate animal than to a Havdalah spice box.

Objection #3: Judaism's rituals and ritual objects tie the ones performing the rituals and using the objects to higher things, which gives perspective to illness, weakness, trial and *tzuriss*.

Answer to Objection #3: The blessing to be recited over beautiful creations of God is, "Baruch Atta HaShem Elokaynu Melech HaOlam Shekacha Lo BeOlamo — Blessed are You, O Lord, our God, Who creates such beautiful creations in this world." Now, if a gorgeous dog or cat or bird doesn't or can't take you to higher spheres (with the help of a blessing), I'm not sure about a Lulav (which is considerably more bizarre looking at that). Please forgive my short temper on this issue, and remember that I am *not* saying using ritual objects are of no importance in this area of human activity. I am just saying First things First.

Objection #4: Some people are allergic to cats and dogs.

Answers to Objection #4: (A) So don't take the cats and dogs to them. This is somewhat like the old joke about the man who comes to the doctor and, lifting up his right arm, says, "You know, Doc, my arm hurts when I go like this." To which the doctor replies, "So don't do like that." (B) Take them to the people who are *not* allergic to cats and dogs. (C) Have the cats and dogs meet those not allergic in some communal room, (D) Use birds, fish, rabbits, cute rodents (if there are such things) such as gerbils and hamsters, ducks, geese, turkeys, capons, ostriches and emus[1], boa constrictors, lemurs, ferrets, wallabies — anything that is alive and pettable — for the visits....Many of these have already been tried with great success. Use your imagination on this one, at least as much as you would use it for other Mitzvahs.

Objection #5: Some people don't like dogs and cats.

Answer to Objection #5: See "Answers to Objection #4".

Objection #6: It's against the law and the health code to have such pets.

Answers to Objection #6: (A) In most, if not most-of-the-most cases, it is *not* against the law or the health code. (B) I once recall even hearing that, if the building was built with the help of federal funds, they *must* allow pets, if the residents want it. Don't hold me to it; just check it out yourself. It's worth checking out. (C) The nastiest response=my most-recently-thought-of response="blood boiling response" — if the Goyim down the street are doing it in their old age home, their hospital, (for example, the San Francisco ASPCA/Humane Society, which has been in the forefront of this project) — they must know something we don't know. Perhaps their laws and health codes are different than ours?

Objection #7: Our insurance policy doesn't cover this.

---

[1]The name "emu" is derived from the Hebrew "Eema", which means "Mother", and the original meaning of this creature's name seems to be something like, "Big Mother Bird." See *The Journal of Biblical Literature*, LXII, pp. 223-228, March, 1974, and *The Biblical Archeologist*, XCI, pp. 19-28, "Big Bird and Big Mother Birds in the Ancient Near East".

Answers to Objection #7: (A) Probably not true in many cases, maybe most cases. (B) See "Answers to Objection #6", subsection (C).

Objection #8: Synagogues — what do we need a cat or dog in the synagogue for?

Answer to Objection #8: Come with me sometime when I am talking to kids. I often ask how many of them have pets, usually cats and dogs. "Holechim Bananot" as the Hebrew phrase has it....They go bananas, and everyone wants to tell me about his or her dog or cat, names, size, type, antics. I would theorize (though no empirical data has been gathered and analyzed as of this date) that we would have a lot easier time getting the kids to religious school if they knew they could play with a cat or dog at the synagogue before and after class or during the break. A Husky, a Persian, a Welsh terrier, a Rex, a Lhasa Apso[1]. Everybody knows that primary and elementary schools have pets in the classroom. It's part of growing up. So this will be part of growing up Jewish.

Objection #9: Some of the staff does not like pets.

Answer to Objection #9: See "Answer to Objection #5" and substitute "staff" for "people".

Objection #10: Who will feed the pet, clean the box, or take the dog on his or her daily walk?

Answers to Objection #10: (A) Feeding and cleaning may be done by anyone on the staff who loves pets, or by volunteers who love pets and who would love to come in and do it because they believe this is important to the welfare of the Jewish community or by kids from the youth group if they get angry enough that no one in the Adult Establishment is willing to do it. (Lots of kids I have talked to are willing to do it. Some synagogues are near Jewish day schools or have day schools in their building, and I am certain there are students there that would love to perform this particular Mitzvah. Most important of all is the fact that, inevitably, some of the residents themselves, whom we all-too-often vastly underestimate will do the feeding and cleaning themselves, with great pleasure and a sense of pride and independence. (B) Walking a dog is more complicated, but I would suggest referring back to the local church that has one and see how the priest or minister manages. Here, too, residents, patients (whatever term you want) are bound to also surprise those who have lost the element of surprise in their work. I suspect they will fight over each other to have the privilege of walking the dog.

III. Some of the Multifarious Benefits

1. Lots of added affection all around.

---

[1]My friends inform me that "Lhasa Apso" is *not* the name of some kind of exotic tea, like Formosa Oolong (which I thought was the name of a spy from the Sino-Japanese War).

2. A sense of responsibility and caring re-instilled in residents, patients (whatever the term). You can't die if you have to get up in the morning to feed the cat and change the litter. You just can't.

3. Lowering of blood pressure (proven by a test of putting cats on the laps of residents of old age homes. Beats the hell out of Apresazide 50/50 and other blood pressure pills and elixirs.)

4. People will feel better.

5. Staff, patients, and anyone else involved will pause and re-perspectivize about the relationship of medicines and technology to human and near-human therapies. The literature of social work, psychology, psychiatry, and general medicine is bursting with articles about this.

6. Miracles major and minor will occur:

A. Some who did not walk will walk again because they have to get out of bed to visit the resident cat in the communal room. Miracles.

B. Some who did not speak will speak. I've been told, and I have read, of many stories where someone hadn't spoken for years, but spoke to the dog. I can't be sure whether or not they spoke to the staff afterwards, but they enjoyed talking to the dog. Miracles.

C. Some whose limbs appear to be frozen and whose muscles have ostensibly atrophied will wow the other residents and staff when they throw a ball for the dog to fetch or bend down to put the bowl of cat food out for the kitty. More miracles.

D. Some will request visits to the animal shelter, pet shops, and zoo to help select other possible candidates for the growing menagerie. In Winter even, in places like Minnesota or Massachusetts even, when it is supposedly too cold to go outside.

E. Many who used to be kvetchy all day and night will not be kvetchy any more, or will turn their kvetchiness to other matters.

F. Loneliness will no longer be the name of the Angel of Death's sword, and uselessness will no longer be the poison dripping from the end of the blade.

G. People who can't sleep in the middle of the night will have somewhere to go, something to talk to, to touch, to play with. (I assume that pets used in these programs are well informed that their sleep patterns will be frequently disturbed. That's part of the job description, Bowser!)

H. Less pills, capsules, shots, enemas, and IV's will be needed. (The point of the whole article is just that: things that breathe and are warm and can be touched are almost universally better than things that come in sterile containers.)

I. The atmosphere, the "feel" of the place may change to up from down, or from up to higher up.

J. More kids will come by to hang out and join the people in their interaction with the pets.

K. Pets do funny things. Lots more people will laugh.

L. Etc., etc. (They even have a horse-ranch in some prison for the inmates to manage. Breaking horses, feeding horses, grooming horses, riding horses must correlate favorably with the recidivism rate.)

IV. The Sad Thing: A Brief Digression

And the sad thing is that so many of the people who want or need contact with animals now — they had pets in their former lives: when they were kids, when they were better psychologically, emotionally or physically, when they had their own roof over their own head.

They may have memories of rolling on the rug and playing with the dog, or throwing a frizbee out on a beach for the dog to catch and bring back, or rubbing the belly of a cat or feeling the cat curl up in bed down at his or her feet or hearing the sounds of the parakeet chirping first thing in the morning. Is it then any surprise when "miracles" happen in the presence of a dog, a cat, a bird? There are probably many reasons for this phenomenon, but is not one of them merely a reconnection with vital resources drawn from past memories? Is not the Irish setter's head on someone's lap the stimulus for so many latent (too long latent) juices and brain connections, nerve jumps, releasing of chemicals throughout the body?

People who become weaker (or what sometimes appears to be) helpless, people who come into the care or under the supervision of others — the last thing they need is to be separated from the familiar, from "home base" as it were, those touches of reality that precede rational thinking. We know people who gave up and died when a spouse and friends of many years pass on. We also know others who began to give up when they first used a walker, a cane, a colostomy bag...or lost their driver's license because their reactions slowed down so much they became a hazard on the road.

And so we compound the hurt[1a] and make harsher the loneliness when we deprive them of pets. All those many years of companionship, fun, protection, innocent play may never be mustered for their restorative powers.

We are not cruel people. I do not believe anyone does this, this warmth deprivation, this denial of contact and companionship, with malice in the heart. Sometimes it may be thoughtlessness, but that can be overcome. Sometimes it is laziness, but that, too, can be overcome. And sometimes it is uncreativity of the

---

[1a]My friend and teacher, Rabbi Marc Wilson, taught me an interesting insight about "compounding the hurt". The Torah tells us (Genesis 21:15-16) that when Abraham sent Hagar and the child Yishmael out into the wilderness, the water ran out, and Hagar "left the child under one of the bushes, and went and sat down at a distance a bowshot away." The text continues, "for she thought, 'Let me not look on as the child dies.'" Rabbi Wilson commented that, it wasn't bad enough that the child was suffering, but sometimes we, too — like Hagar — make things that much worse by saying that we don't want to see that suffering. The situation with Hagar and Yishmael is much more extreme than that of pets in old age residences, but the principle is the same: we are supposed to actively and purposefully see the pain. Who knows? Had Hagar not put herself so far away from Yishmael, had she watched from close by, perhaps she would have come up with some solution to ease or cure the child's suffering.

soul, but that, too, can be overcome with the help of experts in the field, and there are many. Even people who never had pets or never liked animals can understand the grandeur of the idea.

Perhaps it is the simplicity of the doing that is deceptive to those who have never seen it in action. You take a cat, put it in the lap of someone who is depressed, deeply depressed, or autistic or near-dead of loneliness, or frail of body, or apparently paralyzed, and something almost always has to happen, something positive, something lifegiving, something revivifying.

You let the dog into the hospital bed, it lies down, puts its head on the person's lap, and lets the shaking hand stroke its head or side. Something miraculous, something exquisitely beautiful will most surely occur.

So be it.

V. Special Case #1 — Fish

Fish.[1b]

Someone thought it might be nice to buy an aquarium for ALYN Orthopaedic Hospital for Children in Jerusalem. You know, for the kids to enjoy.

I think someone said they had had one a few years back, but no one could recollect what had happened to it. I think that's what I recall.

In any event, I remember seeing that they already had a small zoo out back, including two peacocks (until one was stolen. [Now that is a new low in human indecency, lower than stealing furniture out of a Goodwill box....Stealing a pet peacock from kids who function with the help of wheelchairs. Lordy, Lordy, is there no end to it?])

For a small number of hundreds of dollars the aquarium was purchased, installed, and waiting to be enjoyed by residents and staff alike. A local expert on fish, fish tanks, fish food, and the like helped with the selection, and the staff and kids jointly selected the best location in the building.

End result: smashing success. Kids love it. Staff loves it.

And I have photographs of the kids gathered round watching the fish, looking *very* happy.

VI. Special Case #2 — Birds

My Grandma Annie, may she rest in piece, had canaries and other birds. Mom remembers them even from her childhood.

When the designers and builders of the Westin Hotel on Kauai and the Hyatt Regency on Maui and on the Big Island of Hawaii decided to design and

---

[1b]Any kind of fish, from the most common to the most exotic will do, though the more colorful the better. Any size tank will do, any landscaping. Only make sure to consult the residents about their preferences.

build the Ultimate Playground, besides the golf courses, tennis courts, not-to-be-believed landscaping, breathtaking views, awesome swimming pools, ultra-restaurants, upscale shops, finest chocolates on the pillowcases, and hallways and hallways of exquisite Polynesian art work — besides all those glorious fun things — they stationed in well-thought-out strategic locales all sorts of tropical birds. Macaws, parrots, cockatoos. There are swans swimming in pools all over the place. There are even peacocks sometimes walking around the lobby, and sometimes you can have your picture taken with a macaw on your arm. There are full-time paid staff in charge of nothing more than the care and welfare of the birds. (Laws? Health code? Insurance? — a guest could get bit good and hard. Liability, lawsuits.)

Birds are nice.

They're colorful, they sing, they do other things like sit on your hand or arm or shoulder, they talk to you, at you, and back at you. They let you pet them, too, sometimes. And they are always grateful when you spoon the seeds into their feeding cup.

Now, at the Jewish Community Center in Indianapolis, birds also seem to play an important and fun role. Zack and Zelda and Clifford and Cuddles are two pairs of finches in two separate cages in two different locations in the building. They are the result of Carol Hutton's work. She is a staff member there, and it just so happens that she raises finches, so that when the idea came up to get birds in the JCC (for elderly people having lunches and other activities, for kids hanging out after school, for anyone who wanted to enjoy them), within a week, things were rolling.

Carol's number at the JCC is 317-251-9467.

You can ask her about (A) how easy it is to do, (B) how the reactions have been, such as how, after closing the building for a few days for a holiday and taking the birds home, how many people asked, "When are the birds coming back?" when the building re-opened. You may also ask her about (C) how the JCC's insurance policy only disallows pack animals, and since no one has saddled the birds and ridden them down to the local convenience store to pick up some soda, they're OK to have in the building, and (D) who feeds the birds and changes the papers on the bottom of the cages. She'll also fill you in on (E) all the ins and out of selecting the right birds (hardier for a breezeway, livelier or calmer, better singers and lesser singers, etc.), and (F) how to adapt the ideas to other Jewish communal buildings. You might also inquire about what happened when she gave a 93-year-old volunteer one of her finches to keep.

A recent phone conversation yielded some facts on start-up costs. As I recall, Carol told me that (G) a pair of finches runs $15-30, (H) 3 months of birdseed runs $6-7, (I) by hanging a sign saying you are looking for a bird cage, you'll get three or four calls very quickly. There seem to be a lot of them in people's basements and garages.

Carol has proven that (J) it is easier to do than you think and (K) the benefits keep piling up every day.

That's Carol Hutton, at 317-251-9467.

VII. *Efficiency and Further Logic*

If we worry about how efficient our energy-efficient microwaves and refrigerators are, we should worry — *Kal V'Chomer*, that much more — about how efficient a pet Mitzvah really is.

If we worry about how high a yield our financial investments will give, we should worry — *Kal V'Chomer*, that much more — about the high yield of this kind of Mitzvah. (The "Bang for the Buck Theory of Investment".)

If we worry about about cost-efficiency in the business world, we should worry, should we not? — *Kal V'Chomer*, that much more — about cost factors vs. results in this kind of dogs-and-cats-and-birds scheme. (The "Bang for the Buck Theory of Business".)

Is the time and effort that we put into starting and maintaining such a Mitzvah project going to yield sufficient results to warrant such time and effort?

Results are measured in increments of:

increased liveliness,

miraculous physical, emotional and psychological recoveries,

happiness,

laughter,

relief,

basic joy at being alive,

moderate-to-incredible personality expansion,

warmth,

friendliness,

openness,

sharing,

good feelings,

increased longevity,

to name but a few basic scales of measurement.

I feel confident that pets and animals in the Jewish communal structure will pass these all-important tests, and, on the other hand, I would hate to think — after the appropriate consciousness is raised — that the projects would be ignored just because it is too much of a bother.

If grocery stores, food distributors, restaurants, bakeries, caterers and the like have been convinced that it is better to take leftover food to shelters and soup kitchens (sometimes handled by their own people, sometimes by outside volunteers), then — *Kal V'Chomer*, that much more — should we be convinced that we can bring live, warm, affectionate animals into the worlds of so many people who need them.

The same with shoe stores taking shoes destined for the dumpsters to people who have no shoes or no decent shoes. If they can be convinced to get them somehow to the shelters, then — *Kal V'Chomer*, that much more — we could manage dogs, cats, birds, fish, and other members of the animal kingdom.

VIII. A Summary of the Projects

1. Get literature from the vet, from the humane society, from the pet stores, from your local zoo.

2. Call Carol Hutton if you are interested specifically in birds. That's 317-251-9467 in Indianapolis.

3. Scout around your local community to find other places doing the project already. They will save you time, money, and energy.

4. When we build new buildings, make it standard policy that pets — visiting, live-in or whatever is best for your own community — are part of the guts of the project. Otherwise, what's the building for?

4. After establishing such Mitzvah projects locally, urge national organizations to disseminate literature and have seminars at their national conventions on this topic....with a clearly-defined practical bent to the literature and seminars. After the reading and the lecturing, we want these things to happen. Jewish Family Service organizations, Jewish old age home organizations, Council of Jewish Federations, synagogue groups, all of them.

IX. Aha!

Aha!

One of my contacts in Oklahoma City just sent me a law (Oklahoma State statute 63, section 1-1929, that reads as follows:

Long-term care facilities—Visiting or residential animals

The State Board of Health shall establish rules and regulations allowing the use of visiting or residential animals in selected long-term health care facilities in this state. Long-term health care facilities which want animals shall be required to apply to the State Department of Health for approval for residential animals. Such rules and regulations shall be established giving consideration to disease prevention, sanitation, prevention of injury to patients and animals, and other concerns deemed appropriate by the Board.

Which means that pets are allowed.

We already knew that.

But I thought that making a copy of the law as it appears on the books in one state would add some oomph to the issue. I am sure there are laws in other states, too. Before setting out to get animals into the appropriate places, get a copy of the law for your state.

X. The General Principle

The only thing left to do is to do it.

Let us set the birds chirping, the cats purring, the dogs fetching, the goldfish swimming merrily, and the ferrets and and gerbils doing whatever they do best to make people happy.

The Strange Stories of "Eema" And Pharaoh's Daughter

For Rabbi Matthew Simon,
who taught me this story from Exodus.

I. By Way of General Introduction

Human beings name their children.

I don't know whether or not mother and father geese name their goslings, or cheetahs their cubs, but people do it as a matter of course, pouring some of their dreams and hopes and memories into the names, wishing in the baby's infancy that somehow they will grow well into those names.

I am sure people have named their children for my father, the physician. He is now approaching his 50th year of medical practice, and, back in the Old Days, he and his friends used to deliver babies. Lots of babies. In the Old Days, people sometimes named their babies for the doctor, as a gesture of gratitude for the years of good care he or she provided for the family.

I also know that people have named their children for my friend Janet. She helps them find babies with special needs to adopt. They are so grateful to her for her help, they name the child "Janet", or, if it is a boy, some have named the infant "Louis", for her husband.

And I am convinced that mothers and fathers name for specific heroes of theirs. By that I mean, if one of their children has been saved from drowning or a car accident by some stranger, some someone who appears out of nowhere to put his or her life on the line for the sake of their child — then the next child carries that hero's name. I *know* that will happen many times as the full story of the California earthquake unfolds, the human tales of thousands who put themselves out to dig through the rubble and ruins to rescue someone, strangers, just plain people, exhausted, but still digging, until they pulled someone alive from the wreckage and concrete. And the same will be true as we learn more of the events of Hurricane Hugo and the tornadoes in Huntsville, AL. More names for more heroes.

And, for sure, some babies will enter this world and be called by the name of the heroic pilot who brought down the disabled plane in Sioux City, saving many, many lives by his above-and-beyond skill. Survivors owe their lives to him, and it is the least they can do.

On a much less august plane of existence, people also name their horses, cats, dogs, birds, estates, boats, and (sometimes) cars.

"Tara" — now that's a good name for a plantation.

"Silver" (or "Hiyo Silver" according to some ancient Jewish texts) is an ideal name for a horse, as are "Trigger" and "Scout" and "Buttermilk". And there isn't a horse race around that you don't wonder what some of the owners were drinking the night they named the newborn colt. Weird, weird names.

Cats, dogs, and birds run the range of "Bowser", "Fluffy", "Muffy", "Shayna", "Tweety", and "Fang" to "Mahatma", "Jehosophat", "Manuel", and "Zimbabwe". My friend, Allan Gould, even had a cat named "Dog", with the appropriate sign on the lawn, "Beware of Dog" to keep away unwanted guests and potential burglars. (They were never robbed as long as "Dog" walked this earth.)

As for boats, try the Marina in Sausalito, CA, sometime. Just walk up and down the docks and ponder the Mysteries, from the biggest yachts to the dinkiest dinghies, names that conjure up episodes right out of The Twilight Zone.

The medieval epics even have names for the heroes' swords, though I can't remember any other than "Excalibur", which seems like a reasonable-enough name for a sword if you have to name your sword to begin with.

See the force of name-giving in action. There's primal power, near magic, and ownership in the names...."You are mine, I own you, therefore I dub thee X." Ownership, attachment, affection, love — all these in the power of naming.

II. By Way of Jewish Introduction

Jews kept their Jewish names in Egypt.

That's one of the reasons they were redeemed from slavery, at least according to some of our Jewish sources.

Nowadays we joke about the assimilation of the Jews by looking at the names. We look in the wedding announcements for "Thor" or "Bubba" or something like "Faygie Sue" from some small town in Mississippi to see just how far modern North American Jews have gone to become a part of the outside world. And every time we come up with crazier names in our heads, someone comes up with a real-life example that goes even further. I read the recent award-winner in a newspaper announcement someone sent me. There were wishes for "lots of Nachas" to the grandmother, Helen Reingewirtz, on the birth of the grandddaughter Cheyayn LaToya Belatova, whose siblings are named Lucrezzia Harleigh, Dylan, Ashley, and Beaujon. (It's a good thing they weren't in Egypt millennia ago. They might still be there.)

We have all heard the family feud stories as the innocent parents decide on a name, and then both families begin to tear away at each other as they scream their dismay. "It's supposed to be for *my* mother, may she rest in peace." "No! The first one always goes to the *father's* side of the family. It's supposed to be 'Max' for Uncle Max, Aunt Zelda's Max."

A couple of years ago in my synagogue, they named a baby girl, and just as the name was announced, a grandfather got up and started shouting, "She's supposed to be named for *my* mother!" And while they didn't haul him away physically, he had to be restrained and soothed. They told him "We'll discuss it later".

But those are just aberrations. In the best of times and situations, the naming of names is really sublime.

III. "Eema"

I was in Jerusalem, sitting in the living room of one of my Mitzvah heroes, The Rabbanit Kapach. The Rabbanit is like a one-woman Mitzvah force (and much, more more) for hundreds of people, and I like to listen to her tell me stories. Even though I have known her for more than a dozen years, there isn't a time I go to her apartment when I don't hear something that opens up more glories of the human soul. Just when you think you have heard everything about Redemption from Human Misery, there is yet another story to carry you further.

This particular time, a woman about 50 years old was visiting, and she kept calling the Rabbanit "Eema" ("Mother"). The fact is that the Rabbanit is no more than 10 years older than this woman, and at first I couldn't imagine why she would refer to her as her mother. In retrospect, it makes sense, but initially, it was such a strange feeling for me to watch them relating to each other as mother and child. They interacted so naturally to each other that way, and then they told me why.

Years back, many years back, the woman was abandoned by her husband. She was left with many small children, and essentially nothing else. Then the Rabbanit heard about her desperate situation, stepped in, restored her well-being and dignity, and got her back on the road to recovery, by pure dint of human kindness and her vast network of like-minded Mitzvah people pitching in.

Since then, the woman has been blessed with many grandchildren. The Rabbanit — naturally enough — helped marry off all the children, and, though I haven't met the offspring, I am sure they refer to her with family honorifics. She is "Savta" ("Grandmother") to them, I am sure.

It was one of the most awesome stories I had heard, though I have heard many, *many* stories when I am with the Rabbanit.

"Eema."

Now it all makes sense.

It's the most natural thing in the world.

IV. Pharaoh's Daughter

We Jews are here today as a result of so many narrow escapes. If we go back through history we will see miracles and natural events mixing one with the other so many times that we would be hard pressed to differentiate between the normal and the out-of-the-ordinary.

Striking — in light of The Rabbanit's daughter — is the story of Pharaoh's daughter and the infant Moses.

Pharaoh decrees a death penalty on Jewish males.

Yocheved, Moses's mother, hides the baby as long as she can, then floats the infant down the Nile in a flimsy infant-sized boat.

Pharaoh's daughter, accompanied by her servants, is bathing in the Nile when she sees the boat among the reeds in the distance.

Then the story begins to unfold.

According to the text, Pharaoh's daughter sends her servant to bring the baby to her; and even though she recognizes it as a Jewish baby, she takes it in and raises it as her own, calling him "Moshe", playing on the word "Mashah", "to draw out of the water". Moses then grows up in Pharaoh's household, and we know the rest of the story, we, the beneficiaries of this woman's courage and kindness. We owe our lives to her, because the boat could have most certainly floated further down the Nile, gotten lost in the reeds, and the infant would have eventually died of exposure and starvation.

Our Jewish tradition fills in more details:

1. Pharaoh's daughter had been stricken with some horrible disease, and she was really bathing in the Nile as some sort of cure. And, indeed, her disease was miraculously cured — because she saved the baby. (Midrash Mishlay 31)

2. 7 human beings (other texts read "9" or "11") did not have to suffer the pain of death....they entered Paradise alive. Pharaoh's daughter was one of them — because she saved the infant Moses from certain death. (Kallah Rabbati 3)

3. Though Moses had ten different names, the one he was known by, and the one God used — and that all of us use centuries later — was "Moshe", the name Pharaoh's daughter gave him — because she saved his life. (Leviticus Rabbah 1:3) For all of human history, that would be his realest-of-real names. That was yet another reward for her act, though she sought no cures, nor immortality, nor Biblical fame. A life needed to be saved, and she saved that life. Pure and simple. What more could a human being wish for in life than to know that he or she has saved a human life?

And yet there is one more Jewish tale, the most marvellous of all, I believe, that enlarges on this critical moment in Jewish history.

The Talmud and Midrash mention it; the Targum (the ancient Aramaic translation of the Torah) mentions it, and Rashi mentions it:

The Book of Exodus says, "VaTishlach Et Amata Vatikacheha — She sent her servant, who brought the little boat to her." "Amata" means "her servant". But something bothered the Jewish interpreters. Something didn't make sense — how could Pharaoh's daughter send someone else to do the Mitzvah? *Why* would she want someone else to do it for her? Mitzvahs should really be done personally wherever and whenever possible, not through another person. Second-hand Mitzvahs aren't as solid as first-hand Mitzvahs.

So they reinterpret "Amata", taking another meaning of the word. To them it meant "her hand", and they understood, instead, that "She stretched out her own hand and brought in the boat." *That* interpretation in and of itself is bold and astounding enough. Our teachers are teaching us, "Jews! Don't miss the opportunity to *personally* perform the Mitzvahs. The full impact never comes through a Shaliach, an agent. You have to do it yourself."

There is still one more step in this long, wonderful story of Pharaoh's daughter. One of the greatest Chassidic Rebbis, Menachem Mendel of Kotzk (1787-1859), found one more element of note. He said, "The boat was much farther from her than she could have ever possibly reached with her own arm. [According to some Midrashim, it was almost a hundred feet away when she saw it.] But a miracle happened and her arm became longer, far enough to reach the boat." The Kotzker continues, "But look — when she stretched out her hand, she didn't originally know a miracle would happen. What could have possibly entered her mind to make her stretch out her arm to a place so far away she couldn't possibly reach it?" And here is the real, the ultimate human lesson. "But this is the way of people who do good: whether or not they can do it, they always get so enthused about doing whatever good needs to be done, they don't sit around trying to figure out whether or not they can really succeed. The reward [for this kind of thinking-and-action] is that miracles happen, and these people achieve even that which is normally considered impossible."

So it is with the heroes of the earthquakes and hurricanes and shipwrecks and the man who plunged into the freezing Potomac to save someone from a plane crash.

So it is with the Rabbanit and her "daughter" and the "daughter's" children and grandchildren.

So it is with all those whose hearts and hands are set on doing Mitzvahs not only once or twice in a lifetime, but every day, at all hours of the day and night. Because they are so naive and don't really know that something is impossible, they do the impossible.

Were it not for Pharaoh's daughter — that upper-of-upper-class young woman going for a medicinal bath in the Nile — were it not for this woman, none of us would be here as Jews today to contemplate and imitate her impossible deed. We would still be in Egypt, slaves to her descendants, the new Pharaohs of every generation.

The Babies and the Cribs

I. The Babies

The count is now more than 1,500.

That's the number of babies with Down Syndrome that 1 woman, Janet Marchese (pronounced Mar-Kay-Zee) of White Plains, NY, was helped place in adoptive homes.

She claims — and she has no reason to lie or even exaggerate the statistics — that about 85% of them are Jewish, which means about 1,250 babies. Some of them are much bigger children now, since Janet has been doing this for 13 years.

Her problem is that, though nearly all the birth parents would like to have the child grow up Jewish, Janet cannot find Jewish homes. She has only been able to find 7 Jewish homes thus far.

This is how Janet works (it is very simple): she gets calls all the time from people who would like to adopt infants with special needs, and, on the other side, she gets calls all the time from birth parents who — for whatever reason — cannot keep their infant with Down Syndrome. All Janet does, through her Down Syndrome Adoption Exchange, is link up families to families. The sets of parents and adoption agencies then do the rest.

Janet also counsels parents who have given birth to the children. Of course. She speaks to doctors, nurses, social workers, other hospital staff people about Down Syndrome, of course. But the actual transfer of babies is as simple as I have described.

That averages out to about 1 baby every 3 days and 4 hours that Janet has worked with ([13 X 365.25] divided by 1,500 = 3.17 days).

Janet is an amazing woman. She's been interviewed by Dan Rather for CBS Evening News. She's been recognized in this particular world of special adoptions by a number of groups. She is a dynamo, she is unpaid for this work, and she is uniquely fine.

But this isn't about Janet Marchese.

I write this article because the response to other publicity about her in the Jewish community has not drawn sufficient attention, and I would hope that, with yet another attempt to raise the issue, the Jewish community and its leaders would begin to move on this matter.

To date, the few speaking engagements she has received within the Jewish community have been essentially in religious schools — hardly the hotbed of the movers-and-shakers in the community. And last year Detroit's JARC[1] honored her at their annual dinner. *That* was a breakthrough, but not so surprising, since JARC is in the forefront of working with Jews with special needs.

---

[1]Formerly the Jewish Association for Retarded Citizens, now simply called JARC.

So here is the problem: how do we get our Jewish communities to publicize this matter and to help find Jewish families who would want to adopt babies with Down Syndrome?

The issue is *not* only whether or not all Jewish parents want their children to grow up to be Harvard or Yale graduates. Janet makes no judgments, has no profound, eye-opening explanations for this phenomenon.

The issue is *not* that Jewish women give birth nowadays later in life than other groups. A sizable proportion of the babies she works with have mothers in their 20's.

The issue is *not* that, because she is in the New York area, naturally enough she gets so many Jewish babies. Her network covers the entire United States.

And the issue is *not* that Jews give birth to a higher percentage of Down Syndrome babies than other groups. Statistics just don't support that contention.

Statistics *do* indicate, however, that, until the Jewish community responds, every 4 or 5 days, on average, another Jewish child will be placed for adoption in a non-Jewish household.

Janet recently spoke at the Conference for Alternatives in Jewish Education (CAJE) conference in Seattle, where her presentation and her sense of presence were stunning.

Now she should be invited to speak at: Jewish Family Services, the Federations, synagogues, Jewish Community Centers, Hadassah and Sisterhood groups, National Council of Jewish Women groups, Na'amat groups — in short, any and every group that might possibly be able to change this trend and these statistics.

Call Janet: 914-428-1236.

(One wonders whether there might not be more of an outcry if headlines in Jewish newspapers would read, "1,250 Babies With an IQ of 100 and Above Are Being Raised as Non-Jews.")

II. Update on Janet Marchese's Babies

I asked friends in different cities to try to get this article or any other article on Janet and the babies into their local Jewish newspapers. Some seem to be succeeding, though there was a recent, and hopefully temporary, setback. In 1 community with more than 5,000 Jews — which 1 in particular is not important — the editor rejected it, saying the issue was not applicable for their community. My contact told me she personally knew 1 family who gave birth to a child with Down Syndrome that is raising the child at home, and another family who also gave birth to a child with Down Syndrome who gave it up for adoption, though most likely the process took place through someone else other than Janet.

Those 2 family situations alone would make it important to print the story locally, but, to repeat my purpose in writing this article: we simply want to find those Jewish families that *do* want to adopt[1a] the Jewish children Janet has found. The only way to find out if these families really exist in the Jewish community is to get out as much publicity as possible, and to bring Janet into town to speak on the subject.

Let us hope for better results in the near future.

III. The Cribs

A certain Jeannie Jaybush from Seattle spoke on the same panel as Janet at the CAJE conference. She is involved in St. Joseph's Infant Corner, a project of her Catholic church, and the project is concerned with babies.

Statistics indicate that in 1987 there were 2,000 homeless children and infants under the age of 5 in Seattle, a city recently voted in some polls as 1 of the 10 most desirable cities to live in in the United States. Some other survey even listed Seattle as #1.

In December, 1988, St. Joseph's put a baby crib in their church as a collection point for diapers, bottles, nipples, baby formula, and just about anything else babies might need. Diapers, bottles, nipples — any non-food items — are not covered by food stamps.

The audience at CAJE was shocked by the statistics, and also very much taken by the idea of the crib-in-the-house-of-God.

Now, since there are many synagogue families that still have cribs in their closets, long after their children have outgrown them, it would be relatively easy to get a crib donated.

And since it is relatively easy to call local shelters and soup kitchens to get a more detailed list of specific items they need immediately for infants and very young children, the project could be rolling relatively quickly.

A good place, a logical place, to put the crib is in the synagogue lobby, next to the food barrel.

Diapers. That's what threw the audience when Jeannie spoke to us. These items are so much taken for granted by parents who can afford them. Jeannie told horror stories about babies and diapers. We could eliminate the need for those horror stories.

[1a]One of the questions in a rudimentary survey I am taking (mentioned in another chapter in this book) is whether or not the respondent knows someone in the local Jewish community who might want to adopt a Jewish child with special needs. I noticed recently that one of the respondents had checked "yes". Now, in its final form, the survey will be totally anonymous, but I knew which person had sent me this particular completed form, and I wrote him a letter in reply. I said that — if it were appropriate — he ought to give that family a flyer for Janet's Down Syndrome Adoption Exchange and a word of encouragement to get in touch with her. Another questionnaire also check the Yes column, and the respondent indicated he or she knew 5 families he thought might be interested in adopting a child with special needs...but I don't know who gave that answer.

Janet, T.J. and Louis Marchese

The MITZVAH CRIB, located at Temple Sinai in Sharon, Massachusetts. (Photo by Tom Temin, Walpole MA)

I am pleased to report that the crib project has been enthusiastically received. To give just 3 recent examples: some of the students of the Temple Beth Ami religious school in Rockville, MD, held a most successful "Baby Shower", the Leo Baeck Day School in Toronto accumulated more than 1,000 diapers in a couple of months, and Temple Sinai of Sharon, MA, moved on the Mitzvah idea immediately. Friday night I suggested the project, and by Sunday morning a fine crib was already in the lobby with an appropriate sign explaining the project. At the breakfast we gathered over $100.00 for the first round of diaper purchases. Now that I think of it, I don't recall any place that didn't respond with enthusiasm once they heard of the need. And Jeannie tells me she gets calls from all over to learn details about how to get started.

Call her, Jeannie Jaybush, in Seattle: 206-938-2364.

She expects your calls.

Before I finished revising this article, I thought I would give her 1 last call myself. I wanted to review a couple of articles I had seen about St. Joseph's project. She filled me in on 2 items in particular:

1. About 6 months after the project began, an 18-wheeler truck pulled up to the parking lot of St. Joseph's. The rather large driver — Jeannie is a little short, so I can't vouch for how big he was in Real Life — said he had some diapers to deliver, but he wanted to be sure this was the right place. It was, indeed, the right place, and the man proceeded to unload 75 huge crates of diapers, or, as they estimated, about 11,000 diapers in all. They never found out who made the donation, and no one ever asked for a tax receipt. (It gives new, glorious meaning to the word "anonymous".)

2. As Jeannie put it, "The only money is in garbage." Through concerted lobbying efforts, they have convinced Seattle's King County to channel nearly $100,000 for free diaper service for people who cannot afford it. This money will provide a full subsidy for about 200 families for 6 months. The convincing part of the argument was how much the county would save on landfill costs, beside the other benefits of cutting down on pollution and other potential hazards that might be associated with disposable diapers.

If you want to take on something more than just a crib in the synagogue, call Jeannie: 206-938-2364.

She expects your calls.

IV. In Conclusion

All that needs to be done is to do it.

The Crib Project is relatively simple. Janet's and her babies' needs are more complex, but the problem is clearly-defined, finite, and ultimately manageable.

All that needs to be done is to do it.

Li'at in the Park

I. Shabbas in Jerusalem

Shabbas in Jerusalem, Summertime.
Saturday morning, an early morning walk before going to a synagogue.
It is so quiet.
After synagogue, a lunch with friends, a nap, and another walk.

Jerusalem is quiet, and people are strolling. Hundreds, perhaps thousands of them, are out for their *Shabbas Shpatzier,* the walk which is like no other walk, because you are free, because you are in a Shabbas mood, because it is Summertime and the sun is out and the day is cooling down. And because you will always run into someone you know, either people you didn't get to during the week because you were too busy, or someone you hadn't seen in 15 or 20 years who isn't out looking for you either, but both of you expect to bump into *someone* from 15 or 20 years ago.

It is prime time for Revelation. It *is* Jerusalem, after all, and it *is* Shabbas. I would suspect that a higher percentage of sublime encounters in the lives of Jews take place on Shabbas afternoons in Jerusalem than anywhere else at any other time, but I don't know that for sure. I only know that the odds change radically. And the radical odds stay the same whether you are walking somewhere-in-particular or just leaving your apartment and wandering to nowhere-in-specific. In both situations, something is going to happen. The odds are always in your favor.

The pattern is easy to detect. Just review the computer print-outs of tours to Israel. See how many 8-day, 9-day, and 10-day tours include 2 Shabbases in Jerusalem. Any smart tour operator knows that it's good business: 2 Shabbases, more inspiration and Revelations, more joy in the memories, more cravings to return, more business. Simple.

Shabbas afternoon in Jerusalem. Summertime. Someone has overfed you, and, despite the nap, it takes a while to hit your stride. Waking up, *really* waking up may take 10 minutes or a half hour, but the after-nap haze is a pleasant haze. I believe it sets the tone and prepares the soul for Revelation.

II. A Certain Shabbas in Jerusalem

There is a park down in the German Colony, near the building called Bet Elisheva. It's not a particularly beautiful park, but there are benches to sit on, and things to climb on for little and middle-sized kids, so people are always there, chatting with each other, enjoying the kids at play.

On 1 particular Shabbas afternoon I happened to *Shpatzier* down that way. Well, "happened" isn't really the appropriate term. These things just don't "happen". Let's just say instead that I got there, as I was supposed to get there for whatever reason, though I had made no arrangements to meet anyone in that particular park on that particular summer Shabbas afternoon.

As I sat on the bench, pulling out of my nap, I noticed 1 of the kids climbing on the climbing-thing. (It's actually a bunch of painted-over old tires and made into a kind of sculpture-for-climbing.) Her name was Li'at, which means "You are mine." A lovely name. I knew her name right away because it was written on the back of her T-shirt.

A lovely name.

She climbed up and down and around and up and down again as kids do, and she was having a fine time of it, as kids do. On a nearby bench were 2 women who obviously knew Li'at, 1 of them probably her mother.

In her climbing and turning and jumping, she would occasionally turn my way, and I could see from her face that she had Down Syndrome. She wasn't fat, her tongue didn't hang out, her eyes didn't roll, but her features gave a hint of an extra chromosome in her genes. OK, so she had Down Syndrome, and it was Shabbas afternoon in Jerusalem, and she was climbing up and down and around a climbing-thing, enjoying herself immensely, as kids do.

Other kids were playing, too, and other adults were passing by or strolling through the park, and I stopped focussing on Li'at's climbing. I noticed some stares, though I am not sure Li'at noticed them. She was busy, after all, climbing and having fun. But then, 1 of the other kids, maybe 6 or 7 years old, noticed Li'at, ran down the climbing-thing and over to the other climbing-thing nearby and explained rather excitedly to his little sister not to be afraid.

He said, "She won't hurt you."

But he said it afraid. He said it with warning in his voice and a hint of "Stay away from her." He had that tone in his voice that indicated that Something Different was around. Indeed, when Li'at started climbing near them, they moved away, though I cannot recall now whether or not they left the park completely or whether or not the parents took them away to a "safer distance".

It was and it wasn't a surprise to me. I wasn't surprised because I had heard about this kind of thing, read about it, seen it in movies and made-for-TV movies. But I was taken aback because I was seeing it with my own eyes.

I went over to the 2 women on the bench. They were in their late 50's or early 60's, and I could tell they were religious people since they wore long dresses, long sleeves, and *shaytelach*, the wigs some Orthodox women wear. I introduced myself, and we began to talk about Li'at, and Li'at's mother told me they had found out about her from someone when she was an infant, an infant all alone, and they adopted her. She spoke with such deep passion and love and warmth and naturalness, I knew a Revelation was happening. Li'at's mother was a survivor, and I recognized her accent, Hungarian most likely.

She had other children she had given birth to.

But some child, who happened to be slower than others, had no home, so she and her husband took her in and she became their daughter. I think she told me that Li'at was 14 or 15 (though she looked a little younger).

Now this woman and her husband were growing older and couldn't give Li'at quite as much as they could when she was younger. So Li'at is living in a setting something like a group home. I knew the place she spoke about, a fine place near Tel Aviv, and Li'at was home for the week-end, and this was Shabbas afternoon in Jerusalem and time for a walk and a chance to play in the park.

We talked about the stares, about kids keeping their distance, the other moments of lack of understanding Li'at has encountered, but Li'at's mother assured me that her daughter could manage. (She was managing very well that Shabbas afternoon.)

And then it was time to go. I wanted to spend more time with them some other time, but I have such a bad memory for figures, I knew that I would forget their phone number if I tried to remember it all the way up to the time when 3 stars would come out.

We said good-bye. Before I left, Li'at had come over for a while, and her mother had put her arm around her so she could put her head on her mother's shoulder. It was a lovely mother-and-daughter scene, but I had to go, and we had to say good-bye.

I came back the following Shabbas, hoping just maybe they would be there again, but they weren't. Next summer I will try again.

III. The Daydream

I am taking a Shabbas walk in Jerusalem. It is Summertime and the late afternoon becomes cooler from around 4:30 on.

I leave my apartment with no-place-in-particular to get to and wind up somehow in a small park in the German Colony, near Beit Elisheva. There are painted tires arranged in a kind of climbing-sculpture and kids are playing on it, climbing up and down and all around.

I see that 1 of the kids is wearing a T-shirt that says "Li'at" on it, and she and the other kids are racing up and down the climbing-thing together, laughing.

Mitzvah-Power-Hungriness
Or
How To Save Lives Regularly
Without Being in the Medical Profession

I. My Abba

This July my Abba began his 49th year of medical practice in Northern Virginia.

I am biased, I suppose, both ways: (a) of course, he is The Greatest Physician in the Whole Wide World, the Osteopathic Physician *Par Excellence* and (b) well, since by nature children are supposed to be at least somewhat rebellious, I am supposed to say, "Maybe he's not really "*The* Greatest Physician in the Whole Wide World."

At the ripening age of 45, I can see that statement (a) is *definitely* true. The proof is simple: last June, a few days before heading for Israel for my summer work with the United Synagogue Youth Israel Pilgrimage, I threw my back out of joint. It happens. As usual, Dad fixed my back, but since I had irritated the muscles and nerves, he also had to give me some anti-inflammatory pills.

Now here's the bad part: I was still in pain a few days after he cracked my back into place. He said, "Don't worry, it takes 10 days for the medications to relieve all the pain."

I left for Israel, doubting. I was cranky off and on, aching off and on, in real-live pain off and on, even borrowing a cane from a friend my first Shabbat in Jerusalem.

And I was angry, angry because my Abba had let me down. And I was disappointed that he — after all these years as a doctor — just didn't seem to know what he was doing.

And then, on the 11th day, the Heavens opened up (as they are wont to do in Jerusalem), I arose from my sickbed, threw away my cane, stretched my body full length and walked like a normal, pain-free human being. I was cured, as if by a miracle. And I was, once again, a new man, and, just as important, a no-longer-doubting son. As it was when I was a child and he would cure me by his touch and an assortment of comic books, my Abba was again at once The Healer, Magician, and Miracle Worker...in short, The Greatest Physician in the Whole Wide World.

II. The Jealous Son Who Never Went to Medical School

Of late, I have become jealous of my Abba. I want to have that awesome power that he has, but I am neither licensed to do so, nor patient enough to start The Long Grind of medical training. Long after he forgave me for not being a doctor, I once went to his alma mater, the Philadelphia College of Osteopathic

Medicine, to see what it would take to be a doctor, "Just Like Him". It was too much to do. I was 30 or so, and I just couldn't see myself doing The Long Grind, particularly since I would need a couple of years learning the basic sciences I had never learned in high school and college.

But the jealousy remained...a positive, motivating jealousy. Here was a man who could not only relieve pain, but also, —by his own daily practice and by his referrals to specialists — was responsible for saving hundreds of individual lives over nearly half a century of practice.

I could see this jealousy pop up in my lectures. I would ask my audiences, "Who has saved someone's life?" Hands would go up....CPR, the Heimlich Maneuver, pulling a drowning person from a swimming pool or the ocean just in time.

I had never done any of those things.

I *wanted* to do some of those mighty, heroic acts, but I had just never done anything like it.

And all the time, a certain phrase from the Book of Proverbs (10:2) — "Tzedakah saves from death" — kept playing in the back of my mind.

III. Saving Lives Without Being in the Medical Profession

It is important to establish the fact that it is good for people to want to save other people's lives. I would state it as an axiom, no proofs or anything like that: *It is good for human beings to want to save other people's lives.* It (a) first and foremost, saves a life, (b) feels good for the lifesaver, and (c) is addictive. Saving one life generates a strong urge to want to save at least one more, and then one more, and then another. It makes the lifesaver Mitzvah-power-hungry.

The ways to do it are as numerous as the sands on the seashore or the stars in the heavens. As to the magnitude of it all, in the world of Mitzvahs, this is the Big Time. Someone who might have died, did not, and *you* have been a partner in that incredible flow of events. In the range of human emotions, this particular phenomenon is in a class by itself, different from closing a good deal (though that is important), different from winning a scholastic award (though that is important), different than making the last payment on a mortgage (though that, too, is important and most joyous). And for people who suffer from low self image — what could be a better way to build that image than to save someone's life?

Still, in all, the single most important element of this concept is that a life is saved.

All other benefits are secondary, though I don't think anyone would mind if someone goes into the lifesaving field for the "wrong reasons" of feeling good and building or re-building self-image.

A life is saved.

What could be better than that?

IV. One Way To Do It

Crib death is a horror. I no longer ask my audiences how many of them know a family that has lost a child to crib death. (I prefer that term over SIDS (=Sudden Infant Death Syndrome), which, by dint of euphemism and lengthening of the term covers over the horror. A baby stops breathing in its crib....why, exactly, nobody knows for certain. The parents discover the baby's lifeless body too late. Tragedy so enormous, we cannot find words to comfort the parents.

The medical profession calls this phenomenon "apnea", which means "no breath". Now there are monitors, apnea monitors, which let fly wildly with alarms and lights when the infant stops breathing. The monitor wakes the parents, and the baby. And now there are more sensitive, sophisticated monitors called "cardiac apnea monitors" which pick up on more delicate-to-discover complications. In either case, the family uses the machine until the baby is old enough to be judged out of danger.[1]

Now, in Israel there is this organization called Yad Sarah. They lend medical supplies for free to people who need them. Yad Sarah has won all the Mitzvah awards you can get, plus awards for Unifying the Jewish People and for efficient business operations. They have the highest reputation, and they save lives every day, in addition to "lesser" (if you can use such a term) Mitzvahs of bringing relief from pain for all those people who borrow wheelchairs, oxygen machines, crutches and walkers, vaporizers, whatever....all for free.

Yad Sarah is scattered throughout the country, with more than 3,000 volunteers at more than 60 lending stations, and only a minimal paid staff. *Everyone* in Israel knows Yad Sarah and almost everyone has a Yad Sarah story to tell about themselves using the equipment or their uncle or their son or some friend.

Yad Sarah needs monitors. Over a 2-year period, my small Tzedakah fund purchased 120 apnea monitors. We'd send over about $550.00, Yad Sarah would put in some of their own, and they built up a (not sufficient) supply. Then they felt that the *cardiac* apnea monitors were needed. My friends kept sending money (these were $2,700.00 apiece), and the Fund bought 14 last year, and another 10 thus far this year. We want to buy a total of 15 of them this year.

So here's the proposal: do it yourself or get a group of friends together. Get $2,700.00 and send it to Mr. Charles Bendheim at American Friends of Yad

---

[1]To be honest, there is some controversy in the medical profession: Some experts swear by these monitors, and others aren't so sure they are as effective as the pro-monitor people contend. There is healthy disagreement, and no absolute unanimity of opinion, though those who believe in the monitors have good statistics to prove their point. So for now, monitors appear to be a good answer until some cure for SIDS is found. It is like the Talmudic phrase, "Kulay Hai Ve'Ulye? — Going to all of this trouble, and it is still a case of 'Maybe?'" My unmedical opinion, after a few years of experience with members of Israel's medical teams is that — in a life-and-death situation — the Maybe should be given the benefit of the doubt: monitors should be provided on the decent chance that they will save lives, 2 or 3 or a dozen, 20. And none of the experts disputes that *some* lives have been saved by the monitors.

Sarah, One Parker Plaza, Ft. Lee, NJ 07024, 201-944-6020.[1a] The odds are it will save a baby's life, some person you'll never meet, who will have a long, healthy life because someone or some group from far away decided to be Mitzvah-power-hungry.

Actually, it's more than one life. When the baby that uses the monitor is out of danger, the family brings the monitor back, and it is lent to another family. And the cycle continues.

And it's a cheap price for a life — even for a strong *maybe* life. Kidney transplants, lung transplants, heart transplants, brain tumor surgery are all way up there in the $75,000-$150,000 range. This is a bargain, a small investment with unmeasurable returns.

Is there a need for more monitors in Israel? Yes, for sure. In fact, not until this summer did I actually see one of the cardiac apnea monitors. Just by chance I was at Yad Sarah one day when one had been returned, and was due to be lent out later in the day. As soon as the monitors come in, people on the waiting list are there to get one for their own baby. It is a wondrous little machine, maybe two feet by fifteen inches by eight inches, and with an alarm that would even wake up my friend Mark Stadler who sets 8 alarm clocks before he goes to bed. I know: I accidentally pressed the wrong button when I was examining it, and it went off full blast right while I was standing there red-faced.

It is *very* impressive, truly a miracle of modern medical technology.

V. Not A Time For Bragging

I *am* bragging about my father. I have no qualms about that. If any of my readers want to go into the medical professions as a result of the exalted nature of this Mitzvah of saving lives, Gezunterhayt — well, fine, and good.

But I'm *not* bragging about the part I've played in the purchase of monitors. The fact that my friends give me money to give away (some $725,000 in 15 years) that eventually winds up saving lives is a wonder in and of itself. I am only telling the story to encourage others to feel the same as I do when I get the chance to write a check for $2,700.00, knowing it may very well save a few babies' lives. Even when I am having a "bad day", when it is all diddly work (car needs repairs, Macintosh refuses to work right, laundry lies in a heap undone, plane reservations screwed up, phone machine swallows messages), the day itself is redeemed by this simple act. The other things to do are just that — diddly, insignificant, necessary but of little meaning in The Real World.

[1a] To see the *real* Yad Sarah, just go to 43 HaNevi'im St. in Jerusalem, one block off the main drag (Jaffa Road). Call a few days ahead (244-047) and try to set up a meeting with Uri Lupoliansky, the founder. If you can spare a few hours, have them arrange a Grand Tour of some of their different facilities. It is well worth it.

Here is an opportunity for anyone to step outside of the World of the Diddly, into something more gutsy, more vigorous and invigorating, something to whet the Mitzvah appetite for still more grand and glorious acts.

Everyone is invited.

And if you can't manage to fund a fancy monitor, ask Yad Sarah to name a less expensive item that they might need. I am sure they will be able to name more than a few.

All you need to do is to do it.

An Informal Survey

I. Introduction

In my talks and articles, I toss around a lot of statistics.

Some of them are crowned with authority because they are based on sophisticated studies by the experts.

Other numbers are things I intuit from asking around when I am doing my lectures. These "other numbers" I preface by saying, "Now, I'm not a sociologist or statistician or demographer, but I get the sense that...."

Someday, I want to do a poll of Rabbis' Discretionary funds, to find out how much money they have available for front-line Mitzvahs, how they accumulate the money, how much is in sums of $18, $25, and how much in larger sums, and what the rabbis' choices are for using the Tzedakah money.

Someday, I want to take a poll of kids and adults in sample communities, to find out their perceptions of the local Jewish old age homes, and more specifically, how each rates the Happiness Quotient of the residents. I hear many different opinions between the kids and the adults, kids saying it's not a good place, adults saying it is a fine place. I'd want to see what the statistics would show.

And someday, I'd want to get a statistical sense of exactly what subjects come up most frequently when the question is asked, "What topic did you not learn enough about in religious school would you most really want to learn about now?" It would help us set our curricular for adult education courses.

The following is my 1st attempt at gathering some small quantity of data. The subject is "How much do some Jews know about other Jews in their home community?"

II. The Questionnaire

The following is a brief questionnaire about needs in your local Jewish community. The questions are listed in no particular order of importance.

Please fill out the questionnaire as honestly as you can, but do not sign it. Take your time. I have left a space at the end of the questionnaire to allow for your personal reactions to my questions and to your own answers. Please feel free to be candid in your comments.

This is my 1st attempt at gathering some statistics on Jewish communal needs, so please forgive the crude format and inexact formulation of the questions.

The results may be used some time in the future for articles that may lead to practical changes in the Jewish community.

I thank you for your time and thoughtfulness in filling this out.

Yes   No

____ ____   1. Do you know anyone in the Jewish community
      who is an alcoholic?
      If so, how many? ____
      Approximate age? ____

____ ____   2. Do you know anyone in the Jewish community
      who is a drug abuser?
      If so, how many? ____
      Approximate age? ____

____ ____   3. Does your Jewish community have a program for
      substance abusers (similar to AA)?

____ ____   4. Do you know any Jews in your community
      who are poor? (Your own definition of "poor" is sufficient.)
      If so, how many? ____
      Approximate age? ____

____ ____   5. Do you know any unemployed Jews?
      If so, how many? ____
      Approximate age? ____

____ ____   6. Do you know any Jews who use food stamps?
      If so, how many? ____
      Approximate age? ____

____ ____   7. Do you know any Jews who are one mortgage payment away
      from losing his or her house?
      If so, how many? ____
      Approximate age? ____

____ ____   8. Do you know any Jews who could not afford
      to buy a respectable Passover meal?
      If so, how many? ____
      Approximate age? ____

____ ____   9. Is there a food barrel in your synagogue's lobby
      for collection of food for hungry Jews and non-Jews?

___   ___   10. Do you know any deaf Jews in your community?
                  If so, how many? ___
                  Approximate age? ___

___   ___   11. Have you ever been to a Jewish community program
                  where someone interpreted for the deaf?
                  If so, how many times? ___
                  What was the occasion? _____

___   ___   12. Are there any Jewish children in your religious schools
                  who are in wheelchairs?
                  If so, how many? ___

___   ___   13. Do you know anyone in the Jewish community
                  who might be interested in adopting a child
                  with special needs?
                  If so, how many? ___
                  If so, which Jewish agency would be be most helpful
                  in handling the process? _____

___   ___   14. Do you know anyone who would attend more Jewish programs
                  if someone would provide them with a ride?
                  If so, how many? ___
                  Approximate age? ___

___   ___   15. Do you know any Jewish battered spouses?
                  If so, how many? ___
                  Wife? ___   Husband? ___
                  Approximate age? ___

___   ___   16. Do you know of any Jews from your community who
                  are, or have been, institutionalized for mental illness
                  (either locally or somewhere else)?
                  If so, how many? ___
                  Approximate age? ___

___   ___   17. Do you know of any Jewish children in your community
                  who are missing or runaways?
                  If so, how many? ___
                  Approximate age? ___

____ ____ 18. Do you know anyone in the Jewish community whom
you would consider a Tzaddik, a Righteous Person?
If so, how many? ____
Approximate age? ____

III. Correlation and Application of Results

It will take a while. Having just produced the form, I can't even begin to imagine the results. Once the forms are collected in sufficient numbers, though, I will pass them on to people who understand surveys better than I do.

At that point, the plan of action begins.

The Ziv Tzedakah Fund Annual Report
April 1, 1989

I.   TO THE FRIENDS OF ZIV, SHALOM!

Our work expands, our ability to respond to a variety of needs grows, new-comers continue to inquire about our work. This annual report summarizes the distribution of $141,000 (as compared to $122,951 the previous year) to individuals and projects we have carefully investigated and consider worthy. Each meets our standards: an actualization of Tzedakah as Doing the Right Thing, a personification of the sensitive, human touch, minimal (if any) bureaucracy, low operating overheard, and direct impact on the lives of individuals. "Ziv" means "radiance" and the Tzedakah work we fund embodies that quality. Contributions come from all ages and range from $1 to $22,500, with a continued and gratifying emphasis on small contributions — which is how Ziv began. We are pleased that we remain very grassroots oriented. It is my hope that many of you will explore any and all of these exceptional examples of Tzedakah work.

[*=people and projects previously funded by Ziv.]

II.   ZIV'S THREE SPECIAL PROJECTS: YAD LAKASHISH (LIFE LINE FOR THE OLD), HADASSAH LEVI'S MA'ON LATINOK, AND YAD SARAH ($74,450)

A. Yad LaKashish (Life Line for the Old) ($7,250)*
It is so sad to have to report the passing of Myriam Mendilow, founder and director of Life Line for the Old. Twenty-six years ago, when she was in her fifties, Mrs. Mendilow revolutionized the world of Jerusalem's Elders, opening a bookbindery. The Elders — many of whom begged on the streets, others who lived with a sense of uselessness and enormous loneliness — rebound (and continue to rebind) the schoolbooks of Jerusalem's children. Over the years, Life Line grew to more than a dozen workshops, meals on wheels, and a variety of other services, though essentially remaining a workplace for the Elders. Not a residence, but rather a place to work. Mrs. Mendilow's motto was, "To be is to do", and the Elders did just that — creating everything from wallhangings to the finest kinds of Tallit, jewelry, sweaters, etc., an astounding variety of products sold in their store ("The Elder Craftsman").

Life Line is a palace, a place where the elderly are the Royalty of our People, a Working Royalty, which is what they prefer. Over the years, thousands upon thousands of Israelis and foreigners have come through Life Line (including more than 6,500 United Synagogue Youth Israel Pilgrims from the U.S. and Canada) and have been understandably moved.

The late Myriam Mendilow, Founder and Chairman of Lifeline for the Old in Israel. (Photo by David Ottenstein, New Haven Ct)

Now the labor of actualizing Mrs. Mendilow's vision still further remains ours: to set up similar Life Lines wherever we may be. For example, the Jewish community of Ventnor, NJ, has established a bookbindery on the Life Line model, and a few other communities continue to explore ways of making real still more facets of Myriam Mendilow's Grand Dream.

This year, our contributions went for various pieces of equipment, e.g., fans to cool the workshops and a radio/tape player for the exercise classes.

Life Line products are available in the United States. Contact Helen Goren, 11 Ashford Rd., Newton, MA 02159, 617-965-0691.

[Life Line for the Old, 14 Shivtei Yisrael St., Jerusalem, 287-831 or 287-829. Contributions: American Friends of Life Line for the Old, c/o Florence Schiffman, Treasurer, 1500 Palisade Ave., Fort Lee, NJ 07024. For general information: Linda Kantor, President, American Friends, 203-795-4580. Information for organizing synagogue or group tours: Rabbi Ron Hoffberg, 201-276-9231.]

B. *Hadassah Levi's Ma'on LaTinok ($28,400)**

About a dozen years ago, Hadassah began to gather babies with Down Syndrome from the hospitals in Israel. They had been abandoned, and she took it upon herself to raise them. After a number of years in their own buildings around Tel Aviv, the children were transferred to a place called the Swedish Village in Jerusalem about two years ago. Hadassah's lease had expired. The Village was administered by the government, and the situation was not good, but during the past year, Jerusalem Elwyn Institutes (JEI) has taken over, and things have improved.

JEI operates a wide array of workshops and services for individuals with a range of mental and physical disabilities in Jerusalem, and the Ma'on children are now under their supervision. Hadassah retains her capacity as their "Primary Raiser", in addition to offering her insight and supervisory talents to other aspects of the Village. The transition to Elwyn sets us at ease, and the future for Hadassah and her kids is promising. We can be assured that the Ma'on children will not be "swallowed up" by the larger setting, but, to the contrary, will enjoy many new benefits. So many people from the U.S. and Canada have followed the odyssey of these children! So many have tied themselves intimately with their welfare! It is a sublime coming together of souls and resources, spanning years and great distances! Nothing less than wondrous.

We gave $27,000 to the Ma'on children, and $1,400 to Elwyn's other projects.

[Hadassah Levi, c/o Elwyn, POB 9090, 8 Grunwald St., Kiryat HaYovel, Jerusalem. Phone: 431-051, 052, or 053. Tax-deductible contributions: made out to "JEI". Send to JEI, c/o David Marcu, 111 Elwyn Rd., Elwyn, PA 19063. Please specify in the letter and on the check if your contribution is for Hadassah's kids. 215-891-2007. Consult David for all updates and specific funding needs.]

C. Yad Sarah ($38,800)*

Through a series of more than 50 lending stations throughout Israel, with over 3,000 volunteers (and only about 20 salaried staff), Yad Sarah lends medical supplies free of charge to those who might need the equipment. Founded about a dozen years ago by Uri Lupoliansky, the project has grown and grown, providing an incredible variety of supplies such as wheelchairs (electric as well as manual), crutches, walkers, glucometers, apnea monitors, and oxygen machines. They serve all segments of the population and represent the ability and power of Tzedakah work to cross all factional lines. Bring equipment when you go to visit!

We have purchased 14 sophisticated cardiac apnea monitors at $2,700 each which will hopefully help prevent Sudden Infant Death (SID's). We also contributed $1,000 towards the cost of shipping some equipment over that was contributed by someone in the U.S.

[Yad Sarah, c/o Uri Lupoliansky, 43 HaNevi'im St., Jerusalem, 244-047. Uri's home: 813-777. Tax-deductible contributions: American Friends of Yad Sarah, c/o Mr. Charles Bendheim, One Parker Plaza, Ft. Lee, NJ 07024, 201-944-6020.]

III. PROJECTS FOR INDIVIDUALS WITH DISABILITIES ($17,995)

A. Janet Marchese's Down Syndrome Adoption Exchange ($400)*

For the past 12 years, Janet Marchese has helped place nearly 1,400 infants with Down Syndrome with adopting families. She simply links families who wish to adopt with those who — for whatever reason (no judgments made by Janet) — cannot keep them. She receives no pay for this work, and we help fund her expenses. Amazing woman, amazing work!

[Janet Marchese, Down Syndrome Adoption Exchange, 56 Midchester Ave., White Plains, NY 10606, 914-428-1236.]

B. Computers for Disabled Children in Israel ($1,725)

Sheda Braunhut made Aliya a few years ago, and now designs hardware and software for children with various disabilities. Funding much of her work with her own money, we have assisted her in obtaining necessary equipment. Amazing woman, amazing work!

[Sheda Braunhut, Yerushalmi St. 6/10, Tel Aviv, 03-546-1989.]

C. Dogs for People in Wheelchairs and Hearing-Impaired People ($1,000)

Founded by Bonita Bergin in 1975, Canine Companions for Independence (CCI) has provided over 400 dogs for people with various disabilities (but not seeing-eye dogs). These canines understand nearly 90 commands and perform an awesome number of tasks. Three of the dogs are now in Israel. Cost for breeding, raising and training: $8,000/dog. Each person gets the companion dog for $125. Amazing people, amazing dogs, unbelievable Mitzvahs!

[CCI, 1215 Sebastopol Rd., Santa Rosa, CA 95407, ATTN: Katheryn Horton, 707-579-1985.]

D. ALYN Orthopaedic Hospital for Children ($3,750)*

A shining light for·children with long-term extreme orthopaedic needs, ALYN has maintained the highest reputation for love and care and training-for-independence. ALYN is often a home for years for the children, until they are old enough to move into society as active, participating young adults. Over the past few years, we have provided both equipment for the central facility, and also for individuals moving out into independent or semi-independent living situations. This year, among other things, we purchased an aquarium, much-loved by the kids (and staff). Amazing place, amazing kids, amazing atmosphere!

[ALYN, POB 9117, Corner Olsvenger and Shmaryahu Levin Sts., Kiryat HaYovel, Jerusalem, ATTN: Brenda Hirsch, phone 412-251. Contributions in the U.S.: ALYN, 19 W. 44th St., #1418, NY, NY 10036, 212-869-0369.]

E. Chazon F'taya ($6,750)*

Daily miracles occur in Jerusalem at Chazon...three floors of work-shops (including a full range of printing capabilities) for individuals with emotional and psychological disabilities. Because it is on a small side street, many do not visit. If you wish to see Tzedakah in all its glory and human dignity at its finest, look for Chazon F'taya. The name means "F'taya's Vision", the dream of the late Shaul F'taya, a vision of hope and uplift.

[Chazon F'taya, POB 6070, 6 Shimon Chacham St., Jerusalem, ATTN: Simcha Ovadia, 827-826.]

F. Yad Ezra Sewing Workshop — Jerusalem ($1,250)*

This Jerusalem project, one of a vast array of one Reb Osher Freund's Mitzvah endeavors, gives work to individuals with psychological dis-abilities in a loving, caring atmosphere. They produce gorgeous Challah and Matzah covers, dresses, and other items. From here, as from Chazon, they have a chance to return to society, refreshed, renewed. (4 Kineret St.)

[Yad Ezra (main office), 9-B HaRav Sorotzkin St., Jerusalem, ATTN: Shmuel Katz, 386-416.]

G. Small, Intimate Home for Children with Severe Disabilities ($1,270)

Bet Gil was founded by some parents whose children had suffered severe reaction to the DPT vaccine. Now there are a number of younger and older children there, disabled for any one of a number of reasons. I cannot begin to de-scribe the intense atmosphere, the caring, the love, the hard, long, and rewarding hours expended to develop the abilities of the children. A beautiful place, a haven for the children, a paradigm of devotion on the part of many people.

[Bet Gil, Emile Zola St. 15, Kiryat Aryeh, Petach Tikvah, ATTN: Israel Herzl, 03-923-2663.]

H. Series of Projects in Hawaii - Helemano Plantation ($200)

Right next to the Dole Pineapple Pavilion, 30 miles or so from Honolulu, a certain Susanna Cheung has established group homes, a restaurant, agricultural projects and other work and living projects for adults with supposedly limiting mental and physical disabilities. It was a most fortunate turn of events, stumbling on the Helemano Plantation. Meeting this woman, listening to her, you are forced to redefine your understanding of human potential. Just amazing!

[Opportunities for the Retarded, Inc., 64-1510 Kamehameha Hwy., Wahiawa, HI 96786, ATTN: Susanna Cheung, 808-622-3929.]

I. Congregation Bene Shalom, Synagogue for the Deaf ($100)

This synagogue in Skokie, IL, serves about 140 families. We had learned about Rabbi Douglas Goldhamer's work, sought him out, and had the chance to offer some funding.

[Bene Shalom, 4435 Oakton St., Skokie, IL 60076, ATTN: Rabbi Douglas Goldhamer, 312-677-3330.]

J. Creative Therapy for Children, Jerusalem ($300)

Misholim provides Expressive Therapy for 5 to 10 year old children, children with communications problems. Some have nerve or brain damage, some have no physical impairments but may have emotional difficulties, some are gifted. Misholim has the highest reputation in Jerusalem, and we are pleased we finally had a chance to manage some funding.

[Misholim, 53 HaPalmach St., Jerusalem, ATTN: Noa Eran, 699-765.]

K. The Work of Curt Arnson ($1,000)*

Curt Arnson is involved in many projects for individuals with developmental disabilities. Each year he points out a few more of these to Ziv, and each year, we are pleased to fund an additional aspect of the work. This year we again provided equipment for his programs.

[Curt Arnson, c/o AKIM-Jerusalem (not the same as the national AKIM organization, with whom we are not associated), 42 Azza St., Jerusalem, 631-728. Home: 416-277. Contributions: AKIM-Jerusalem.]

L. For Jewish Individuals in Pennsylvania Mental Institutions ($250)*

For years, the late Rabbi Leib Heber used to visit Jews in mental institutions in and around Pittsburgh, providing loving and warm Jewish experiences for those living there. His work is being carried on by a group of volunteers who want his marvellous work to continue.

[Western Pennsylvania Auxiliary for Exceptional People, 281 Sharon Dr., Pittsburgh, PA, 15221, ATTN: Rabbi Moshe Goldblum, 412-271-1578.]

IV.   INTEREST-FREE LOANS ($2,800)

A. Gomel L'Ish Chessed Interest-Free Loan Society, Jerusalem ($1,500)*
We continue to support the efforts of this fine, small group of people providing loans with no interest to people in need. We have been involved because of a friend and teacher, Dr. David Weiss, a prominent immunologist, who serves on the board of the free-loan fund.

[Gomel L'Ish Chessed, 56 Ben Maimon St., Jerusalem, ATTN: Dr. David Weiss, 669-363.]

B. Ziv extended two interest-free loans this year. ($1,300)
We also continue our membership in The Association of Hebrew Free Loans, an umbrella organization for this work. Contact Julius Blackman, 415-982-3177 for information.

V.   ETHIOPIAN JEWS ($1,700)

A. The Association of Ethiopian Immigrants ($400)*
A grassroots, front line group of Ethiopians in Israel working for the benefit of Ethiopians who have already arrived, and for those still trying to get to Israel. Fine work.

[Association of Ethiopian Immigrants, 23 Hillel St., Jerusalem, 248-722.]

B. North American Conference on Ethiopian Jewry (NACOEJ) ($1,300)*
Among NACOEJ's many projects (besides hard-working trips to Ethiopia) is an Adopt-A-Student project. Funds are provided to allow Ethiopians in Israel to stay in college or some other institution of learning that would help them integrate more fully into Israeli society. We helped fund this program, besides contributing to other NACOEJ work.

[NACOEJ, 165 E. 56th St., NY, NY 10022, ATTN: Barbara Ribakove Gordon, 212-752-6340.]

VI.   PROJECTS FOR ELDERLY PEOPLE ($7,600)
A. Project Ezra ($4,550)*
Working for a number of years with the elderly Jews of the Lower East Side of New York, Project Ezra exemplifies the best of Tzedakah. We funded holiday needs, purchase of computer equipment, and the all-important homemaker program which brings in help to take care of cleaning and personal needs of the elderly. Make a point of seeing this work if you are in NY.

[Project Ezra, 197 E. Broadway, NY, NY 10002, ATTN: Misha Avramoff, 212-982-3700.]

B. DOROT ($1,700)*

Working on a personal basis with elderly Jews on the Upper West Side of Manhattan, DOROT covers a broad span of programs: regular visits by volunteers, holiday programs, food deliveries, and their Homelessness Prevention Program (HPP) — a transitional shelter for homeless Jews. (Homeless Jews?!) These are people who "fall through the cracks". Of 52 people who came to HPP last year, 32 were successfully relocated into more permanent housing.

We provided for holiday needs, and $1,100 went towards equipment for HPP.

[Dorot: 262 W. 91st St., NY, NY 10024, ATTN: Judy Ribnick, 212-769-2850. HPP: 316 W. 59th St., NY, NY 10025, ATTN: Sarah Peller, 212-666-2000.]

C. Work with Chronically Disabled Elderly People ($1,000)

Because of his insistence on remaining low-key, I will only mention that Dr. Martin Kieselstein's work with chronically ill and frail individuals covers many areas that directly benefit them and enrich the quality of their lives considerably.

[HaAguda LeEzra Ve'Iddud VeShikum Keshishim VeCholim Birushalayim, POB 7843, Ibn Ezra St. 24 Jerusalem, ATTN: Dr. Martin Kieselstein, 633-805.]

D. Watchdogging, Gadflying, Ombudspersoning — Shishim Plus ($350)

Shishim Plus (=Sixty+) is a recently-founded group of older people in Israel keeping an eye on the government, making certain that it delivers its promised benefits to elderly people. They lobby on housing, health insurance issues, and services, as well as acting as intermediaries for individuals who have justifiable claims. We purchased a phone answering machine for their just-opened office.

[Shishim Plus, POB 71061, 1 Diskin St., Jerusalem, 690-747, ATTN: Ya'acov Kurtzman.]

VII. PROJECTS CARRIED OUT BY SPECIALLY-APPOINTED AGENTS ($1,430)

During the course of any year, Ziv needs to call upon certain individuals to carry out what are, by their very nature, a number of quiet projects. We undertook six such projects this year, each one managed with dignity and the requisite anonymity. Si Levine, for years a most reliable Mitzvah-messenger in Israel, has asked us to relieve him of this work due to lack of time. We wish him a Yasher Koach — Strength and More Strength — for the years he has served Ziv.

VIII.   FOR HUNGRY, POOR, AND HOMELESS INDIVIDUALS ($8,300)

A. The Ark — Chicago ($200)*
Now over 15 years old, The Ark represents one aspect of the Chicago Jewish Community's work with Jewish poor people. For me and others who know this project, The Ark has always been the way Tzedakah can work when performed with sensitivity to the dignity of others. Aside from the quality of services they provide (miraculous at times), I am always struck by how many Chicagoans immediately understand what is meant by Tzedakah. They say, "The Ark", and no more need be said. Other cities would do well to visit and to imitate their work.

[The Ark, 2341 W. Devon Ave., Chicago, IL 60659, ATTN: Renee Lepp, 312-973-1000.]

B. Bet Tzedek — Los Angeles ($200)*
Founded a few years ago by a small group of Jewish lawyers, Bet Tzedek set out to do *pro bono* work for Jewish poor and elderly people. Nowadays, because of their incredible success, they have expanded at an unbelievable rate, now using non-Jewish as well as Jewish lawyers and paralegals, and handling non-Jewish as well as Jewish cases. There are few paid staff attorneys, and it seems that lawyers and paralegals flock from everywhere to be a part of their sublime-yet-very-mundane work. Bet Tzedek (like the Ark) is the best of the best in their field: bringing justice to those who otherwise might not have found it, merely for lack of funds.

I am pleased to mention that a similar group is starting in San Diego, and I would hope that similar groups would be established in other cities.

[Bet Tzedek, 145 S. Fairfax Ave., #200, L.A., CA 90036, ATTN: Ralph Gottlieb, 213-939-0506.]

C. MAZON-A Jewish Response to Hunger — International ($100)*
Now only in its 4th year, MAZON is taking in hundreds of thousands of dollars a year, and is able to make a much more significant number of allocations to projects involved in feeding Jewish and non-Jewish hungry people. The sad part is that the number of applicants has grown at a still faster rate....so many places requesting funding, so much need. Starting with a simple idea of asking people to add a 3% Tzedakah Surcharge to the food costs of their celebrations, the project has taken hold in an ever-growing number of places. I am certain I speak for many when I say that MAZON has brought this Problem of Hunger out of the realm of the abstract and into our much more immediate consciousness. The growth of MAZON, the sheer enormity of the need...the work is at once exhilarating and frightening.

[MAZON, 2940 Westwood Blvd., #7, Los Angeles, CA 90064, ATTN: Irving Cramer, 213-470-7769.]

D. *Project ORE - Services for Homeless Jews, NY ($200)*

Project ORE has a shelter for homeless Jews on the Lower East Side. They also have a number of other projects for these Jews, including a hot lunch program and other services. *Jewish* homeless people. *The Baltimore Jewish Times* published an article on that city's homeless Jews. Undoubtedly, more should be done in this area. We are not "exempt".

[Project ORE, c/o Educational Alliance, 197 E. Broadway, NY, NY 10002. ATTN: Peter Fine, 212-420-1150. Contributions: "Educational Alliance", but indicate that the funds are specifically for Project ORE.]

E. *Trevor Ferrell — The Kid in Philadelphia ($2,150)**

It is now more than 5 years since Trevor Ferrell (then 11 years old) went out on the streets with his family and handed a blanket to a homeless person. Since then, Trevor's many, many volunteers, his friends, and the staff of Trevor's Campaign have continued the make the rounds of Philadelphia's homeless people every single night. They have served more than 200,000 meals since that night in December, 1983.

Furthermore, the shelter (Trevor's Place) has been fully renovated, with a continuing success rate of finding jobs and more permanent housing for over 80% of the people who come to the shelter. I am angered when people use the catch-all word "band-aid" for many kinds of Tzedakah projects. One could learn well from the previous statistic what kinds of things are band-aids and which ones are much, much more.

The book about Trevor's work (Trevor's Place) is particularly moving, as is the video. Ziv, besides contributing towards other needs, has underwritten the purchase of 200 blank tapes, and Torah Aura Productions in L.A. has reproduced the 200 videos, free of charge. This video has become the single most powerful educational tool in my teaching of Tzedakah, and is a "must" item for educators, synagogues, and anybody else involved in sensitizing people to the realities of hungry and homeless people. Both the book and video are available from Trevor's Campaign, and we request (on Trevor's behalf and on behalf of homeless people) a $25 donation for each item.

[Trevor's Campaign, 137 E. Spring Ave., Ardmore, PA 19003, ATTN: Frank Ferrell, 215-642-6452.]

F. *Shoes in Denver — Ranya Kelly, "The Bag Lady of Arvada" ($100)*

One day, Ms. Kelly, a suburban woman in her late 20's, needed a carton to mail something to someone. She decided to check the dumpsters in a local shopping center. In one dumpster, much to her astonishment, were 500 perfectly good pairs of shoes (each were marked with a little bit of yellow paint)...obviously thrown out by a shoe store. She took them home, gave some of them to friends and relatives, and still found an incredible number left over. So she went down to a shelter and donated the rest of them. Seeing the harsh realities of poverty and homelessness face to face, she became determined to keep looking in dumpsters and simultaneously asking the shoe companies to give the shoes to her (rather than throw them away), and she would take them to shelters. After a three-year struggle, Ranya Kelly won: since last April has gotten over 12,000 pairs of shoes. This enormous number of shoes does not include the ones she had gathered on her own before April, and these 12,000 pairs are from less than 20 stores. Imagine how many shoes would be available to people who need them if more people would do what she is doing. Try it: the dumpsters, the stores. Call Ranya Kelly first for logistical advice.

Ms. Kelly receives no salary for this work. Our contribution helped pay for gas and other expenses. (She's also getting linens donated from various stores around town.)

[Ranya Kelly, 7736 Hoyt Circle, Arvada, CO 80005, 303-431-0904.]

G. Shelter at Hebrew Union College — Cincinnati ($100)

The students at Hebrew Union College in Cincinnati took it upon themselves to establish a small shelter for homeless people on the grounds of the school. When I was at HUC this winter, I was very taken by the students' commitment to this project.

[HUC Shelter, 3101 Clifton Ave., Cincinnati, OH 45220, ATTN: Matthew Eisenberg.]

H. Tova's Kitchen — Jerusalem ($150)

For the past seven years, Tova Cohen has been rising early on Wednesday mornings to provide a hot, nutritious meal to some 30-35 elderly Jews from the neighborhood. She serves the food in a nearby synagogue and provides enough for people to take some home with them. This is another example of our following up on a newspaper article we had read. Tova's Kitchen is very real, more than just notices and articles in *The Jerusalem Post*. It is an example of carving out some small part of the world and fixing it up just right (Tikun Olam).

[Tova's Kitchen, Yosef Karo St. 26, Jerusalem, ATTN: Tova Cohen, 823-572, ask for Nechama.]

I. Mitbach Yitzchak (Yitzchak's Kitchen) — Tel Aviv ($200)*

This is a small Hungarian restaurant in Tel Aviv where patrons are served in the normal fashion: those who pay, pay the regular prices...but those who cannot afford to pay, order from the same menu, and eat the same food, but for free. Mitbach Yitzchak is still there, with additional food programs quietly going on besides. Very quietly.

[Mitbach Yitzchak, 48 Montefiore St., Tel Aviv.]

J. Passover Food — Washington, DC ($500)*

We gave our annual contribution to B'nai B'rith Project Hope, Washington DC's most extensive program for providing Passover food packages for those who might need the food to make the holiday a joyous occasion. B'nai B'rith does this project in many cities.

[B'nai B'rith Project Hope, c/o Len Elenowitz, 8801 Post Oak Rd., Potomac, MD 20854, 301-983-1345, evenings; daytime, 261-1402.]

K. Three Extraordinary Food Banks ($2,400)*

We have stayed in close touch with three food banks. The food they provide would have been thrown out by the stores. Each director's concern is food-with-dignity.

1. Gleaners (Las Vegas) ($1,250)*. 400,000 pounds of food a month; 20,000 hungry people a month. The food is free. Customers may pay if they want to, whatever they can afford. Many pay something; they want to. Dignity. There is no limit on most items — you take as much as you need. Because of one Celeste McKinley and her husband, David.

[Gleaners, 3120 S. Highland, Las Vegas, NV 89109, ATTN: Celeste McKinley, 702-731-FOOD.]

2. Gleaners (Youngstown, OH) ($1,000)*. Joseph Lordi, founder of this foodbank, knew from experience the often-degrading aspects of "the system". In need of food himself, he felt pained enough to take one of his public assistance checks and fly to Las Vegas to learn how to set up a program "just right"...from the Rebbi-of-Foodbanks: Celeste McKinley.

[Youngstown Community Food Center, Inc. and Gleaners Food Bank, Inc., 82 Sugar Cane Dr., Youngstown, OH 44512, 216-726-9591.]

3. Toledo (OH) Seagate Food Bank ($150)*. Alice Mosiniak (age 65+) handles 1,000,000 pounds of food a month, distributing to 20 counties in Ohio. She does it, she does it right, she does it with dignity, at an age when many people would retire. Awesome.

[Toledo Seagate Food Bank, 526 High St., Toledo, OH 43609, ATTN: Alice Mosiniak, 419-244-6996.]

L. Sister Margaret — Shreveport, LA ($1,750)*

Heating bills, clothing, food, housing, counselling, job searches...just about anything that falls on the shoulders of people suffering hard times in Shreveport — also falls on Sister Margaret McCaffrey's shoulders. We admire her and her work immensely, her caring and devotion, her vigor, how she draws so many (though never enough) people to work with her.

[Christian Service Program, POB 21, Shreveport, LA 71161, ATTN: Sister Margaret, 318-221-4539.]

M. Reverend Steinbruck — Washington, DC ($250)*

Luther Place N St. Village is Reverend John Steinbruck's complex of projects in a difficult and poor section of Washington. A man of great compassion, he not only serves poor, hungry, and homeless people with Grandeur-and-Humility-of-the-Spirit, he shares his wealth of experience and insight with the Jewish community quite frequently, thereby opening the listeners' hearts and minds to the very immediate problems on the streets of Washington.

[Luther Place N St. Village, 1226 Vermont Ave., NW, Washington, DC 20005, 202-667-1377.]

IX. JEWISH PROJECTS FOR BATTERED WOMEN AND VICTIMS OF RAPE ($7,200)

A. Jewish Battered Women's Shelters ($6,200)*
   1. Jerusalem — Beit Tzipporah-Isha L'Isha ($5,000)*.
Our fund has supported this particular shelter for years. Fine and, unfortunately,
necessary work. We have learned much from their devotion and wisdom, their patience and insight.

   [Isha L'Isha-Beit Tzipporah Battered Women's Shelter, POB 10403, Jerusalem, ATTN:
Dvora Leuchter, 381-587 or 382-009. Contributions made out to "Woman to Woman" or through
The New Israel Fund, 111 W. 40th St., #2600, NY, NY 10173, 212-302-0066. Indicate that you
recommend the contribution be for Isha L'Isha.]
   2. Baltimore ($1,000). One of less than 10 *Jewish* battered
women's shelters in North America. Rebbetzin Chana Weinberg has been our
contact, and a mainstay of this project. There is also a non-crisis domestic hotline
in Baltimore called "Eitsa": 1-800-533-8TSA (within Maryland), 1-800-622-8TSA
(outside of Maryland).

   [Rebbetzin Chana Weinberg, 401 Yeshiva Lane, #2D, Baltimore, MD 21208, 301-521-
3600 or 486-0322. Contributions made out to: Chana Weinberg Tzedakah Fund.]
   3. Chicago — Shalva ($200). Founded by some of the
Mikvah women in Chicago, Shalva (which means "Peace of Mind"), is a most
worthy project. We only hope that they will be successful in encouraging other cities to launch similar programs. They have a new hotline number: 312-583-HOPE.
They accept collect calls from anywhere in the United States.

   [Shalva, Box 53, Chicago, IL 60660, ATTN: Sherry Berliner, 312-583-HOPE.]
**B. The Linda Feldman Rape Crisis Center — Jerusalem
($1,000)***
              This too — rape — is, all too sadly, an issue in our communities.
We again support the efforts of the Jerusalem project, this time helping to purchase
a much-needed phone answering machine, and providing funds for additional
poster publicity around the city.

   [Linda Feldman Rape Crisis Center POB 158, Jerusalem, ATTN: Maisoun Karaman,
245-554.]

X.   *A MISCELLANY ($13,525)*

A. Relief for Victims of the Armenian Earthquake ($250)
   [American Jewish Joint Distribution Committee, 711 3rd Ave., NY, NY 10017, 212-
687-6200.]
B. The Rabbanit Bracha Kapach — Jerusalem ($8,000)*
              The Rabbanit is an all-around Mitzvah Wonder Woman, taking care
of hundreds of people throughout her neighborhood, Nachla'ot, and other areas of
Jerusalem. Wedding dresses for brides who cannot afford their own, summer
camping for kids, Shabbat provisions for families...so many activities. Her

Passover food program reaches more than 2,000 families, and we contribute towards that, as well as other of her activities. Meet her; bring a wedding gown.

[The Rabbanit Bracha Kapach, 12 Lod St., Jerusalem, 249-296.)

C. Dr. Simon Wiesenthal, Nazi Hunter ($100)*

[Dokumentationszentrum, Salztorgasse 6/IV/5, Vienna, Austria, ATTN: Dr. Simon Wiesenthal.]

D. ZAHAVI-The Association of Rights for Large Families ($3,000)*

Our good friend, Dr. Eliezer Jaffe, told us of ZAHAVI years ago: an Israeli national organization dedicated to assuring the appropriate benefits and solving the unique problems of families with four or more children. It is a wonderful, dynamic grassroots organization, and we have been involved in many aspects of their work, among them: partially funding home reference libraries for children in large families (the family pays a portion, the local municipality a portion, Zahavi a portion), and interest-free loans. For a $400 contribution to ZAHAVI, we were able to "invest" in two such home reference libraries. $1,800 of this contribution is from the will of Howard Levy, longtime friend of mine and other Washingtonians. Howard loved children and wanted to provide for them in some useful, direct fashion. This sum will be used as an endowment for the ZAHAVI children.

[ZAHAVI-Jerusalem, 1 Metudela St., Jerusalem, ATTN: Dr. Eliezer Jaffe. Jaffe's home: 37 Azza St., 637-450. Contributions (Minimum=$25) through PEF-Israel Endowment Funds, 342 Madison Ave., #1010, NY, NY 10173, ATTN: Sidney Musher, 212-599-1260. Ask about PEF's many other projects. Fine Mitzvah people!.]

E. AACI-Jerusalem Scholarship Fund ($500)*

This project has always impressed us: providing non-tuition scholarships for all kinds of necessities to help children and young adults remain in school and college...children who had a parent killed in a war or terrorist attack. There are regular individual evaluations and a very real sense of care for each student selected, which is why so few of the students drop out. Our $500 is a small endowment for one student.

[AACI-Jerusalem Scholarship Fund, 6 Mane St., Jerusalem, ATTN: Michael Bargteil, 660-772.]

F. Relief for Jewish Substance Abusers — JACS ($100)*

JACS (=Jewish Alcoholics, Chemically Dependent Persons, and Significant Others Foundation) is a national organization trying to (a) get Jewish communities to recognize that there *is* indeed a problem in this area, and (b) to organize local groups to begin dealing with it. Where they *do* succeed in establishing a group, the benefits are many, though all too many communities still deny that there is a need for JACS (or similar group) in their town. We contributed to the local Northern Virginia group. Many cities fail to establish groups. The claim: "No need."

[JACS (national group), 197 E. Broadway, NY, NY 10002, 212-473-4747.]

G. LZ Birmingham — Vietnam Veterans ($1,000)

Loren Levson, a Jewish Vietnam veteran, has set up in his own home a national computer bulletin board for Vietnam veterans. He is attempting to get veterans to stay in touch, to talk about their difficulties, to prevent depression, despair, a sense of futility, and worse. Loren explained to me how the suicide rate among Vietnam veterans is frighteningly high. He is just trying to get them to talk, to make contacts, to link up with others, to work things out. ("LZ" stands for "Landing Zone", a safe haven.) We have helped pay for some computer equipment and other expenses. It's just a simple, straightforward operation: one person's attempt to set things right.

[LZ Birmingham, 24 Richmar Dr., POB 130444, Birmingham, AL 53213, 205-870-7706, Computer number is 205-870-7770.]

H. John Fling Takes Care of a City — Columbia, SC ($568)*

Mr. Fling is a one-person all-encompassing Mitzvah project: father-brother-uncle-grandfather figure for hundreds of children in difficult family situations, friend of many of the city's blind people, fixer-upper for hundreds of other "just plain folk" who find themselves in trying circumstances. I spent a day with him this year, and another day last year, and it is easy to understand why he is legendary in Columbia. A retired auto parts delivery man who knew poverty and hard times from childhood, he just wants people to have a fair chance in life.

[John Fling, POB 5491, 2916 River Dr., Cayce, W. Columbia, SC 29171, 803-256-7195.]

I. Ziv's Annual Tree, planted with my own hands in the Jerusalem Peace Forest, in honor of all those who support our work. ($7)*

XI.   DAVID MORRIS: ZIV'S EDUCATOR AND AGENT IN ISRAEL ($6,000)*

David Morris has been serving us well the past few years: carrying out specific Mitzvah missions on our behalf, teaching Tzedakah and showing many people our projects, opening up new areas of interest for us, and giving me updates on the status of the people and projects we support. Our work — so involved in direct, grassroots programs in Israel — would be simply impossible without his help. David helps us only part-time (he is a [super] licensed tour guide as his main occupation), but always works above and beyond his "part-time" label. He is exceptionally sensitive on all matters that demand our attention and does not hesitate to press issues when he believes we should be moving in new directions. We are privileged to have him work with Ziv.

Last year we funded his work as follows: $5,000 for his part-time involvement, plus, mid-year, a $1,000 special grant to develop a program to organize bus loads of individuals to take all-day tours of our programs. This year we would like to engage his services for $5,500. *As always, no funds for David's work are taken from our general account. Only contributions specifically recommended for David's work will be applied to this aspect of Ziv's program.* If you would like to help support David's work on our behalf, please indicate as such when you contribute.

To contact David for information on Ziv's Israel activities: David Morris, Shabtai HaNegbi St. 69, Apt. 8, Gilo Alef, Jerusalem, phone: 767-894.

XII. SUMMARY OF ZIV'S FINANCIAL ACTIVITIES

	4/13/81-3/31/88	4/1/88-3/31/89	Total to Date
Allocations (including Ziv Agent/Educator)	$443,804.50	$141,000.00	$584,804.50
Expenses (including last year's printing and mailing, but not this year's)	$7,541.17	$3,926.35	$11,467.52

XIII. ADDITIONAL MISCELLANEOUS INFORMATION

A. During the summer of 1988, Nina Targovnik of Phoenix, AZ, served as our Tzedakah apprentice in Israel, investigating new projects for us, lending insight to the day-to-day operations of Ziv in Israel, leading tours. Many of the new "discoveries" we owe to her work, and we wish her a Yasher Koach as she continues to speak of our work in Phoenix.

B. As Ziv grows, more and more people assist us on a volunteer basis. They wish to remain anonymous, but I have made it clear to them that, without them, we would be stuck back at some level considerably below our present capabilities. A public, anonymous Yasher Koach!

C. We have received a special grant which will allow us to send everyone an updated mailing or two (though not a full report, which will remain annual). It will also afford us the opportunity to send additional materials about special projects to selected portions of our mailing list.

D. People who want to get occasional Tzedakah educational materials, please contact Kate Kinser, 1323 W. Albion, Chicago, IL 60626, 312-764-6955. (The CAJE Tzedakah Network.)

XIV. CONTRIBUTIONS NOW; FUTURE PLANS

A. This will be my 14th consecutive summer in Israel as Tzedakah Resource Person on the USY Israel Pilgrimage. Once again this affords me the opportunity to continue Ziv's personal and direct approach to our projects over there.

Contributions should be made out to "Ziv" and sent to:

Bena Siegel, Treasurer
Ziv Tzedakah Fund
11818 Trailridge Drive
Potomac, MD 20854.

Last summer we had nearly $60,000 to distribute.

B. As always, we cannot accept earmarked funds. <u>The only exception, as
mentioned previously, is if you wish to *recommend* funding for David Morris's
work for Ziv in Israel</u>.

C. All contributions received between now and my departure for Israel in
late June are used exclusively for programs in Israel. After the summer, any new
contributions are used for our work in the United States and other countries, as well
as for Israel.

D. The one negative side of the work is that we are inundated by requests
for funding. Even though we receive help from friends who volunteer their time,
we cannot possibly keep up with examining these requests. Ziv's Board of
Directors has set the following policy: <u>Ziv is not accepting requests for funding of
new projects and individual work</u>. Any new programs we support are found
through our own initiative. Please be understanding. We are overwhelmed.

Through my travels and Tzedakah talks and seminars, I continue to find
growing enthusiasm for our work. At synagogues, JCC's, Federations, education
days and retreats, people seem to be taken by our seeking out individuals (Mitzvah
heroes) and projects that embody the highest goals of this Mitzvah. I would hope
that more and more people would more aggressively seek out such people and
places, locally, and wherever they may travel. They are not difficult to find, if we
would set our minds to looking in the right places. There is uplift and, of course, a
sense of presence, a radiance when engaging in this work.

I am privileged to be your Shaliach-Messenger, and grateful for the privilege. You have entrusted Ziv with great sums of money which must be carefully
and insightfully distributed to benefit others, and to prove that Tzedakah (Right
Acts) and Tzedek (Justice) can function in this world, can touch people, can allow
for simple human dignity to prevail. It is so high-sounding, but, I think you will
agree, we have seen it work to whatever extent we are able to help make it happen.

To all of you, our annual wish: Yishar Kochachem — All the more strength
to you to continue such exalted work. Or, as the Rabbanit Kapach customarily tells
me, "Nizkeh LeMitzvot — May we be privileged to share this kind of Mitzvah
work for many years."

Danny Siegel, Chairman

Ziv Tzedakah Fund Update
December 1, 1989

I.   Ziv Contributors and Friends, Shalom!

Forgive me — I have become money-hungry.

For Ziv, that is.

The demands on our fund keep growing, which is why we are asking for additional contributions at this time.

While it is true that we have given away a little over $80,000 since April 1st, at the present rate, we will not have much more money available for Tzedakah projects than last year, when we had $141,000. Our Mitzvah people and projects need more than $141,000.

I think it is time we had $200,000-$250,000 a year to give away. Yes, we continue to find new contributors, and yes, our friends of long standing continue to give nicely, generously. And yes, we even have some synagogues giving Yom Kippur appeals on our behalf, and more and more of our contributors are sharing our annual report with some of their friends. But all too often I have this feeling that, when it is time for us to write a check for $1,000, it should be $2,500, or $2,000 should be $5,000 or more. We simply have so much more to do. That is the reason for a second mailing this year.

This mailing has been funded entirely by a special, anonymous contribution. We will continue to keep our promise to you to keep our overhead as low as possible.

And we have always promised you that we will not flood you with flyers and reports and appeals, so this will serve as an update and a suggestion list for further Mitzvah work, *and* the only other appeal you will get from us until the annual report is issued in April.

We are keeping this brief, and writing in an A-B-C format to get straight to the point.

Contributions to Ziv are to be sent to (as the enclosed envelope indicates):

Bena Siegel,
Treasurer, Ziv Tzedakah Fund
11818 Trailridge Dr.
Potomac, MD 20854

II. Updates, Suggestions

A. Emergency Bone Marrow Transplant Testing: A special project — See the enclosed flyer.[1]

B. Yad Sarah: Lending medical supplies free of charge throughout Israel. We have purchased 10 cardiac apnea monitors @ $2,700 each since April 1st. This machine will hopefully prevent many crib deaths. We are committed to purchasing 15 of them by April 1st. In addition, they need a large supply of pyjamas and nightclothes — cotton, extra large — and sheets, for their special project providing laundry service for families where one of the family has become incontinent. Do not mail them, but rather take some with you when you go. [Yad Sarah, 43 HaNevi'im St., Jerusalem, 244-047, Uri Lupoliansky.]

C. Adopting Families for Jewish Babies with Down Syndrome: Janet Marchese of White Plains, NY, has placed more than 1,500 babies with Down Syndrome in adopting homes throughout the country. Over 1,250 of them are Jewish, and she has found only 7 Jewish homes. We know there are many more Jewish families out there who would want to adopt the children, if they only knew they were available for adoption. Please (1) spread the word to friends in your communities, (2) invite her to come speak in your communities...synagogues, Federations, JCC's, or Jewish Family Service, (3) call her just to learn more about how to correct this difficult situation for the Jewish people: 914-428-1236.

D. Life Line for the Old (Yad LaKashish): Many have inquired about Life Line since Mrs. Mendilow passed away. I was there all summer with the USY Israel Pilgrims, taking tours shortly after the new director, Nava Ein-Mor, assumed her responsibilities. We still feel the pain and loss of Mrs. Mendilow's passing, but the work continues, things are running smoothly, and the Elders are well. For more updates, contact Linda Kantor, President of American Friends of Life Line for the Old, 203-795-4580.

E. Charleston, SC, Jewish Community: Those of you who would like to assist Charleston's Jewish Community in rebuilding after Hurricane Hugo may send contributions made out to "Charleston Jewish Federation", c/o Michael Wise, Director, 1645 Raoul Wallenberg Blvd., Charleston, SC 29407 and indicate on the check that it is for Hurricane Relief. Assistance to the San Francisco general community may be channeled through the normal agencies mentioned in the media.

---

[1]Ziv attached a flyer requesting that people be tested in their local communities for a possible bone marrow match. Allison Atlas, a 20-year-old woman in Washington needs such a transplant, and Jews of Eastern European descent have a better chance of providing the match. A massive campaign was underway in the Washington area with an incredibly fine response from the Jewish community. After the mailing went out, people called me on a number of occasions to tell me about similar programs in their communities for other individuals. For information, call LIFE-SAVERS Foundation of America, 1-800-999-8822. If you wish to speak with the person who organized the project in Washington, call Fern Ingber, 301-496-0572.

F. For Homeless, Poor, and Hungry Jews and Non-Jews [note: for the following items, remember that there are *Jews* in your community who need these items, too. Seek out Jewish groups that will accept the items.]:

1. Cribs in Synagogues and Other Jewish Communal Buildings: We feel it is important to address ourselves to homeless and poor babies, both Jewish and non-Jewish. Based on a project undertaken in Seattle, we suggest placing a crib in the lobby to collect diapers, bottles, pacifiers, formula, and other items which would help solve this problem. Contact Jeannie Jaybush for more details: 206-938-2364. Teen-agers and younger kids keep telling me that they assume there have always been, and will always continue to be, this many hungry, poor, and homeless people. We must prove them wrong.

2. Shoes — Ranya Kelly, Denver: Ms. Kelly has accumulated more than 15,000 pairs of shoes in a year and a half, which she has distributed to shelters and other projects in her city....All of them were destined for some landfill, all of them thrown out by local shoe stores. She now gathers 500-1,000 pairs/month from only 5 shoe stores in Denver. Try it yourself. Call Ranya Kelly and find out how to do it: 303-431-0904.

3. Leftover Food from Jewish Events: A group of Jewish women in Worcester, MA, has created Rachel's Table, which picks up leftover food from Jewish communal events, private parties, and secular institutions and restaurants, and then delivers the food to soup kitchens and shelters. A paradigm of front-line Mitzvah work. Contact them at 508-799-7600 to find out how to do it in your community. *You are not liable if someone gets sick from the food you donate. Nowhere in the U.S. are you liable. I repeat — nowhere.* So, it is only a matter of logistics. In any event, make it a practice from your local events to take the leftovers down to an appropriate Mitzvah project.

4. Other Leftover Food: Try a bakery, a fruit and vegetable stand. Ask what they do with their leftover baked goods or fruits and vegetables. Tell them you will pick it up, take it to an appropriate agency, and have the agency send a tax receipt. (I tried it at a bakery. It worked! About $300-400 worth of baked goods just from that one asking.)

G. Soviet Jews: Massive efforts are needed for the re-settlement of our Soviet Jewish brothers and sisters. Besides the fund-raising, it is clear that we need to increase our local efforts to help welcome the new arrivals into our local communities with the particular necessities of the moment, and most of all, with warmth, encouragement, and a sense of sincere welcome. The money will be found — through long hours of tough fund-raising work — but it is the human, Jewish element that will be needed to make a good, pleasant home for the new arrivals. We, children, grandchildren, and great-grandchildren of immigrants need only picture our own ancestors coming over on the boats to understand this situation.

H. Ethiopian Jews: We welcome the news of the re-establishment of diplomatic relations between Israel and Ethiopia, tuning in for all the latest reports, hoping that this is the opportunity for the final release of the remaining Ethiopian Jews and their safe passage and re-settlement, and — in so many instances — reunification with their family members in Israel who have waited too long for their release and arrival.

I. Materials — Newsletters, Videos, Etc.

1. Trevor Ferrell, The Kid Who Feeds So Many Homeless People (and Finds Jobs and Housing for Them): We continue to fund the video about Trevor (about 6 minutes). We find it to be the single most effective piece of educational material on Tzedakah for all ages. I urge you to order it not only for syangogues, Federations, and schools, but for your own home. It is a *must* item. $25.00 contribution to "Trevor's Campaign", c/o Frank Ferrell, 137 E. Spring Ave., Ardmore, PA, 19003. (215-642-6453) The book is also fabulous, readable down to age 11 or 12. Add another $25.00 contribution for the book.

2. The Giraffe Gazette: Giraffes are people who stick their necks out to bring some Tzedek and Tzedakah into this world, some justice, decency, quality of life, caring — you pick the translation. The Giraffe Gazette is a quarterly, 32-page-or-so newsletter that tells the stories of these Mitzvah heroes who take all kinds of risks. The newsletter is inspirational and instructive to read. I *always* use it for my lectures, and, whenever possible, track down some of these Giraffes, to meet them, learn from them, attempt to imitate their work. $25.00/year. Call 1-800-344-TALL. A *must* item.

3. Mitzvah Dogs: Canine Companions for Independence (CCI) — the dogs that follow 89 different commands for their owners who function in life in a wheelchair or are hearing-impaired. I love cats. I hated dogs. I still love cats, but now am a dog-lover, a Mitzvah dog-lover. I was even invited to speak at one of their graduations. Fabulous video (a "20/20" segment — make sure to ask specifically for that one), $10.00 check made out to "CCI". Contact Katheryn Horton, c/o CCI, 1215 Sebastopol Rd., Santa Rosa, CA 95407, 707-579-1985. They have 5 centers around the country (Northern CA, Farmingdale, NY, Orient, OH [near Columbus], San Diego, and Orlando). See if you can arrange to have them come out and do a demonstration for you. If the Talmud had a phrase like, "This will wow your sox off", our sages would have certainly used such a phrase for CCI.

4. Additional Tzedakah Resources: Kate Kinser is the CAJE Tzedakah Network chairperson. She may be called upon to provide materials and insights into specific projects you may wish to launch. Ask to be put on her mailing list: 1323 W. Albion, Chicago, IL 60626, 312-764-6955 (h), 708-328-7678 (w).

5. Jewish Directories Relating to Accessibility for Individuals with Disabilities: The United Synagogue of America has published a section in its new directory indicating which Conservative synagogues have specific kinds of access for individuals with disabilities. Only about 10% of the congregations are represented. Call 212-533-7800, ask for the United Synagogue, and request a form to fill out so your synagogue will be listed in the next one. For Reform, Orthodox, and Reconstructionist congregations — request that your national organization do the same. And have your local Jewish community's directory list access for their buildings and events.

III. In Conclusion

I have been asked to do a monthly column for the *Baltimore Jewish Times*, which allows me the opportunity to pass on new ideas and projects to a wider readership. It helps....It helps a lot. Still, the best way for the word to spread about these Tzedakah people and projects is through you, the people involved in Ziv. We have come a long way since our early days, and I feel that we are on the verge of major expansion. Yasher Koach to all of you. The more complete report follows in April, as always.

Danny Siegel
Chairman,
Ziv Tzedakah Fund

Anything Worth Doing
Is Worth Doing Poorly

I. The Mind Goes

I know I heard it at a conference last Summer — "Anything worth doing is worth doing poorly." I think.

And I know I heard it at a bat mitzvah a few weeks later — "Anything worth doing is worth doing poorly." I think.

The first time from my old friend, Beth Huppin; the second time from my old friend Malka Edelman.

I know, without thinking twice, that that is the exact quote — "Anything worth doing is worth doing poorly."

And I know (I think) they both attributed the quote to someone else, now lost to me.

And I don't remember the contexts either one of my friends was making reference to.

And I know I have mentioned the quote in passing in another place in my writings.

And I know that the Talmud tells us we are supposed to quote our sources, that it brings Redemption to the world. I even know that that principle is on page 15a of the section of the Talmud called Megillah, and that Rabbi Elazar said it in the name of Rabbi Chanina, "Whoever says something in the name of the person who originally said it, brings Ge'ulah-Redemption to the world."

So we'll have to work with what my memory dredges up, and proclaim (for a specific case) The Huppin/Edelman/Anonymous Teacher's Ultimate Rule of How to Begin a Tzedakah Project — "Anything worth doing is worth doing poorly."

II. Examples

1. Cough drops: It is late Fall in the Northern United States. The needs of hungry and homeless people grow as the temperature drops. Sara Cohen, a Mitzvah person in Chicago, says she needs cough drops for people in a shelter. The fastest growing population of homeless people is children. One child gives the cold to another, to a parent, to others in the shelter.

You need cough drops *now*.

So you find money to buy cough drops.

Sooner or later you ask: (a) Where can you can get them wholesale or donated? (b) Are sours balls and similar candies as effective and cheaper, and, if so, where can you get them in bulk, wholesale, or donated? (c) Should we get religious schools to adopt the project, since they should learn to identify with children who have to suffer long-term colds and irritations — merely for lack of cough drops? (d) If money is limited, is food more important than cough drops, are blankets more important, sox? (e) Beyond residents in shelters, shouldn't cough drops also become standard items at food banks? People who come to food banks aren't usually homeless. They just live on very precarious incomes, and if they can't buy all the food they need, they may not be paying heating bills, or may keep the thermostat down so low, colds plague them more frequently. (f) Jewishly, recalling that there are — just to mention a few examples — 15,000 Jews in Toronto living at or near the poverty line, 37,000 in Chicago, 65,000 in Los Angeles, how do we mobilize cough drop projects into the Jewish Mitzvah programs?

All of these questions are significant, and all of them will, in the end, provide greater, more all-encompassing relief to more people, but *now* is when cough drops are needed. Planning and figuring and calculating are secondary to the *now* of the Mitzvah.

2. Ron Barshop of San Antonio had an idea, "SA-25". Besides other Tzedakah work he might be doing, he pulled 25 people together (counting himself), they each put in $25/month, and then invite a representative of a local Tzedakah project to their meeting. After the presentation, they contribute the month's pool of Tzedakah money to the project that they had just heard about. It's working, though some have dropped out and others have come in, and sometimes it might not number 25 people. As they continued to meet, they got a chance to refine their approach, re-examine the kinds of projects they wanted to support, learned through simple give and take whether or not they wanted privately to give more money to a specific project. It wasn't long after I spoke with Ron that the project began. It was his idea, and he wanted to start soon. He just wanted to bounce some ideas off of me. So, with a minimum of expertise and a maximum of Tzedakah-vigor SA-25 got its start.

Barshop's idea has worked, works, and continues to work. The local food bank, an innovative literacy project, and the Special Olympics — to name a few — have been beneficiaries of their contributions in the range of $600. And I think part of the success of it was that, after a certain amount of thinking, it was clear to him that the rest of the thinking had to wait. It was time to actually do it, to start the Tzedakah money flowing.

The idea is replicable anywhere, and the money/month and numbers of people and frequency of meetings can vary according to the specific group: 10 people, 18 people, $10/month, $18/month, monthly, weekly, bi-monthly. It is a variation on the idea of Tzedakah Collectives.

3. Others have done what the cough drop people do and what the Barshops do. They continue their work in relatively modest proportions or on a grand scale, they work with different kinds of Mitzvahs, different people who need the Mitzvahs benefit. What so many of them have in common is that they have followed the basic rule of doing it *now*, even if it is done poorly. After a while it is done better and better, but it might never have happened if they hadn't started then and there.

III. Implications of The Huppin/Edelman/Anonymous Teacher's Ultimate Rule of How to Begin a Tzedakah Project (Taking Careful Note of the Frequent Use of the Word "Sometimes")

1. Sometimes there's no time to delay or procrastinate when some act of Tzedakah just *has* to be done.

2. Sometimes it is a matter of life and death, and we *certainly* cannot delay. It may be that a few dollars or hours or a few hundred of both are wasted, but by doing it *now* you may have saved a life, for which there is no price tag nor a Book of Hours to tell us just exactly how many hours of effort a human life is worth.

3. Too much planning is occasionally the excuse for putting the Mitzvah work off indefinitely.

4. Sometimes too much planning is a malicious euphemistic catch-all for never wanting to do it at all. "Making a study" is an ugly phrase to people in need.

5. "Something done at just the right time is as wonderful a human experience as can be imagined"[1] is an important Jewish principle. Waiting may spoil the time co-ordinates, bringing ruin, suffering, or dismay to the people who need the Mitzvah done sooner.

6. Sometimes...planning means you have to call in planners. Planners have their place in the Mitzvah world, but sometimes the fine texture, blessed uniqueness, and primal energy of the Mitzvah work are preserved only if the initial steps are taken by the Mitzvah doers.

7. The Big World feels the tension, too. My friend, David Hirsch, tells me of a business approach called "Ready, Fire, Aim", coined by an entrepreneur named Chris Whittle. Another friend informs me that on the other end of the spectrum is the "Rolls Royce Syndrome" — don't do it unless you can do it first-class, top of the line.

8. Not allowing for poor performance sometimes deprives good Mitzvah people from plunging in and doing Mitzvah work. The pioneering aspect and feeling of breakthrough are fresh only when you catch the sparks and fire of the first moments. This is the power and the glory of the first few words of the Torah, "Beraysheet Bara Elokim-When God began to create...." And in the scientific realm, this is somewhat like the fascination of some astrophysicists and cosmologists with the Big Bang. The mini-second after the Big Bang is a little less fascinating than the First Moment of the World.

9. People who jump into a Mitzvah project spontaneously — because a need is staring them right in the eye — will last longer at the job and have a slower burnout rate because they were the founders of the project. It is their vision that made it happen, they saw it work, the magic of the Mitzvah act face to face. They know, as no late-comer can know, how much Mitzvahs work.

---

[1]My translation of Proverbs 15:23.

10. The ones who do it, even poorly, stumbling, failing, muddling through, inevitably find that others are attracted to their sincerity, forthrightness, and action-oriented approach. Among the others who join are those who bring with them their own large and small expertises which will help develop the program, stabilize it, and allow it to flourish even beyond the initial dreams of the founder. It always happens that way. There are so many good people around and so many good ways for them to link themselves to Mitzvah work, they will find you.

11. Sometimes...sometimes, Mitzvahs done poorly still bring relief, critical relief that might never have come at all because of the delay in preparing to do it well. Additionally, the things that go wrong by doing the Mitzvah poorly are more often than not relatively minor and certainly not disastrous.

12. Strategic planning can proceed simultaneously with the actual Mitzvah work. Indeed, the strategic planning proceeds better as the planners watch the work-in-action from the earliest stages of activity. In Mitzvah work, you learn not only from your mistakes, but even more so from the *first* mistakes. You learn from the right things you do, but even more so from the *first* right things you do.

13. Sometimes (I would estimate almost always) there is more warmth and humanity to Mitzvah work when it begins spontaneously, immediately, and directly, with rules-of-thumb instead of hard-and-fast rules, and with Mitzvah people (even Mitzvah-fumblers) instead of experts taking the lead. Being on the front lines from Day One gives more insight, sometimes, and different insight, than beginning with studies and statistics.

14. Goodhearted people who want to do good should *never* be held back from doing good.

15. There is never any real, absolute guarantee that doing Mitzvah work well accomplishes more than doing Mitzvah work poorly. Quantitative and qualitative studies would be worthwhile in this area — if they don't take too much time away from front-line Mitzvah work.

IV. The Plan

The only thing left to do is to do it, even poorly.

The Giraffes
And The Jews

I. The Mitzvah Zoo

There's a whole zoo-full of these things: there's cats and rabbits and other creatures that do their Mitzvahs by visiting old-age homes and all kinds of institutions; there's horses to be broken and trained and groomed in prisons to help inmates find some self-image; there's seeing-eye dogs of course, and dogs for hearing-impaired people, and the Canine Companions for people in wheelchairs; birds in Jewish Community Centers so people who come to the local JCC's to break their loneliness can have a non-threatening friend to talk to, to listen to, to play with; there's all kinds of raptors — eagles and hawks and owls and falcons — that are brought to Boy Scout and Girl Scout troops and schools that show people how human beings hurt them by gunshot and poison and accident, and how human beings can fix them again, even if they might not always get well enough to go back out into the wild.

And now there's the Giraffes.

Giraffes are people who stick their neck out.

In Jewish terms, they are people who stick their neck out to perform acts of Tzedek and Tzedakah, Justice and Righteousness, who fix up the world in small and big ways. They take risks, sometimes very personal, heavy risks, to set things right where a mess has been left by people, by nature, by whatever.

Trevor Ferrell is a famous Giraffe: he's the kid in Philadelphia who feeds, houses, and finds a permanent home and employment for the street people of his city.

Janet Marchese of White Plains, NY, is a Giraffe: she has helped place over 1,500 infants with Down Syndrome in adoptive homes.

Ranya Kelly is a Giraffe: she has gotten hold of more than 15,000 pairs of shoes — shoes that were being thrown out by shoe stores in Denver — and given them away to homeless and poor people.

Another Giraffe blew the whistle on Agent Orange and its relation to cancer while working in a VA hospital, for which she was fired.

Another Giraffe went to Hebrew High School with me in Arlington, VA. He also blew the whistle, in this case on the Environmental Protection Agency. I think the eventual outcome was that they couldn't fire him, but he's in some sort of dead-end job with the EPA. And I imagine he's still blowing whistles on government senseless blunders, horrible waste, and blatant and gross injustices.

A fourth, a certain Jim Walsh, is a high school football coach in New York who noticed that one year his players were, well, somewhat puny. He pleaded with the league to move his team into a different, safer league — *so his kids wouldn't get hurt.* When the league refused to make new arrangements, right before a big game, Jim Walsh forfeited the season...*so the kids wouldn't get hurt. He didn't want them to get hurt* (how many times must he have said it to the league supervisors?) — competition/winning-spirit or no competition/winning spirit.

A fifth Giraffe fights river-polluters, so his and his neighbors' river won't die, and a sixth decides a nuclear reactor just doesn't belong in her town's back yard, organizes, fights, and wins the fight.

There's even one Giraffe, a certain James Boren of Falls Church, VA, whose self-founded organization (The International Association of Professional Bureaucrats) gives out awards called "The Order of the Bird" to companies and bureaucracies that beat people down. (I would have called it the Doofus of the Year Award). One of his prime awards went to an agency that made another Giraffe (Guy Polhemus of New York) go through every single can being recycled by homeless people, to make sure they were all from the recycler's home state. There's a racket in recycling of cans, people are profiting where they shouldn't be profiting, and — as is to be expected from projects that Giraffes do — the Big Boys, i.e., the ones responsible for paying out the refunds, found less than $5.00 worth of cans that were from outside New York...out of thousands and thousands of cans. And all this Giraffe wanted to do was to allow homeless people to gather cans, bring them to his project, where he would give them their refunds so they would have some measly spending money. And the Big Boys would begrudge them even that, for the mere sake of a little greed, those few or few thousand or few million extra bucks. Imagine![1]

There are already about 450-500 Giraffes, and more being discovered every few months. And very few of them, if any, are larger than life. To the contrary, they are as close to life-size as anyone could be. They are normal people, and by learning about them, we can re-define for ourselves what normal ought to be.

II. The Giraffe Project and "The Giraffe Gazette"

A short ferry ride from Seattle, a certain Ann Medlock and her crew of searchers and researchers and writers are determined to tell everyone they can about

---

[1]This, in a world where the average A-list woman spends an average of $111,500 a year on dresses. (*The Washingtonian Magazine*, January, 1989) The A-list is the aggregate of people in the innermost social circle in Washington. This little fact, this $111,500/year budget for dresses, in a world where poor people are lambasted for their laziness. (It's the well-trounced theory, "If they would only apply themselves, they would succeed. We did it, and they should do it.") The fact is, 25% of homeless people work for a living, but can't make enough money to put a roof over their heads. And it's not the extravagance itself that rubs; it's the flip-side arrogance that says that all poor people are spongers and are living off the hard-earned sweat of others, the hard-working people. There was a time, I believe, when it was considered bad form to bad-mouth poor people, when High Society folk had better taste and a little more discretion, or at least had the decency to keep their distasteful opinions to themselves in the sancta of their domestic dens. One final jab — in reality, the High Society people probably still have that discretion. It's the Upstarts who have made it acceptable to opine their theories, compartmentalize their prejudices, and are never seen on the front lines to really get a look at who poor people really are. Theories degrade people, foster suffering, and can be as effective a killer as the drug dealer with a gun.

Giraffes. It's her idea, and it's one of the best I've seen. It's simple, powerful, inspirational, and — most of all — useful. I try to make a point of meeting Giraffes when I am out on the road for speaking engagements or just visiting people.

What Ann does is this: she gets people to be Giraffe Spotters. The Giraffe Spotters are people from everywhere and anywhere who send her articles, or write letters, or tell her by phone or face to face that they know a Giraffe, or they heard or saw some radio or TV spot about a Giraffe-type person. Ann and her gang then track down the Giraffes, check them out, and if it is determined that the person does indeed perform these large or small acts of Right and Just and Good Things, and *if there is an element of risk involved*, she and her committee award them the title of Giraffe, complete with certificate. But there's no money with the award.[1a]

Ann then publicizes the Giraffe's work in *The Giraffe Gazette* and sends out 30-second news releases to local media in an attempt to get their work publicized. She wants — we *all* want — the Giraffes to gain greater support, to be strengthened in their ever-so-important work. (In Yiddish we would say, their "Giraffekeit".) It's not that the Giraffes are seeking fame, fortune, or ego-strokes. Indeed, most of them are *not* that kind of person, but they need the publicity so that they can take their work further, alleviating yet more suffering and getting more decency and fairness plugged into communities or states or the country or the world.

Now *The Giraffe Gazette* is a wonderful newsletter. It comes out 4 times a year, and each issue is 20 to 30 pages long. It keeps growing, and it keeps getting better and better and more and more astounding: so many good people willing to stick their necks out, so much variety in everyday people doing such good things. You can trust me on that one: I have mild dyslexia, and a 20-to-30-page newsletter is very daunting to me, but it is the first thing I read when it arrives in the mail. I read and underline, sometimes write "Wow" in the columns, or "Wow!!", or "Wow!!!", sometimes write "awesome", and usually annotate which city the Giraffes live in, so I might have a chance to visit some of them. (I think I know about 10 of them. I feel privileged that about a half-dozen names I suggested have been adjudged Giraffes, and as a result of the publicity, a few of them have won other awards with some money involved, which will go to support their projects. It feels good to be a Giraffe Spotter.)

Ann has sent me a zip-code-order list of Giraffes, so I can easily find the ones in communities where I am visiting, so I can meet them, and, if I have the opportunity, even join in their work, maybe take on some of the spots, long necks, far-seeing eyes of the Giraffe. Everyone could do the same: get the list, visit, get involved.

[1a]Because The Giraffe Project runs on a shoestring budget, they do not have funds to make cash awards. The publicity the Giraffes get from the project will hopefully bring their work to the attention of foundations and other groups that *do* give money, so the Giraffe's work can continue and grow. It is nice to be able to report that this is beginning to happen more and more, as the word gets around.

If you are a member of The Giraffe Project, you also get occasional sheets of media releases, the short texts of Giraffe projects that are sent out to the radio and TV stations, little summaries you can use to read to friends or teach your classes or memorize like you would a good poem.

And, of course, you can get Giraffe T-shirts and sweatshirts and coffee mugs. (One Jewish day school in the Washington area had a retreat for one of the classes and gave each student a Giraffe T-shirt. A capital idea.) It's elementary fundraising, but it seems to work. Ann and her people are honest and responsible with the funds. No one's getting rich on the backs of Mitzvah people, on the long, gracefully slanting backs of these Giraffes.

III. What To Do

Here's what to do:

1. Call 1-800-344-TALL.

2. Send in $25.00 for membership. You'll get the newsletters and press releases, and discounts on regalia. (My Giraffe T-shirts get a lot of attention when I am out walking.)

3. Ask for copies of the "Giraffe Sighting Report" so you can be on the look-out in the media for Giraffes, so you can pass on the information to Ann and her gang, so the cycle can continue: more Giraffes, more people learning about Giraffes, more people joining in in Giraffe work.

4. And don't forget to tell them how good it is — for a change — to read some good news in the news. Thank them for reminding us that besides all the government corruption, the scandalous scandals and outrageous unfairnesses we read and hear about every day that lots of good things are happening and that maybe we can win the good fight, the right fight, be #1 where it *really* makes a difference.

5. Do it.

As they say on the radio commercials, "That's right. The number is: 1-800-344-TALL".

IV. In Sum

Ann's way out near Seattle, in a place called Whidbey Island, Washington. There's a Giraffe office in New York. I like that: Coast-to-Coast, with all kinds of people in between spotting Giraffes so they can tell others.

For those readers who follow my writings, let me add this: they're on the up-and-up. No wasted money, nothing dishonest about them. The Giraffe Project is just exactly what they say they are. You can trust me. Ann came to the Conference for the Advancement of Jewish Education (CAJE) in Seattle in August and wowed the crowds. She is what she says she is.

V. Postscript: Giraffes and the Jews

An ideal course for adult education classes would be "Jewish Giraffes throughout History." A classic case would be Queen Esther, who risks her life to save the Jews from Haman's plot. At one point (Esther 4:16) she agrees to broach the subject to King Ahashueros, saying, "And if I am lost, I am lost." Starting with the Bible, the teacher could cover material through the Talmud, Medieval Jewish Literature, on into modern times.

Modern times, modern Jewish giraffes....

The Detroit and San Antonio Jewish newspapers have already done it: they have featured local Mitzvah heroes. Perhaps some other Jewish papers have done the same, but I have not heard about their efforts. Again, these people are not seeking the publicity, but *we* need to know about them. The Giraffe Project includes the specific element of risk, but for the Jewish community, the local paper need not necessarily follow that lead. They may choose to feature the local Mitzvah heroes whether or not there is a risk factor, though if there is this element of risk, the local Jewish community could also submit their names to The Giraffe Project.

As for the Jewish ideal that these kinds of Mitzvahs are best done quietly and anonymously, I would counter that we are living in trying times. Egocentricity, egomania, and ego-gratification are unfortunately the rule of the day in many sectors of the community, and Jewish tradition allows the suspension of some rules *LeShaym Chinuch* — for educational purposes. (Jim Beatty, a Giraffe who is a *pro bono* lawyer for Atlanta's homeless people, turns the idea of egomania completely around when he says, "Deep down I'm really a hedonist, and this work feels so good I wouldn't think of doing anything else.") I would think that suspending the rules is justified in America in this latter part of the 20th Century, with one proviso: if the Mitzvah hero or heroine gives his or her permission. Without that, we have no right to intrude.

What to do:

1. Call The Giraffe Project: 1-800-344-TALL and read *The Giraffe Gazette*.

2. Call Arthur Horwitz, editor of the *Detroit Jewish News* at 313-354-6060.

3. Ask for a copy of the insert from February 3, 1989, on Mitzvah Heroes.

4. Bring a copy to your local Jewish paper and encourage them to do a similar project.

5. Do it.

It's good for them, and it's good for us.

It's good for the Jews, and it's good for the world.

If it is true — as some people maintain — that "it's a jungle out there", let's make the jungle a friendlier, more beautiful and decent place to live.

The *Giraffe Project* logo.

The Woman Who Has More Shoes
Than Imelda Marcos Ever Had,
And Other Interesting People

For Mrs. Trude Holzmann

I. A Day in Denver

Nothing really could go wrong that day.

Even if something had gone wrong, it wouldn't have mattered: I was on the way to Hawaii for a week, my tickets compliments of United Airlines and its Mileage Plus Program, fancy-schmancy hotel half-price, compliments of the same program. Glorious sunshine, tennis courts, beaches, horseback riding, snorkeling, dawn walks, sunsets over the neighboring island of Molokai....nothing could go wrong on "The Day Before".

There ought to be a blessing Upon the Occasion of Meeting the Person Who Thought Up the Airline Mileage Programs, the programs that send you to Paradise for a week for free or near-free, and even allow a stopover on the way over or back.

Denver was my way-over-stopover this time: there were a number of Mitzvah people I wanted to meet in that city, and with the help of my friend, Megan Marx, we set out to visit as many as we could in the one day time frame we had. We met four of them, which I believe is a new personal 24-hour record.

For the sake of this article, I am breaking the chronological order, but I want others to know about these people, to call them up, to meet them, too, some day. These are not simply nice stories. They are being reviewed for very practical purposes.

II. Daddy Bruce

At the age of 89, Daddy Bruce Randolph still sits at a table in his restaurant ("Daddy Bruce's Barbecue", located on East Bruce Randolph Avenue) making plans for the big Thanksgiving dinner. For many, *many* years he has been feeding thousands of hungry people on Thanksgiving. It's an event in Denver. *Everyone* in Denver knows about Daddy Bruce's Thanksgiving, Christmas, and Easter dinners, and nearly as many people know about his famous barbecued ribs and barbecue sauce, though not everyone has tasted the gourmet goodies....They are somewhat outside and beyond the bounds of even the most liberal interpretations of the Kosher laws.

He talks about the hours he and his people stay up cooking the ribs and the turkeys and fixins. He talks about the people who help him out, and he speaks with especially great pride about the dinners they deliver to people's homes with the

Daddy Bruce Randolph, age 79, of *Daddy Bruce's Barbeque,*
with the author.

help of the Denver cab companies, holiday meals for people who just can't get out for the celebration at the restaurant. I see pictures and posters of the Denver Broncos all over the walls, and I see certificates and awards and plaques covering the rest of the walls, including an award from one of the local synagogues. Daddy Bruce tells me someone once wrote a book about him, and I said I would like to get a copy of it, and he tells me he thinks he's got one upstairs (he lives above the restaurant). He takes his 89-year old body up the steps — not with any particularly great difficulty — up the steps, doesn't find the book, comes back down, asks some of the people working in the restaurant if there's one downstairs, they say no, and he goes back upstairs again — again, without any particularly great difficulty — to look once again. Finally he finds one and signs it for me.

And I keep thinking: this man was almost born in the last century, and he's looking really fine, probably about age 60, and what's on his mind is the big Thanksgiving dinner for hungry folks two months down the road. I remember the oft-quoted line, "If I'd have known I was going to live so long, I'd have taken better care of my teeth." When you listen to age-89 Daddy Bruce, you'd probably want to say, "If I'd have known I was going to live so long, I'd have started planning Mitzvahs early on, with big plans way, *way* into the future."

I remember from one of the radio interviews with Daddy Bruce I had heard on tape that he has a childhood memory that motivates him to do this. He remembered that Santa Claus used to come visit all the neighbors' kids when he was a child, but, for some reason, he didn't come to his house. It seems that Daddy Bruce wants to make up for that somehow and he's doing a fine job of it.

Daddy Bruce, c/o Daddy Bruce's Barbecue, 1629 E. Bruce Randolph Ave., Denver, CO 80205.

III. Shorty Zarris

J.C. Penney in Denver gives out a humanitarian award annually. It's called the Golden Rule Award. In 1988, one of the recipients was Ernest "Shorty" Zarris, and the $2,500 award money went to the city's Senior Support Services. He was being recognized for delivering meals to homebound elderly people for the previous 9 years, in every kind of Denver weather. He does his volunteer work through Denver's Senior Support Services, and he has a crew of other volunteers that give him a hand on his rounds.

You can always count on Shorty. And if you are hungry for that hot meal and lonely for human contact, it is that much more important that you can rely on Shorty to come, bring the food, and visit. And though I didn't ask him, I am sure he's saved a number of lives when he discovers some of his people in desperate health and calls the rescue squad.

Shorty has just turned 70.

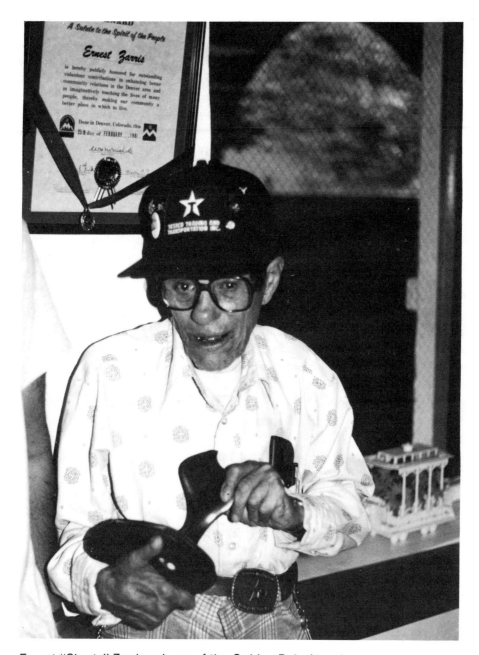

Ernest "Shorty" Zarris, winner of the *Golden Rule Award*.

He wears a baseball cap, and a belt with a giant buckle, and his physical stature justifies his nickname. That is, of course, only his *physical* stature. In human terms, he is a giant or at least the size of a husky lumberjack or longshoreman for all the effort and energy he puts into getting through the lousy Denver weather to deliver the meals. And for all his recognition and fame, he is really quite a regular man, very pleasant and unassuming, as is often true about people who deliver meals on wheels.

What I liked about the articles I had read about him, and which led me to go visit was this: Mark Wolf of the *Rocky Mountain News* said, "He wandered into the Senior Support Services office nine years ago....He asked for something to do, *found people who seemed to need him* [italics mine] and has never left."

That's the key to Shorty and a lot of Mitzvah work, the loneliness-breaker and antidote to low self-image: being needed. If more people felt needed, more good things would happen in this Woeful World and less people (both Mitzvah-doer and recipient-of-the-good-acts) would feel lonely, and neither would feel less than grand on the Human Scale of Grandeur.

There's one other thing Mark Wolf mentions that caught my eye. It's in the caption accompanying Shorty's picture. The caption begins, "Shorty Zarris has worked for nine years as a volunteer for Senior Support Services, delivering Meals on Wheels. The 69-year-old mentally disabled man...."

So Shorty is slower than most of us. If you would want to use other terms, you could say "mentally disabled", or "retarded", or "with special needs" or "developmentally delayed". Pick whichever one seems appropriate to you, and decide whether or not it is a relevant fact in the life story of Shorty Zarris.

I make reference to this eye-catching fact on occasion during some of my talks. My notes read "Shorty and the Pacemakers".

You already know about Shorty.

"The Pacemakers" part is from a clipping a year or two ago from the Associated Press indicating that Cordis Corporation and four of its former executives had been indicted on charges of knowingly releasing faulty heart pacemakers on the market. They weren't working right, plain and simple. (The pacemakers-that-wouldn't-pace have since been withdrawn, of course, and Cordis sold off its pacemaker division.) Attorneys for Cordis pleaded guilty to 11 felony and 13 misdemeanor counts.

The comments in my talk go generally something like this: on the one hand, some bright individuals covering up the facts about life-and-death medical instruments, and, on the other hand, someone with a much lower IQ (half that? 40%? 57% of the IQ of the former Cordis executives?) delivering Meals on Wheels in all kinds of weather to hungry, lonely people. And then I ask them, "If you had six weeks to spend with someone, which would you pick? Shorty Zarris or the Cordis executives?"

The point is clear. Enough said.

IV. The Eagle Repair Shop

Sigrid Ueblacker repairs eagles. And hawks and owls and falcons and other birds of prey. There have been a couple of thousand she has taken care of since 1984, nearly all of them victims of gunshots or traps or poisons or other unfortunate encounters with human beings.

Some of them get well enough to return to the wild; others can never go back. Some have to be taken care of in her Intensive Care Unit, and others need relatively less dramatic attention: basic veterinary care, good food, and a huge cage to practice flying again. And of course constant human care.

They've even flown eagles down to her from Alaska to take care of. I saw seven or eight golden eagles and one bald eagle when I was at her Birds of Prey Rehabilitation Foundation (BPRF) project outside of Denver. One of them was no more than a foot away from me in the I.C.U. when I looked into the cage.

Magnificent birds.

A giant repair shop, with cages built with the help of volunteers that are 10 or 20 or 50 times larger than I would have ever imagined, because the birds need huge spaces to really fly better, to get stronger, to imitate the distances they will need when they go back to their real home.

But BPRF isn't just another repair shop for raptors. (That's one on those College Board words. It means "Birds of Prey"). The secret, if there is one, is that Sigrid seems to not only know everything there needs to be known about taking care of these birds, but she also is a thinker, a creative, insightful person willing to risk things, to try out new approaches, to make breakthroughs. To use the hackneyed phrase, she is "on the cutting edge" of this field.

I suppose she is a fanatic, but she is a low-key fanatic. She didn't scream once about the injustices of human beings towards their environment, nor about the cruelties and stupidities of poisons and shotguns. She knows her stuff, and she is slowly winning her battles because of the way she *does* things.

Sigrid gives each bird a name: Ludwig Leucocephalus (a bald eagle, the second name meaning "white-headed"), Amadeus, Papageno, Ajax, Myranda, Othelia, Stripes, Kabob, to mention a few. But they are not her pets; she doesn't want to own them. For Sigrid, "owning" these birds means sending them back out into God's Country to live their lives in the wild. There they can be wild once again, Genesis/Garden-of-Edenlike, as they were meant to be.

Sigrid's newsletter is called "The Windwalker".

What must it be like to walk on the wind?

The photographs alone, even without accompanying text, are very moving.

But it is the birds themselves — how do you describe them, their magnificence, this majesty they wear with such natural dignity?

There's a picture in another article I have about Sigrid. In that photograph she is holding (cradling?) an eagle in her arms, some wounded eagle that was sent her way. I think that is a more complete picture, one that communicates magnifi-

cence and majesty much more: a human being respecting this world, awed by the
wonder of it all, and working long, hard, painful, and often dirty hours to keep it
wondrous and majestic.

*Sigrid Ueblacker, Birds of Prey Rehabilitation Foundation, POB 261145,
Lakewood, CO 80226, 303-460-0674.*

V. The Woman Who Has More Shoes Than Imelda Marcos Ever Had

15,000 pairs of them.

All of them apparently destined for some landfill. Leftovers, unsellables,
mismatches, a few of them slightly damaged.

Baby-sized shoes, middle-sized shoes, adult-sized shoes, sturdy boots,
sandals, thongs, slippers, party shoes, sneakers, every kind of shoe imaginable.
Almost every single one of them eminently wearable.

I have written about Ranya Kelly before, the woman with all these shoes,
but when I wrote about her a year ago, I hadn't met her. I had spoken with her on
the phone and read articles about her, but on The Day in Denver, I finally got to
meet her, all barely-five-feet-tall-and-absolutely-unpretentious Ranya Kelly, who
looks just like her picture.

With ultimate brevity: three or four years ago, when Ranya was 29, she
needed a box to mail something to someone. She didn't have one in the house, so
she looked in a dumpster in a nearby shopping center. In the dumpster were 500
pairs of shoes.

She took them home, starting giving them to friends and relatives, and realized there were far too many for her circle of contacts. So she went to a shelter and
gave the the rest of them away. Never having seen real-live poverty before, she
was stunned, and determined to continue looking in dumpsters. And she continued
to find shoes in the dumpsters, and continued distributing them to places that reach
poor and homeless people. (Her friends began calling her "The Bag Lady of
Arvada" [the Denver suburb where she lives and found her first shoe-filled dump-
ster].)

When she was caught, the shoe store made sure to shred the shoes before
throwing them away. When she called the company, they threatened to have her ar-
rested.

She fought the Big Boys, the corporate Bad Folks who run the entire chain
of stores.

And they gave in.

Finally....

After the protracted and senseless struggle we expect to hear in these kinds
of tales.

Now she picks up the shoes regularly, sorts them, makes out the appropriate forms which will assure tax benefits for the shoe store, and then distributes to

Ranya Kelly, The Denver Shoe Woman.

just about every place you can imagine, to all those people who might not have decent shoes because they couldn't afford them. Her five-year-old son accompanies her whenever possible, as he has done ever since she began this simple redistribution of shoes.

She averages 500-1,000 pairs of shoes a month, *from only five shoe stores*. She would go to more stores, but she doesn't have enough volunteers to help her sort and distribute more shoes. She is doing this as a volunteer, of course, taking no salary for the work. None whatsoever.

The most striking story of all is the five pairs of shoes that went to a woman, victim of some disease, whose feet were very much different sizes. The woman survived the recent Denver winter in thongs or sandal-like shoes. She just couldn't afford buying two different-sized pairs at a time. Ranya and this woman went through the inventory and found 5 pairs for her.

On a philosophical level this is a Classic Case of:

1. Righting of a senseless wrong (Tzedek/Tzedakah) — though Ranya is not one to philosophize about this; it just doesn't seem right that these shoes should be thrown away when people who need them could get them,

2. Fixing up the world a little better (Tikkun Olam) — though her day-to-day thinking doesn't operate in such grand terms,

3. Goodheartedness, simplicity, straightforwardness, and innocence (Temimut) victorious over the forces of stupidity and mean-spiritedness — though Ranya would not put it so strongly,

4. A latter-day David(ess) conquering the Goliaths of Greed —though she would not express it so harshly.

The problem is that Ranya Kelly embarrasses easily, does not like all the publicity and big to-do about what she does. I have two enlargements of pictures of Ranya we took when we visited her at her shoe storage room: one has her alone, looking, well, "normal". The other is of me and Ranya together, each holding two pairs of shoes, with cartons of other shoes fuzzy in the background.

Best of all, beyond the philosophizing and the symbolism is the very real reality of hundreds and hundreds of people who might not have had decent shoes...who now have decent shoes.

And it's all so simple.

Time-consuming, yes, but simple.

Many people from around the country have called Ranya to try something in their own cities with their own shoe stores.[1]

She welcomes the calls.

Call her: 303-431-0904.

---

[1]One of the teen-agers from Calgary, Alberta, who attended the recent United Synagogue Youth convention in Philadelphia proudly reported to me that he had already gotten 5 shoe stores to donate their shoes, with more to come once he and his friends could get to other stores. He had heard about the project at BBYO Camp during the summer, decided it was a worthwhile project, then went home and did it.

Try it once.

Just one trunk-load of shoes and you might very well get hooked.

Ranya Kelly, 7736 Hoyt Circle, Arvada, CO 80005, 303-431-0904.

V. Update On The Woman Who Has More Shoes Than Imelda Marcos Ever Had, Fall, 1989

Ranya Kelly, her husband, and son took a week off for vacation. They were heading from Denver down to the Glen Canyon-Lake Powell area on the Arizona-Utah border, via Grand Junction, CO, where they visited Ranya's mother. The trip took a week and they covered more than 1,000 miles. A vacation. Naturally enough, they put 60 or so pairs of shoes in the trunk of the car before hitting the road.

It seems that an old roommate of Ms. Kelly's who now lives in Utah had heard on the radio of the work she was doing, and asked her to stop by because people down her way needed shoes. She was in a town where a plant that processes some by-product of Uranium had closed down and people were unemployed and feeling hard pressed to make ends meet.

I had been at Glen Canyon in 1970; it is a marvellous part of our country, a wonderful vacation spot, and I was eager to hear from her about the beauty of the scenery, the vistas, the fresh air, the incredible sky.

But when she got back, Ranya's travelogue was a little out of the ordinary. She told me the names of towns they had visited that were hard to find on my map. So I asked her to send me copies of her own maps, with the routes they had taken clearly marked. Mack, CO, Blanding, and Hanksville, UT, Window Rock, on the border of New Mexico and Arizona, and Page, AZ (near Glen Canyon) are all circled and have Ranya's comments written near the circles:

Window Rock — "Shoes".

Mack — "Shoes, 15 pair, 2 families, plus extra".

Blanding — "Shoes, 2 families, plus extra, 28 pairs".

Hanksville — "Shoes".

Page — "Shoes, 5 pair, 2 family".

What happened was that, besides delivering the shoes in the town where Ranya's roommate was, they struck up conversations along the way with gas station attendants and other people they came across and as a result found other places where shoes were needed along their route.

So they delivered the shoes.

Ranya Kelly sent me one other document, a letter from Fr. Simon Conrad, the Pastor of the St. Michaels Mission in St. Michaels, Arizona. In part, this is what it says:

Dear Ms. Kelly:

At this time of Thanksgiving, we want to thank you in a very special way for your generosity to the Navajo People of our Mission. We are speaking in the name of the Mission staff and all those who were helped through your donation of 150 pairs of new shoes.[1a]

Again this year on the final Friday of October the Coors truck brought to St. Michaels Mission on the Navajo Indian Reservation in northern Arizona your gifts from the Denver area....

Throughout the next week we were able to distribute most of the clothing. Some of the food items and some heavy winter coats we keep for free distribution to the needy as they come in need throughout the year.

We are confident that the clothes distribution accomplished its purpose again this year. An old Navajo couple told me they hitch-hiked fifty-five miles from Steamboat Rock, Arizona, to avail themselves of the clothes. They had heard about it on the radio. Many of the older Navajos who can not speak English thanked us in their own native language for the clothes and food....[1b]

[1a]Ranya shipped that order separately on a Coors truck that was sent from the Denver area to deliver clothes and other items for various Mitzvah projects.

[1b]One final note, too painful to put in the main text of this article. As I think and think again about my childhood stories about America the Beautiful, the Land of the Free, the good things we learned in school, it is just so sad, and so hard to believe that an elderly Native-American couple has to hitchhike 55 miles in this glorious country of ours to get clothes, shoes, and food. Forgive my naivete and sentimentality, but it *is* sad...but correctable.

What Do Paul Newman,
Bruce Springsteen, and Kenny Rogers
Know About Mitzvahs
That We Don't Know?

I. Paul Newman

What started as a half-joking venture has mushroomed beyond all expectations. Paul Newman used to whip up some homemade salad dressing for his guests. Then he'd make a little more and give them some to take home. Then he and someone else decided to market it. Then spaghetti sauce (actually "Newman's Own All Purpose Industrial Strength Marinara Sauce), then popcorn. Then he started with his lemonade.

All profits from the venture go to Tzedakah (the label reads "to charity"). He gives his money to many Mitzvah projects, but his favorite is his Hole in the Wall Gang Camp for kids with cancer, which he founded.

It's a bit of a fluke. At first, it seemed like a fun venture, something his company would handle on the side. He could do it with a minimum of time and effort, so what was the problem? He is, after all, still a full-time actor and part-time race car driver. It wouldn't hurt to do this one other thing, since it didn't interfere much with his other activities.

First it was $3,000,000, then $7,000,000, then $9,000,000. Then, as I kept reading more and more articles, I saw it had grown to more than $20,000,000, which, in Yiddish would be called *a sach Gelt*, a nice piece of change.

What Paul Newman knows about Mitzvahs that we don't know is that they are so easy to do, if we'd only let them be easy. A little oil, a little spices, a few secret ingredients, and $20,000,000+ later kids in great distress are having the time of their lives which they wouldn't be having were it not for Newman's understanding of how easy it can be.

And what Paul Newman knows about Mitzvahs that we don't know is that once you start, lots of people will join your good efforts. I am sure his company can't keep statistics on something like this, but a noticeable percentage of the sales must be from people who decide to buy his products specifically because the money goes to Tzedakah...besides how good they taste. On the one hand — of all the good-tasting marinara sauces, or all the crunchy popcorns, of all the overwhelming number of salad dressings that sit on the grocery store shelves — if his stuff didn't taste good, the products would still be sitting on the shelves. On the other hand — of all those products that sit on the shelves — if so many of them taste good, there are many, many people who choose his products because they know the benefits that the profits will bring to other people.

More and more companies are beginning to grasp this, but some others just don't seem to have caught on yet. They don't understand that, if it were known that they donate their unsold shoes to shelters, many people will *consciously* choose to but their shoes from that store. They don't understand that, if word gets out that they make seats on their airline available for runaway kids to return home free, then people would *consciously* choose to travel on their planes. Some clothing stores now say, "Buy a suit from us, bring in your old suit, and we'll give you a $50 discount." The old suit goes to homeless people. (Sport jackets get you a $30 discount.) The Cynics' Response, "It's a good marketing strategy, a ploy, no more than a scheme to rake in more dough." Siegel's Reply to the Cynics, "You ought to consider that, somewhere down in that suspected grungy morass of greed, perhaps there is some little, drowsy craving to do good for others."

And what Paul Newman also knows about Mitzvahs that we don't know is that he really didn't need that extra $20,000,000+. He gets by on his other income. He has his house, he has his race cars, he has food on the table. All he seemed to need was a camp for kids with cancer and a few other Tzedakah projects, and the price in money was so little, the time and effort so minimal, there seemed to be no reason not to do it.

II. Bruce Springsteen

Sometime in October, 1984, a certain George Cole, director of the Steelworkers Oldtimers Foundation in Denver, gave Bruce Springsteen a steelworker's hat. It was right before his concert, and this simple act stirred something in The Boss's memory. He recalled that there were times when his own father was unemployed and there wasn't any place for him to go for assistance.

So Springsteen wrote a check for $10,000 for their local food bank project.

And on that particular tour, he wrote *another* check in the *next* town for a similar local project. And he did it again, at all his concerts on that tour, in sums of $10,000 and $25,000, totalling almost $500,000 by the time the tour was over.

What Bruce Springsteen knows about Tzedakah that we don't know is that we all had to come from somewhere, and that our memories fog very quickly, and we forget that somewhere in our own past there was need. Sometimes other people responded to that need, and we should show our gratitude by extending ourselves to others, and other times — as in the case with Springsteen's father — when the response wasn't there, we need to make sure that such unresponsiveness doesn't happen again. Success can short circuit these memories, but it doesn't *have* to. Flushed with money and fame, we could leave people lying in the dirt, but we don't *have* to. We can remember and respond.

And what Bruce Springsteen knows about Tzedakah that we don't know is that when an *immediate* need presents itself to us, we, as human beings, can respond *immediately*, and that *that* is what makes us human. For The Boss, "I'll send a check" wasn't good enough. The memory of a depressed, out-of-work father made him understand better that Now is when the Mitzvah has to be done.

Right now.

III. Kenny Rogers

I grew up on country music, Virginian that I am.

Sunday nights were the best times. The airwaves seemed to clear up, and I could pick up WWVA in Wheeling, West Virginia.

Fine country music. All those fiddles, the guitar strings stretching on the neck, and all the Great Themes of Life: Momma, the railroads, luv, prison, broken hearts, drinkin and brawlin. As I said, all the Great Themes.

I favor Johnny Cash, Willy Nelson, Emmylou Harris, Hank Williams, Sr., and Dolly Parton, to name a few. The music of Kenny Rogers is in the second rank in my ratings, but I still like some of his stuff, like "The Gambler".

A few years back, Kenny Rogers would put a letter in the local papers before his concerts, telling his fans that the price of admission was the ticket — plus a can of food. The letter usually began something like, "My wife, Marianne, and I are concerned about hungry people in America...." By the time he had done 71 of those concerts, local food banks had benefitted to the tune of more than 2,000,000 pounds of food. I assume he kept doing it for a number of other concerts, but the article I have ends at 71 performances and those 2,000,000 pounds of food.

In the world of country music, you don't get much more famous than Kenny Rogers. There's ego-gratification in fame, there's lots of money, and power. Imagine, announcing that you are coming to town to play some music, and 25,000 people buy tickets to fill a stadium (a small stadium at that). It is hard to imagine.

The twist is that the audience is a captive audience: they are there because they want to hear you. You give a little nudge in the direction of Mitzvahs, and the results are so staggering — in this case 2,000,000 pounds of food — it is just awfully difficult to comprehend. What does 2,000,000 pounds of canned, bagged, boxed food look like? How many hungry people will it feed, and for how long? How many pregnant women will give birth to healthier babies because of their better diet during pregnancy? How many people will be tided over just long enough to get another job? How many people will sit down to a decent meal with the whole family and say, "We're going to make it through this one"?

Because of Kenny Rogers and his simple idea.

So, what Kenny Rogers knows about Mitzvahs that we don't know is that the power that comes with fame can be harnessed to Mitzvahs. In the Big Time, that includes such stars as Liz Taylor, who taught us that AIDS is not to be ignored nor shuffled under the rug, and that money, enormous amounts of money for research and care will somehow bring relief, sooner or later.

That's fame in the Big Time, of course. But scaling it down to whatever level we find ourselves on, the principle is the same: we have power according to our status as parents, as children, as spouses, as business people, as professors, as journalists, as members of religious groups. Kenny Rogers teaches us that we should use that power at least sometimes to make good things happen...and that we'd be surprised just how much we can accomplish with that fame.

We should assess for ourselves how large our network is. We should take more time to consider what we could do if now and again we would but channel our efforts into the area of Mitzvahs. And seeing the results of one country singer's project, we ought to think big, bigger than we used to think.

2,000,000 pounds of food.

IV. Ongeshtupped

The old Yiddish joke goes, "There's 4 levels of rich: *reich* (rich), *ongesh-tupped* (loaded), *Rotschild* (Rothschild), and *oif mir gezogt* (It should only happen to me).

The Big Boys I am writing about are at the very least *ongeshtupped*. We, poor fellow creatures of the super-stars, could make long lists of synonyms and colloquialisms for how rich they are....Everything from "Ah!" to "They have money up the wazoo" to "If some people fly first class, they probably charter the whole plane just for themselves." (Elvis supposedly once sent one of his cronies to some distant town on his private plane, just to pick up some special peanut butter to satisfy one of his momentary cravings.)

I sometimes get lucky and get to fly first class. I have upgrade coupons from the airlines, or the plane is overbooked and they bump some of us up to the fancy part of the plane to make room for the overbooked, huddled masses yearning to get home any way they can...back in coach. I like to see who really *is* up there. Do they dress differently, handle their forks with a different grip, read the *Wall Street Journal* or *People Magazine?* About 6 months ago I had a young couple sitting in front of me. The woman kept glancing back to the first row in coach. I pieced it together somewhere over Omaha: in coach were her kid (about 2 or 3 years old) and the *au pair*. Now, that's not *really* rich. *Really* rich is flying the whole gang in first class, instead of skimping on the other tickets.

Cynics in my audiences get their chance after I talk about The Big Boys. They say it is easy for The Big Boys like Springsteen to toss around $10,000 or $25,000 at a shot. It's the same for them as $10 or $25 is for us, they say.

Well, no and yes. No, 10 grand is still 10 grand, and you can certainly buy a lot more toys and stay at fancier suites at the Plaza and have your salmon flown in direct to your door much easier with $10,000 than you can with $10. Yes, the comparison is valid in a nasty sort of way when you think that — at that eye-opening concert in Denver sometime in the Fall of 1984 — Springsteen passed the hat for the needy that the food bank and he were supporting. The crowd pitched in: $900. Now, there were 15,493 fans in the audience, and simple math brings you to the conclusion that that averages out at 5.8 cents/person. So, to tell the truth, for the cynics, the ratio of $10,000/$10 isn't entirely true. It's more like $10,000/5.8 cents.

And the cynics continue, "Well, they came to a concert to be entertained, not to be asked for money" and "Well, they probably spent so much on the tickets" and "Well, they probably aren't carrying much cash". (How do they buy the records, albums, T-shirts?).

To quote the prison warden in "Cool Hand Luke", "What we have here is a failure to communicate."

And it is a sad lesson for fundraiseers. If Springsteen, The Boss Himself, makes the pitch, and the Tzedakah pickins are so slim as a result, one has to wonder how lesser mortals could possibly get others to part with their money for some worthy cause.

It is a very sad lesson, and that is one of the other things Springsteen knows about Mitzvahs that we don't know: Tzedakah means the *actual* act of giving. You have to as-literally-as-you-can-think-of part with money that is in your own possession and transfer it to the possession of others who need it more.

And another thing Springsteen knows that we don't know: Tzedakah means money in absolute dollars. Put very simply: if each person at the Denver concert had given $1, that would have made $15,493 plus The Boss's $10,000, for a total of $25,493, which would have offered considerably greater relief to hungry people than $10,900, which is what was actually taken in.

And one more lesson from Springsteen: sadly, even at the lowest level of cynicism, using the principle of "$10,000 for him is like $10 for us", they should then have actually given $154,930 (plus his $10,000 makes $164,930), but the blowhards in the audiences don't even come up with their "fair share".

If Springsteen understood Hebrew, we'd say "Yasher Koach to you! All the more strength to you". And we'd have to urge him to keep his spirits up in the face of disappointment and tell him to go right on doing what he's doing, giving away his money, making his pitch, and hoping that somewhere along the way, more people will put their money where their mouths are.

I just wish the reporter for the *Denver Post* had interviewed him afterwards to find out how he could handle (a) the good feelings for his own donation, (b) the bad feelings about the crowd's tightwad response, and (c) the mix of those feelings, which is the hard part.

V. In Conclusion

The fact is that we probably *do* know all these things The Big Boys know, but we keep it too much in the back of our minds. Perhaps the real lesson these guys are teaching is that we should take it out of the back of our minds more often, and move ourselves to act, more frequently, right now.

I write and talk quite frequently about what I have learned from Paul Newman, Bruce Springsteen, and Kenny Rogers. I usually take one or two of the themes as a point of departure for some particular insight into Mitzvah work. But I think tying them all together in one essay really increases the power of what they have done and what we can do, they, The Big Boys, and we, the Lesser Folk.

There is one trap: we could say, "It's easy for The Big Boys." Or "It's so much easier for The Big Boys.

But that's just not true.

Somewhere deep inside we know that's just not so, and all we have to do is just do it.

A Letter to the Editor

I. A Summary of the Letter

From the *Chicago Tribune*, September 7, 1989:

Since April, 1986, the Defense Department has been conducting research at Louisiana State University on head wounds.

"Hundreds of cats have been shot in the head to figure out how to get wounded soldiers back to the front lines quickly," according to the Physicians Committee for Responsible Medicine.

"The main conclusion," the group said, "is that cats stop breathing as a result. Though the cats are given an anesthetic before they are shot, they are given no pain relief if they survive."

The research is scheduled to continue through September, 1991, unless cancelled.

II. Comments

1. You have to read the letter twice to believe they are really doing this. The first time you doubt that you have read it right.

2. With bizarre stories like these, you need to make sure that the source is a good one. It is — The Physicians Committee for Responsible Medicine.

3. You really have to wonder if there might not just be another way to conduct tests to solve this battlefront problem.

4. You ought to wonder what kind of university is so desperate for research funds that they would take on such a project.

5. You really should wonder what kind of people-who-are-called-scientists actually conduct the tests, fire the guns, handle the mess, record and correlate the accumulated data.

6. You could wonder just exactly how often the scientists conducting the tests say to themselves or their colleagues, "Now this particular shot has the following direct and immediate implications for our boys on the front lines."

7. If you have children, you might wonder how the scientists explain their work to their families, what words or euphemisms or jargon they use to have it all make sense to them.

8. You would do well to wonder what kind of people thought up this idea at all, and what other kinds of ideas they come up with.

9. You wonder what kind of people designed and refined the specifics of the test.

10. You wonder why the tests have been going on for so long without protesters stopping it, like cosmetics companies did with all kinds of foreign substances on bunny rabbits' eyes for the sake of testing their products.

11. You wonder — as a Jew — if there is any Jewish term or concept that could conceivably justify this practice.

12. You wonder — if, in fact, there is no such Jewish term or concept — if anyone among our own people has become assimilated so much that, for the sake of science and the welfare of our soldiers, they would take part in this test.

13. You wonder where the cats come from and whether or not they are buried with some form of dignity, the buriers reminding themselves that these, too, are creations of the Lord.

III. *The Writer of the Letter to the Editor*

This letter was written by a young woman, a teen-ager, as I recall.

14. You wonder what she thinks her world will be like when she is a full-fledged adult, and just how much harder she's going to have to fight to bring a little more decency into the world.

15. You wonder whether or not she will turn against All Adults, become an anti-social drop-out, deciding she wants nothing to do with a world that can be so grisly and unfeeling.

16. You wonder if she will pursue The Humanities instead of The Sciences or, to the contrary, pursue The Sciences, in order to try to clean up their act.

There's a lot to wonder about from this little letter to the editor.

GI95T

I. The Letter

Several years ago someone told me his daughter and granddaughter had a joint *pushka*, a Tzedakah box they both contributed to regularly. It was nice to hear about, so I sent them a small contribution. In return, I got the following letter from the mother:

Dear Danny,

Joanna and I gratefully received your $5 for our Tzedakah box. Our theory is that we are so fortunate, she and I, that it behooves us to share our good fortune. So when we get a nice phone call, see a good friend, get invited out to dinner, have an especially good day, receive a compliment, or whatever, we put some money in our pushka. It's been going for 3 months now. We are far from rich, so the amounts are not large, but each month we decide where to send our contributions.. Some places may not even be appropriate, in terms of the greatest need, but it's instilling in my daughter the right idea about life. The first month we sent it to Greenpeace, an environmental organization working against whale, seal, and dolphin slaughter. The second month we sent it to the nursing home where my grandmother (and Joanna's great-grandmother) is a resident. This month it is going to the Pine Street Inn, the Boston Shelter for homeless men and women, the street people of our city.

The experience of giving is a total joy to us.

Shalom,
V.U.

II. Commentary

The letter was written some time during or before 1982, which will prove to be significant as we analyze the contexts of Ms. V.U.'s words. I found the letter so meaningful for teaching Tzedakah, I included it in a previous book, published sometime in 1982, and have since read it to many groups of students, asking for their comments. In my notes, I refer to the text as "GI95T" which means, "*Gym Shoes and Irises: Book One*, page 95 at the top". I think it is important to record some of the comments that have accumulated over the years as a result of the groups' discussions:

...we are so fortunate, she and I, that it behooves us to share our good fortune: V.U. has not revealed her level of income. However much money she makes, she feels that her life is a good one. I point out to the students the Halacha, the Jewish law, that, "Even a poor person who is supported by Tzedakah funds must give Tzedakah from what he or she receives."[1] A discussion usually follows

---

[1] Shulchan Aruch, Yoreh De'ah 248:1.

on the topic of human dignity, and how important it is for those who have to receive because of tight financial conditions, how very important it is that they, too, retain the fundamental human power to be a giver.

...*when we get a nice phone call,....:* We often associate Tzedakah with a gesture of Thanksgiving. In gratitude for some major event in our lives — a birth, wedding, bar or bat Mitzvah, anniversary, etc. — we share with others. When I read the letter to my students, they (and I) are impressed by how V.U. selects important life events to be marked by Tzedakah. To her, seeing a good friend, just plain having a good day, and similar moments *are* major events. They are more common that anniversaries or births, but not to be ignored or forgotten. At first glance, they seem to us to be relatively insignificant events, but to V.U., they are moments of great importance, worthy of being singled out and celebrated. It is a very striking insight.

...*we put some money....we decide where to send....we sent it to...:* The key to the family Tzedakah activity is that it is done jointly. The daughter — whose age cannot be determined, but I imagine to be "young" — puts money in when her mother does, helps decide where to send it, and helps send the contribution to the recipient. It is the repetition of the word "we" that makes the point so strongly.

...*each month:* Mother and daughter allocate the money on a regular basis, rather than wait too long and thereby run the risk of losing the rhythm of the Mitzvah. Maimonides addresses this approach to Tzedakah by saying that "if someone gave to an appropriate recipient 1,000 gold coins on a single occasion, and, as a result, none to another person...this single great act does not allow the giver the full opportunity to acquire the personal quality of generosity — not as much as if one gave 1,000 gold coins on 1,000 different occasions, giving each coin generously. The repetition of the act of generosity 1,000 times reinforces and secures for the giver the personal characteristic of generosity. Using the other [one-time] approach, the person's soul has been stirred greatly only once to do good, and then the feeling may pass."[1a]

...*it's instilling in my daughter the right idea about life:* That is to say, "and reminding myself about the right idea about life". And "tying my daughter and me together in this great endeavor of giving." Jewish educators are inundated with the laments they hear from parents who say they have nothing in common with their children. Here is a classic opportunity to create a common, long-lasting bond around a human act that reaches into the highest spheres of life.

...*the right idea about life:* Namely, that Life=giving, Life=sharing, and that human beings have this in common: they are all human and have needs, and some have more in life than others do, and the ones who have more should take some of what they have and give to others, so that they, too, might have a fair, decent, stable life also. The essence of V.U.'s lesson to her daughter is that she is not just mouthing philosophies and ideals, but that she and her daughter are *acting* on those

---

[1a]Commentary to Pirkay Avot, Chapter 3, Kafach Edition, Mishna 18.

ideals, which is the Jewish way of doing things. Philosophies and ideals make sense and penetrate our thinking only when they come alive through the way we do things.

...*Greenpeace...whale, seal, and dolphin slaughter:* By the time we reach this part of the letter there is generally a lot of tension in the air. I try to loosen up the crowd, mentioning that fact that Greenpeace has added "religious school teacher slaughter" to their list, that Greenpeaceniks are so troubled by how the poor teacher suffers from the antics of the students, they have taken on this cause, in addition to all their other important environmental work. I get some laughs, humor-laughs and sad-knowing-laughs.

...*the Pine Street Inn, the Boston Shelter for homeless men and women...:* The irony is that V.U. implies that the Pine Street Inn is the *only* shelter for homeless people in Boston. This may have been true when V.U. wrote this letter around 1982. But, sadly, in 1989, how many shelters are there in Boston? How much the situation has changed, how devastating, how extensive the problem of homelessness has become!

...*a total joy:* Exactly as it should be. Or to use the Talmudic phrase, they feel a sense of Simcha Shel Mitzvah, the joy of doing Mitzvahs. The daughter is learning early on that there are many kinds of joy in life. The mother is teaching that one of those joys — in a class by itself — is the unique joy a person gets from performing acts of Tzedakah.

III. A Talmudic Principle

The Talmud teaches that "One who review a certain text 101 times is bound to gain more insight than one who has gone over it only 100 times.[1b]

That line dredges up many unpleasant memories from our early schooling...all those times we went over poems or historical dates or the lists of British kinds and queens from the time of William the Conqueror and the Battle of Hastings. By the 27th time, we hate the poem or list, and this is most unfortunate. There are many ancient and modern texts that can and do provide enrichment and insight the more we review them, but our school-acquired distaste for that method keeps us from trying it again as adults. Maimonides' comment on giving frequently and V.U.'s letter are both prime examples of what review and re-review might yield, and I and my students are still not through with either of them, though we have been through them time and again. The key is to review the passage a few times, let it sit for a while, pick it up again and discuss it with someone else, let it sit again, then pick it up once more and discuss it with yet another person.

I would think that if we found 18 or 25 or 36 such texts in a lifetime, they would provide a solid basis for day-to-day living. Whoever or wherever this Ms. V.U. is — she has given us one of those texts, and we are grateful.

[1b]Chagiga 9b.

Amazing, Normal Kids
Or
Someone Should have Told Us
A Long Time Ago
What We Should Have Wanted To Be
When We Grew Up

I. Four Cities

It all begins in Rockville, MD, Chicago, Philadelphia, and Toledo.

I travel a lot, maybe too much.

I catch planes and trains, and use my car to get to speaking engagements where the topic is "Tzedakah — The Theory and Practice of Mitzvahs"[1] : how we can all get more involved in making the lives of other people more decent, more dignified, more pleasant. My theme is always, "What do we want to be when we grow up?" And it makes no difference if I am talking to 15-year-olds or 45-year-olds or 70-year-olds. "What do I want to be when I grow up?" really means "Who do I want to be, what *kind* of person?"

What has happened recently is a discovery (really a re-discovery) — that "kids" are sometimes the best teachers. "Kids" can and *will* do things that amaze the so-called "adults", and, as a result, they get everyone, young and old, to re-think this "What do I want to be when I grow up?" thing.

Enough theory! Let's get down to the real stuff:

1. Rockville, MD — a confirmation class at Temple Beth Ami. My friend, Phyllis Greene, is the educational director, and she has prepared the kids well for the event, laying the *Jewish* Jewish foundation for the evening's activities. We have $100, $150, maybe $200 of their Tzedakah money lying on the table in one dollar bills — and during the evening, we all throw in some more of our own money. I start rattling off projects:

  A. Buy $10 worth of Tzedakah food to take down to one of the local food pantries.

  B. Find two overcoats, take $10, get them dry cleaned, take them to a shelter. (If the dry cleaner won't give a discount, the "kid" has to come up with the difference on the dry cleaning costs.)

---

[1]My hosts are forever wanting catchy titles for the talks. I find it easier to write a book than come up with a catchy title. It's a totally different skill. One basic rule of thumb, though, is to use the more neutral term "Mitzvahs" rather than "Tzedakah"....Otherwise it might understandably scare some people away because they would think we were asking for money, which is rarely the case. To date, the most popular title is "What do Bruce Springsteen, Paul Newman, and Kenny Rogers Know About Mitzvahs That We Don't Know? — Mitzvah Heroes", with second choices running to "Everyday Miracles", "Mitzvah-power-hungriness", "Everyone a Miracle Worker" and "116 Practical Mitzvah Suggestions".

C. Buy $10 worth of flowers and deliver them Friday afternoon to the Jewish old age home in Rockville, wishing the people a Shabbat Shalom.

D. Buy $10 worth of thermal underwear (it is late Fall, Winter is coming, it will be very cold[1a]), take the underwear to a shelter.

E. Ask some woman for her wedding dress and arrange to have it delivered personally to the Rabbanit Kapach in Jerusalem, a woman who lends them to brides who can't afford their own. ($10 — to give to Tzedakah in honor of the woman giving the dress, perhaps a first payment on sheets or towels or a table-cloth for the newlyweds.)

F. $10 or $15 towards the purchase of a copy of *Gates of Prayer* in large print, so visually-impaired people can enjoy the services. As for the rest of the money for the prayerbook — the "kid" has to find it.

G. $10 to a kid to do any secret Tzedakah project — we don't want to get a report. Just do it.

This whole amazing and normal process goes on for over an hour with only a short break.

Amazing — the projects are enthusiastically accepted by different teen-agers. Almost all of them are grabbed without a moment's hesitation; more often than not, bunches of teen-agers raise their hands for one of the projects. I was amazed — there was so much electricity in the air that evening.

Normal — I shouldn't really have been amazed. I had ignored, or forgotten about, the awesome Mitzvah-power of "kids"; I seriously underestimated them and their enthusiasm. (I should have remembered a previous visit to Beth Ami — I had made only passing reference to a similar group a year or two before — just a quick mention about clothes for homeless people. At that particular session, we hadn't assigned it to anyone yet — but one of the confirmation "kids" picked up on it and started a massive clothing drive in the synagogue.) This is what kids do, can do, want to do, were they given more opportunities to do so. They love to do it.

2. Chicago — I am invited to a bar mitzvah party. Ranan, the son of my friends Larry and Marlene Engelhart, is celebrating his coming-of-Mitzvah-age. I'd say there were about 150 people there, and Ranan has asked them to bring a can of food, which will be taken to The Ark, a Kosher food pantry[1b] for Chicago's Jewish poor people. He also asks them to bring any extra overcoats they might have. Someone in Chicago has arranged to have them dry-cleaned and distributed to people in need of them. Mitzvah-totals from the party: 150 cans of food, and *80 overcoats*. (Does a Ranan Engelhart grow up to be a Richard Gelfond [Great Neck,

---

[1a]I had read an article that reported that, by mid-Winter 1987/1988, 13 people had frozen to death in Washington, DC, most of them on the streets of the Nation's capital, some under other circumstances.

[1b]The Ark is essentially a range of front-line Mitzvah projects for poor Jews, the food pantry being just one of them. It remains the paradigm of a community's direct Mitzvah-involvement in the immediate needs of Jews living on the edge.

NY] who cleaned 14,000 kids' overcoats in New York when the Salvation Army conducted a massive clothing drive for poor children? Free of charge.)

Amazing? (I'm beginning to get used to amazing kids.)

Normal? For sure. Ranan spent a lot of time being normal when I was with him. And when he described (in a very unassuming manner) the Mitzvah-goods that had been distributed as a result of his announcement, he sounded particularly normal.

Normal? There's a natural follow-up....Ranan's synagogue decided to have a clothing drive the next year. They needed an experienced chairperson, so they picked the one who had the most experience in gathering coats for poor and homeless people: Ranan. (By then I think he was 14.)

Amazing? (They gathered 100 overcoats. We most certainly expected nothing less.)

Normal?....Well, you know by now I think he's normal and that it is perfectly OK to spend your early teen-ager time doing these things. And I am sure Ranan thinks it's normal for a 14-year-old to have racked up 180 overcoats for people in need of them by the time a 14-year-old is 14 years old.[1c]

3. Philadelphia (by now I am beginning to think *Very* Big) — Akiba Hebrew Academy, about 150 9th and 10th graders. We do lots and lots of what have become by now "the usual" Tzedakah projects: someone assigned to find 3 sweaters, 3 overcoats, 3 pair of shoes, 3 blankets, and get them to a shelter. I have become educated; I know they'll raise their hands quickly...very quickly. We begin moving into the Big Time: someone is to go to a bakery and ask what they do with the leftover bread and other baked goods. If the manager says the bakery throws the items out, the "kid" has to arrange to find a soup kitchen or some such place, pick up the bread and cakes and pastries, take them down to where the hungry people are, and get a tax receipt for the bakery. (Big Time, but Easy Stuff.) Then we hit it just right, Really Big: it is about a week and a half before Purim. We study Maimonides' text[1d] that says that we should spend more on food for poor Jewish people on Purim than for our own celebrations. One of them volunteers to find 10 Jewish families who might not have a decent Purim because they cannot afford it (however they locate them is up to "the kid" — and "the kid" is supposed to find the money [from classmates, friends, wherever]) and make sure they have the food and other Purim extras to make it a special Purim for all of them.

Amazing? By now, I know I don't have to check up in a few weeks to see if it is done. I know it is done.

[1c]Ranan's younger brother, Ari, became "of Mitzvah age" in November of 1989. His particular bar mitzvah-related projects included food for The Ark, used eyeglasses for the Lions Club to distribute, and books for Keshet, Chicago's special program for children with a range of limitations. Call the Engelhart's to find out how to do it: 312-588-5024. If you are a kid, speak to Ranan or Ari, if you are a parent, speak to Larry or Marlene *and* Ranan or Art.

[1d]Mishnah Torah, Laws of Megillah, 2:16-17.

Normal? For sure. Why shouldn't a teen-ager worry about people not having a decent Purim (Passover, Rosh HaShana, any Wednesday any time of year) — *and do something about it?*

4. Toledo — all kinds of youth groups, religious school kids, age 10 or 11 to 18, about 65 of them. We start off with "the usual", and with "the usual" reaction — every Mitzvah is grabbed quickly: clothes, blankets, the bakery, whatever. Then I tell them I bought 6 necklaces at the local Jewish old age residence, nice necklaces made by the people who live there. For a few dollars each (to Tzedakah) they can have one, *if* they promise to wear them around school and with friends and tell the story of where they came from. I am sure every kid who takes one has fancier jewelry at home, but these are special items. You can see in their faces that they understand why the necklaces are so special. I have this feeling that, 10 or 15 or 25 years down the road, if I run into any of the necklace kids, they'll still have this exquisite jewelry and still talk about The Night of the Necklaces.

Amazing that they should be so enthused about such baubles? You already know my answer by now.

Normal? You already know my answer by now.

II. More and More Examples

It's not really fair giving only those examples. It doesn't give you a big enough picture. Here's some more 1-2-3:

1. Baltimore: a "kid" raises money (babysitting, allowance, etc.) to buy the synagogue a TDD (=Telecommunications Device for the Deaf), a machine that connects to the phone and allows you to communicate with deaf people through a typewriter device....so that hearing-impaired Jews in Baltimore can be more active in the synagogue and community.

2. San Jose, CA, and environs: a young, young "kid" gives his grandfather a tree in honor of his birthday. The grandfather is so impressed, he calls the synagogue and asks what they need. They say, "A Torah." He buys them a Torah ($10,000? $15,000? $20,000?)

3. Near Philadelphia: a "kid" sends Trevor Ferrell $597.50 from her Bat Mitzvah money. You know Trevor: he's the one who on December 8, 1983 (at age 11) took a blanket down to a homeless person, right on the streets of downtown Philadelphia, and he, family, and friends kept doing it and kept doing it — food, clothes, blankets, even a shelter called Trevor's Place. Trevor's Mitzvah summary to date goes something like this: By now they have fed more than 300,000 meals to homeless people. As for the people who have come out of the freezing cold and into the shelter — Trevor's Gang has helped find permanent housing for 84% of the the residents, found jobs for more than 80% of them.

Amazing or normal? Trevor's my friend, my teacher, my hero, but too normal to believe. His taste in movies runs to flicks like "The Fly". By now, these facts and figures shouldn't be so amazing to anyone, once you are in the groove of

seeing normal Trevor-type people in action. What is unsettling is that we should be
so amazed at how normal this is.

The irrefutable proof of the Amazing/Normal Principle came on December
26, 1989, when Trevor delivered a triumphant speech to the United Synagogue
Youth International Convention in Philadelphia. Trevor — in all his 17-year-old-
ness, addressed the nearly 1,000 teen-agers and 200 staff and told them essentially
that anyone could do it. Trevor — speaking kid to kid — made plain and simple
sense. Trevor — failure at public speaking in school — had them on their feet, not
only giving him an ovation of admiration, but cheering him because they now know
they can do it, too.

John Holt, the American educator, says it as eloquently as I have seen it
said, "Charismatic leaders make us think, 'Oh, if only I could do that, be like that.'
True leaders make us think, 'If they can do that, then...I can, too.'" What Trevor
lacks in charismatic speaking abilities, he makes up in authenticity. The kids and
the staff at the USY convention could see that clearly. Here was an authentic human being.

4. Thousands upon thousands of bar/bat mitzvah "kids" have twinned with
Soviet Jews, talking of them in their speeches, writing letters to their twin, praying
and hoping for their happy exit from the Soviet Union (some of them meeting their
twins).

5. Anaheim, CA, (June 1982): Older sister's bat mitzvah — Marcia Levin
twins with a Soviet Jewish child her age, gives a speech on Tzedakah, sends me
$54 for my Tzedakah fund for "elderly people who need it in Israel", pays a half
scholarship for a recently-arrived Soviet Jewish immigrant "kid" to go to camp, and
gives her younger sister (she's 10) $206 from the bat mitzvah money towards the
younger "kid"'s goal of $3,000 to help an Ethiopian Jew get safely to Israel.

Anaheim, CA, (May, 1985): The younger sister, Meryl, has her bat mitzvah, having reached her goal of $3,000 to save a Jew from captivity.[1e]

6. Chicago: the bat mitzvah invitation invites friends and family to join the
"kid" the day after to bring bag lunches down to the corner of Halsted and Madison
Streets, where they will distribute them to homeless and hungry people.

7. Philadelphia: Temple Sinai in Dresher requires bar/bat mitzvah "kids" to
have a Tzedakah project. One of them likes to visit the old age residence, and invites a resident to the bar mitzvah. (Compare that to an article in Parade Magazine,
August 16, 1987, where they caught 16 nursing homes testing new and unap-
proved drugs on residents without their consent. What do we want to be when we
grow up? People who invite the elderly to our celebrations, or using them as
guinea pigs for drug testing?)

[1e]It's been more than 7 years since I got Marcia's bat mitzvah invitation in the mail.
I've had a chance to see the sisters on occasion, and frequently speak with their mother to see how
they are doing. They are doing fine: As best as I can tell, neither has become emotionally
damaged nor even remotely a basket case as a result of their bat mitzvah projects. They seem to
be, for lack of a better term, quite "normal".

8. Dundas, Ontario: a Sweet Sixteen where the "kid" says that in place of presents she'd prefer contributions to Ma'on LaTinok, a home for 38 kids with Down's Syndrome in Israel all of whom were left behind in the hospital...a place I have known since it was founded 10 or 11 years ago. (Results, over 500 much-needed dollars. Another kid in Wisconsin asked the same for her bat mitzvah. Results, over 4,000 much-needed dollars. Princeton, NJ, bat mitzvah "kid" gave 10% of her bat mitzvah money to Ma'on LaTinok, Hadassah Levi's residence in Israel for children with Down Syndrome. In California, another one does the same for her celebration.)

9. Newport Beach, CA: instead of a bar mitzvah reception, a "kid" has a concert for the family and friends. A concert by "The Hi Hopes", a band composed of disabled (?) individuals who play marvellous music. (Of course. Why would they have the concert if the music weren't so good?)

10. BBYO in four cities has special needs chapters for children with disabilities, with a lot of mainstreaming into the so-called "regular" BBYO programming.

11. Jacksonville, FL: young, very young, 5 1/2 years old, Ellen Goldstein sends me a $5.00 money order for Tzedakah, one of seven she distributed, with her parents' help. She had to choose seven out of ten possible places. (An early, good, normal, non-amazing introduction into the world of Mitzvahs.)

III. *Just Exactly What Do We Want To Be When We Grow Up Up*

There are more, so many more, examples I could give: the hundreds of kids who, when they go grocery shopping with their parents choose one extra item for Tzedakah, to give to hungry people; the kids in Minneapolis and Washington, DC, who chose to perform the Mitzvah of *Shemirat HaMet*, sitting up with the body between the time of death and burial (such an important Mitzvah), the kid in Texas who by age 17 has already worked 4 Thanksgivings serving dinner at the Salvation Army, the ones who are changing the policies of old age homes to allow pets — so many more.

But I'll close with one last example: a certain Stephen Katz on Long Island who started a project called G.I.F.T. (=Generous Intentions Feel Terrific). He and a friend gathered over two thousand items for shelters for the homeless in New York. That's the good, normal, un-amazing news.

The bad news is that when he went for a college interview and told the interviewer (a college senior) what he was doing, the so-called college-educated whatever-name-I-might-think-of-for-him said, "Do you think that's really practical? Aren't you just prolonging their suffering?" And he went on and on cutting down Stephen's Mitzvah work.

Stephen thinks he did rather poorly at the interview.

I think he's wrong — *he* did wonderfully. *The other guy* blew it.

Stephen knows what he wants to be when he grows up: a normal, un-amazing person who does Mitzvahs. The other guy apparently hasn't caught on yet. Three and a half or four years of college don't seem to have given him much of an education.

And for everyone who loves these Mitzvahs, who might read this or that article, one final note: Don't ever doubt that you are right. (That is, after all, what the word "Tzedakah" means — "The Right Things To Do".)

Just do it.

And enjoy it.

In fact, if you want 116 different ways to do these Mitzvahs, call 212-533-7800 and ask for the USY office. Tell them you want a copy of the article "116 Practical Mitzvah Suggestions." They'll send you the list, besides the other Mitzvahs you already enjoy doing.

Pick another one now and again. Add to your Mitzvah repertoire.

And most of all, just continue to be normal and amazing (or un-amazing).

Sending Your Jewish Kid
Off to College

I. Preparing for Life

The old-fashioned way of thinking was that a college education might instill wisdom in the student and provide some measure of guidance for a well-thought-out and upright life.

Which is why, I imagine, the Columbia University library has the names of many great geniuses carved into the stone over those very imposing Greek pillars. Socrates, Plato, Demosthenes, ~~Rabbi Akiva and Beruria~~, Cicero, ~~The Baal Shem Tov~~, Homer, Herodotus, ~~Maimonides~~. In short, all The Heavies.

On the other hand, the Nasty '80's gave us this strange trend that kids go to college to get degrees to get good jobs, which yield happiness and security.

And the Nasty '80's gave us this unsettling idea that a "better" college means stronger, more broadly-accepted and resilient degrees in the job market, and therefore, better jobs, more happiness and security.

That's just plain silly.

Good degrees and good jobs don't *necessarily* yield more happiness.

And better degrees and better jobs don't *necessarily* provide security, other than increasing the odds for *financial* security.

II. What I Hear

For 14 years I have worked with American and Canadian teen-agers during my summers in Israel. I often see them a few or many years later. I want to catch up, to find out where they went to college, what they are doing now, what kind of jobs they have. Most of all, I want to know how they are. When I zero in on the college questions, I hear some things that are tough to digest:

1. Frequently they tell me that they have few mentors, professors who are role models for them, who share their wisdom in addition to their scholarship.

2. At best, they infrequently have courses that are intimately concerned with living life with ideals and meaning.

3. Frequently, children of Jewishly-involved parents drift away over the years from intense, average, or even fringe Jewish involvement.

4. Many kids who were active in Mitzvah work in high school — generally through their Jewish youth groups — drift away from Mitzvah work at The University. At best, involvement in Tzedakah programs becomes peripheral in their thinking and in their time schedules. (On the other hand, I get very excited when I meet medical students who are in the thick of "extra-curricular" Mitzvah work unrelated to their medical studies. The myth is that Med School takes *all* your time. So much for that myth.)

5. While the memories of earlier Mitzvah work may be present in their minds, what I hear is that there is no reasonable guarantee that they will pick up on this work later on, once they are "secure". The hiatus of higher education — that long, interrupting time-frame in the flow of life — is deadly to Mitzvah work.

6. The draw and pull of other things, from Medieval studies to future plans in corporate law, are so strong, we have almost nothing to counteract the sheer force of it, including 12 years of a day school education. Even the childhood experiences of everything from equestrianism to outdoor camping sometimes carry a greater weight in the long run.

7. We are unable to keep our best-of-the-best and most-involved-of-involved Jewish kids in Jewish professions. This is true even for those who attend Jewish institutions of higher learning.

8. Few, if any, of them speak of being inspired.

III. *Paltry Suggestions*

Do not misunderstand.

They're not bad kids. Not at all.

In fact, so many of them are pleasant, decent individuals.

But if we are concerned about the future of the Jewish community, we have to re-orient ourselves and re-educate ourselves and remind ourselves of what college life may bring. These suggestions are so weak in the face of the vast numbers of our Jewish students emerging out into the Big World unattached and uninvolved in their Judaism, that I would hope others would pick up on the theme and get down to more thorough, more intense, and more well-funded practical suggestions:

1. Parents — find out whether or not the place you are paying so many, many thousands of dollars to educate your child offers much *in* the classroom itself. There's this great [read:lousy] throwaway line I remember, "It's not what happens *inside* the classroom as much as what happens *outside* that counts." Then, the logical conclusion would be that — for a lot less money — you could have them spend a few years working for a Jewish Family Service's Meals on Wheels program or the JCC's after-school program for latchkey kids, or the synagogue Tzedakah committee, and at the same time have them take courses for a degree from a less expensive "worse" (as opposed to "better") school.

2. Parents — ask if the colleges your kid is applying to have any inspiring teachers. And ask what they are inspiring them about. Find out if there are any mentors, and whether or not you would want them as mentors for yourself.

3. Parents — check out what Mitzvah activities are available on the campuses your kid is considering. Are there facilities to tutor learning-disabled Jewish kids in the local synagogues? Can they do work-study by being a big brother/big sister to Jewish kids who need a big brother/big sister? Can they participate in the activities of the local Hebrew free loan society? Is there a local Mitzvah hero they

can work with? Push the Jewish organizations on campus to publish a guide to such activities.

4. Parents — see if there are Jewish studies courses being offered that are somehow related to ideals and action, Menschlichkeit and caring. Ask if the courses are essentially scholarly examinations of Jewish texts, handled and taught the same way Shakespeare or Homer would be taught. Some are, some aren't. If they are Shakespeare/Homer types, then understand that they are not necessarily geared to inspiration and guidance.[1] (Jewish institutions of higher learning are particularly guilty of this compartmentalization.) Do not be misled. For example, there would be a difference between a course called, "A Philological Analysis of Isaiah 40-66" and "The Craving for Justice and Equity in Isaiah 40-66". The former is scholarship and has its place; the latter offers us all more hope and comfort in a world of many injustices and ever-growing numbers of despairing human beings. Speak to students who have taken these courses and mark which courses fall into which category: pure scholarship or life-related, or if they combine both. Urge Jewish institutions of higher learning to offer more courses in the 2nd category, the one about life.

5. Parents — ask yourselves exactly what you would hope your child would be like as a human being and as a Jew when he or she graduates 4 years down the road. Don't be afraid to discuss it with your child, this Jewish thing. Don't be afraid to say, "Now is the time when you can integrate your Tzedakah work with your other training and education more fully." It is *their* choice to listen or not, but it is *your* obligation to raise the issue. Discuss the relationship of wisdom and knowledge with them and how both subjects will be presented at college. Discuss the relationship of thinking to action, philosophy to life-style, and all those other issues you *really* think are critical. Begin intensive discussions from the moment College Board exams become a necessity. That would be a good time to ask your kid exactly "what he or she wants to be when he or she grows up". Compare Profession to Life; discuss Success, Happiness, and Security in depth.

6. Institutions of Higher Jewish Learning — when a Golden Child comes your way, don't blow it. Golden Child does not mean "great intellectual genius" or "budding scholar" — they are a dime a dozen. Golden Child means "Great Jew". Accommodate, bend over backwards, tailor-make — do anything — to foster that Great Jew's Jewishness. Accommodate, bend over backwards, tailor-make — break all the rules — to urge them to go into Jewish work. With great pain I recall a Golden Child and an institution that blew it. Some other secular field became much more attractive, despite numerous pleas to the school that they were not accommodating, bending backwards, tailor-making whatever the Golden Child would

---

[1]Some professors of Jewish studies marvellously combine their scholarly tools with a real desire and ability to transmit sublime messages to their students. Whether there are enough of this type of university faculty, I cannot say, though, from what I hear from the students and former students, the answer is, sadly, no.

need. Oh, she'll be a good professor of something, or lawyer, or doctor, an involved Jew, but we won't have her full time.

It is our loss, and our fault.

7. The Jewish Establishment — pour any and all money into anything that will stem the tide (it is really a tidal wave).

Enough breast-beating (which seems to be a national Jewish leadership pastime).

Do it.

IV. *Collegium and Chevrah*

Cassell's Latin-English and English-Latin Dictionary records the following definition: "*Collegium*.....colleagueship,...a body, guild, corporation, college...."

One of the best Hebrew translations for *collegium* would be "Chevrah". Chevrah is your friends, your gang, the people you do things with; it also means "society in general". It would be hoped that college would create a Chevrah for your child that is a Mitzvah-Chevrah, a group of friends who stay together throughout life for the purpose of doing Mitzvahs. Perhaps 20 or 30 years down the road, they will still stay in touch, still join forces to take care of the needs of the Jewish community and humanity at large, insuring happiness and *real* security for those who would never have such blessings were it not for their Mitzvah work.

"University", of course, is from "universitas" which is from "unum" which means "one", "total", "whole". "Wholeness" in Hebrew is "Shalom".

Our Gift
To the Next Generation

I. Our Gift

I think they will thank us in a few decades.

They will be grateful that TV ads on the screen will say, "Batteries not included" and "Each piece sold separately".

They will thank us for unit pricing in the grocery stores, so they don't have to stand there figuring how much per ounce 4.63 ounces of crushed pineapple cost @ $.79 compared to 9.07 ounces @ $1.35...and for the ingredients on the package, listed according to percentages (by weight or by volume), so they'll know how much of it is salt or sugar or junk and what borderline-dangerous additives, preservatives, and chemicals that might be invisible to our eyes.[1]

And I think they will be grateful that merchants will no longer use bait-and-switch tactics with their customers. They might wind up in court. You know bait-and-switch. The advertisement says, "Brand Y Dishwasher for only $259.99", and when you get to the store, they tell you they are out of them, but that instead they *happen to have* another model at just $459.99. They'll thank us because they will know this is not fair, not acceptable, not legal, and that they have rights, and can take steps to keep from being cheated.[1a]

II. Injustices, Scandals, and the Jewish Response

Injustices and scandals nowadays range anywhere from overstated claims about the health benefits of oatbran to unsafe generic drugs to faulty parts in military and civilian vehicles to outrageous stealing in the Department of Housing and Urban Development. Everyone could make a list for himself or herself of what is most irksome, horrifying, wrong, and he or she *should* make such a list as a point of departure for changing things in this world. A recent radio advertisement indi-

---

[1]Red M&M's are back, if you notice these things. They were off the market for many years because the dye was dangerous to our collective and individual health. Now they've figured a new way to make those little munchies-for-chocoholics safer, and you'll find them any time you open the bag. There are many of us who are grateful for this small — but significant — victory.

[1a]While no single individual can be considered the Father or Mother of the Consumer Rights movement, most people would agree that a landmark case in our day was Ralph Nader Vs.General Motors. He wrote a book called *Unsafe at Any Speed* about how the Chevrolet Corvair was a lethal vehicle for the common driver, breaking up and burning in relatively simple accidents. In the "good old days" of corporate high-handedness, the manufactuer used all kinds of tactics, including personal intimidation, to stop Nader. I have seen old newsclips of the Chairman of General Motors delivering a public apology to Mr. Nader in front of a Congressional committee.

And while we may or may not agree with Mr. Nader's tactics on all issues nowadays, historically speaking, his actions back then had enormous impact on future activities in the movement to make products safer for the consumer.

cated that a certain automobile company uses something like "Product Z and rebuilt parts" when their mechanics fix your car. Those words "and rebuilt" (sometimes they say "reconditioned") are very interesting. Did the company get caught using not-new parts without telling its customers? Did a furor raise its lovely head and the company give in? It was a curious little phrase, worth looking into. (In general, the media are particularly helpful in this area: Jack Anderson's columns, Ann Landers now and again pointing out some senseless or indecent goings-on, investigative reporters digging deep, deep into what's happening that should not be happening.)

As we read about and hear about these injustices, it is hoped that we, as Jews, will respond by recalling the Biblical phrase "Tzedek Tzedek Tirdof-Pursue Justice." (Deuteronomy 16:20)

As Jews, we are supposed to go beyond being merely bothered or distraught about these injustices. We are supposed to get involved, and to fight the good fight to add some more Justice to life.

Within our own limits, of course:

Some people have more time than others. A group of friends in Dallas is taking on a grocery store chain because they are throwing out too much outdated bread instead of donating it to shelters and soup kitchens. Until the issue arose, my friends didn't think they had time for it, but they made time. There was no need to re-arrange their *entire* schedules; they only shuffled their hours a little bit here and there, and now the Battle for Bread is on.

Some people have more skills and stamina and courage than others. They are good at making flyers and posters and organizing campaigns and rallies, and they can get by on 4 hours sleep a night.

And some people just like jumping into a fray more than others, if the outcome of the battle is of critical importance to the welfare of others, or what might be called The Good Fray.

Furthermore, I think people feel a need to be tied to something bigger and grander than themselves, so beyond themselves that it extends for miles and maybe for years and generations. There may be too much of the humdrum in their lives, or they have a deep down unlocatable idealism and yearning for a different meaning to the words "The Good Life". This idealism and yearning is a key to mustering resources.

We could tap into young people's minds and energies before they consider settling into cynicism. We could fire them up, instead, for The Good Fray.

We could take some elderly people, stir their memories of earlier days when they organized labor unions and fought for more decent working conditions.

And we can take the generation of the civil rights sit-ins, the anti-war protesters from the 1960's, and the ex-Peace Corpsniks, and listen to their tales of how the world changed.

We could learn from all of them and fortify our own resolve to enter The Good Fray.

III. Some Things You Do and Don't Need
in Order to Give The Next Generation More Gifts

You *don't* necessarily have to be a paralegal or lawyer, though you may want to know someone who likes doing — and is licensed to do — this kind of legal work.

You *don't* need to become a full-time consumer advocate, Tzedek consultant, or career whistleblower, but you *may* need to write more letters of complaint or protest.

You *may* need specific skills in complaining and persistence, and you *do* need just a little time now and again.

You *don't* need to risk your health, livelihood, job, or security. You *don't* need to be a hero.

You *might* need to work on your abilities to be gentle but firm and gentle-and-firm.

IV. Interpretations of "Tzedek Tzedek Tirdof"

The Biblical verse repeats the word "Tzedek" in order to emphasize how important this Mitzvah is, as if to say, "Become *intensely* involved in matters of Justice in this world".

I would read, "Tzedek #1" — be involved in small-scale Justice, "Tzedek #2" — as well as large-scale issues. We never know how the small issues radiate outward and cause greater and greater changes.

And I would read, "Tzedek #1" — aggressively look for injustices to be corrected, and "Tzedek #2" — and also...do not run away from injustices that come your way.

Do not do it because you think you are a Tzaddik, a Righteous Person, but rather because, in your own quiet way, you believe injustice is just that — injustice — and that there is no place for injustice in this life. Plain and simple.

And do it to reaffirm the basic truth that you can make a difference.

V. Justice and the Law

I think we are all pretty much weary of hearing things like, "We're not talking about Justice here, we're talking about the law." The phrase is usually bandied about when something terribly disturbing and unfair has happened, and we people-in-the-street ask why the law didn't correct the situation.

If it is true that there are so many situations where the law and Justice don't coincide, then it might be helpful to begin conducting a series of seminars and talks and retreats everywhere we can and as frequently as possible where experts can give us details, cases, day-to-day instances. They will have to show us when and where the two didn't match up and still don't match up, and where the two "didn't used to" match up in the past, but do now, and how the changeover took place. And those same experts would do well to lay out eminently practical strategies for how we can do just that: change the situation.

If we are to look to the Mitzvah of Tzedek Tzedek Tirdof-Pursuing Justice, this would be the first step.

The next step, of course, is to pick an injustice or two, and then to get down to removing it from the list of All the Things That Are Wrong in This World. If it is letters that have to be written to the appropriate authorities or bosses or heads of state, we can write one or two of them. If it means not buying a certain product until the manufacturer sees the light or is brought to his or her knees, so we'll do without the product for a while.[1b] If it means going with our families[1c] and friends to a rally, then, we should go to a rally.

The only thing left to do is to do it.

[1b] A classic case in the early 1970's was the meat boycott. Americans felt that the meat industry was engaging in the time-honored tradition of price gouging. So they bought fish and fruits and vegetables. A more striking case is Nestle's and their baby formula product. A few years back the company was heavily marketing this product in Third World Countries without giving appropriate instructions to the mothers. The results of that approach were disastrous, including serious injury and even death to infants from various complications. American women organized a long and massive boycott. Nestle's wouldn't buckle under the pressure, the boycott dragged on, and the company finally gave in.

You can always pick a smaller, one-on-one issue, such as asking the store manager to see proof of what the regular price of a sale item is. You want to see with your own eyes that the product was, in fact, marked down as much as the tag says. Time and again, studies show that the more the customer complains, the more the merchant has to give in. The opposite of "Tzedek Tzedek Tirdof" is "Let It Ride".

[1c]Going with your family means including young children. These are the exactly the childhood memories we want the next generation to remember well into adulthood.

"Mom, You're Embarrassing Me In Front of My Friends!"

I. "Aw, Mom!"

It's a familiar scene.

It's your kid's bar or bat mitzvah party.

Someone asks the band to play some Golden Oldies, and, all of a sudden — without malice or aforethought — you are up on the floor doing the Mashed Potatoes and the Twist and the Monkey. They switch to Elvis moaning, "Are You Lonesome Tonight?" and you and your husband sway real slow around the dance floor, whispering sweet nothings in each other's ears, perhaps even getting a little weepy.

Your son/daughter is having a fit. Usually it happens when the band lets fly with "Everybody Loves to Cha-Cha-Cha" and you let your hair down and let go.

By making faces at you from the head table, the kid tries desperately to get you to stop, and, failing that, runs right into the middle of the dance floor and says, "Aw, Mom! You're embarrassing me in front of my friends! Act your age!"

II. "Now, Dear, Just Sit Right Over Here While I Get You Some Hot Chocolate and Then You Can Soak in the Tub."

It's a familiar scene.

It is early Fall, the trees are turning russet and golden.

Your kid is 15 and has a chance to make the basketball team.

You say the near-fatal words, "Come on, I'll shoot a few hoops with you and take you on in a little game of one-on-one."

[Sedentary 48-year-old males and females display Ultimate Dumbness from this point on.]

You crawl back into the house after an hour of being wiped all over the court, and your spouse says (chucklingly, knowingly), "Now, dear, just sit right over here while I get you some hot chocolate and then you can soak in the tub."

III. Life-Time Schedules

The law student figures that by age late-20-something he or she will be a junior partner, early-mid-30-something, senior partner.

The intellectual, scholarly child figures that by 24, PhD. 25 — assistant professor. 29 — associate prof, 35 (with a little luck) — full professor.

Age 18-21, "I'll suffer through student housing", 22-24 — rent an apartment, 25 — buy condo, by 28 (with a lot of luck) — a house.

That's good, but there's also a little warping. You can read any of the recent polls. They ask the business-track students, "By what age do you plan to make $1,000,000?" It is more than somewhat appalling to discover what percentage of the students figured that they'd be rolling in dough, I mean *really* rolling in it by age 30.

Which is OK.

If it is just one of many goals, and only one of many goals that would be nice to reach but not by sacrificing everything else that comes in the way such as family, personality development, sensitivity.

The kids are embarrassed when Mom and Dad cut loose on the dance floor[1] and we're a little embarrassed when we see a 70-year-old relative traipsing around town dressed like someone age 25[1a] or a 50-year-old male trying to act cool or hip with a teeny-bopper earring hanging from one lobe[1b].

We say they should act their age.

And that is the issue.

IV. Acting Our Age

The issue is acting our age.

For Momma on the dance floor, it's a harmless bit of "letting go" for a few moments, and a most pleasant one at that.

For the over-the-hill basketball jock, it was fun, a good bonding of parent to child, and the soreness will go away in a few days, unless The Jewish Michael Jordan of Canton, OH, was dumb enough to really rack up his knees or ankles.[1c]

But there are more serious time-gaps and time-lags and time-lapses to be considered. Time lines for the budding professional or businessperson or professor can be useful, but within limits....But they can also be a set-up for future frustration and failure. It is OK to want to succeed — Lord knows how famous some actors, writers, musicians wanted it, want it — by such-and-such an age, but (a) at what cost? and (b) what about other goals?

"At what cost?" is for others to deal with in other articles and studies.

"Other goals" is more to my liking. Let us consider some "other goals".

By what age should we want to be able to give away $1,000 to Tzedakah? $2,000, $5,000? I see it when I review the accounts from my Tzedakah fund: friends who used to give me $18, $25, $36 now give $500, $1,000, even $10,000 and more, and not necessarily because they have suddenly gotten an enormous raise

---

[1]Kids, be nice. Go easy on them. They're just having fun. Be thankful they forgot how to Shimmy. If you pick on them now, they'll bear a *very* heavy grudge and will get back at you when you do your ridiculous dances at your own kid's bar/bat Mitzvah. You have been warned!

[1a]Everyone has at least one of these in the family. They're harmless.

[1b]A little sad, perhaps a little pathetic, but think of them as "colorful".

[1c]No sexism is intended. Just substitute "*her* knees or ankles" for "*his* knees or ankles" if Mom is dumb enough to try a work-out with the kid.

in salary or because their business magically boomed. No, they realized that there was a time-gap, and that they had been giving amounts appropriate to a period of their life 5 years previous, and that they needed to catch up with themselves. Now their line is, "What's good for my business is good for your fund." (Which is a far cry from "What's good for General Motors is good for the country.")

How far along should we be in life in order to say, "I'm old enough....I can set up a scholarship fund all by myself for some kid to go to a Jewish camp"? Or that we can tell the rabbi, "Buy 5 shelves of books for the library, any books you think are best for the congregation, and send me the bill"? Or that when new immigrants arrive in town and they need a couch, a bedroom set, appliances, bookcases, — we can tell Jewish Family Service, "I can handle that"? Or that we'll buy 30 Passover food packages instead of just a couple of them.

This is one of the main reasons why rabbis have a campaign going to get bar and bat mitzvah kids to give away a portion of their money. Many of them are suddenly rich for the first time in their lives, and they want the new-Jewish-adult to get the feel — right away — of how much can be done with Mitzvah money.

V. Letting Go

The other side of acting our age is all about the act of letting go.

By a certain time of life, the urge to acquire things should become less important to us. We don't really need to buy so much from the multitude of catalogues that come to our mailboxes. We can say to ourselves, "We have enough."

We can open the pantry and draw the line, recognizing that there is enough food there to feed the 8th Army if the troops happened to drop in. We say to ourselves, "We have enough." And, as a family, we can take a percentage of the overstocked pantry items down to the shelter or soup kitchen.

We can open the closets and see an overabundance of shirts, blouses, suits, sweaters, shoes, coats, and we can say, "We have enough." And we are surprised, when we lay out all the things we will give away (because we have enough of them), we are astounded by just how many items there are in our closets and cupboards, how many things.

I have never understood the phrase "an embarrassment of riches". If we are embarrassed by the overflow of things we have, and if we do not like being embarrassed, we can relieve that feeling by divesting ourselves of the sheer quantities of goods that are embarrassing us.

The same goes for our investments and our bank accounts. We look at them, these figures and charts and documents, and, taking into account future security and financial long range planning, we can say, "We have enough".

Then we start giving some of it away.

And that is as it should be, when we begin acting our age.

VI. The Frivolousness/Tchatchka Factor

All this Acting Our Age theory still needs to take into account an element of fun. As I have described the problem and solution above, it is all-too-serious, too heavy.

Enter The Frivolousness/Tchatchka Factor.

Recognizing that everyone's idea of "within reason" is different, we could say that, within reason, everyone should have some percentage of things that are a bit frivolous. We don't really *need* these things — that extra suit, the 2 crates of fancy fruits at triple the price shipped from Somewhere Out West, the ultra woofers and tweeters in the car stereo. But they're fun, or they give us a little added pleasure, and — within reason — they're all right to have

And we most certainly *ought to* have fun.

And we most definitely *should* own *tchatchkas*, all kinds of things that are fun things.[1d]

It is the Frivolousness/Tchatchka Factor in life.

In sum, acting our age means, I suppose, that we have reached a point in life when we outgrow acquisitiveness and greed. We tell ourselves that we no longer need everything our hearts ever desired, because our hearts have become softer, and we have learned not to desire so many things. Another *tchatchka* — one more toy — doesn't really make much difference. Craving 10 more *tchatchkas* at age 41 isn't acting our age.

And if we show the children that we simply *must* have those 10 more *tchatchkas*, do they know enough to say, "Mom, you're embarrassing me in front of my friends?" or "Why don't you act your age?"

And if they don't say it because it doesn't seem unusual to them, what will become of them when they grow up? Will they know how to act their age?

[1d]There's an irritating side-issue that ought to be mentioned. When kids grocery shop with their parents and select that 1 extra item for Tzedakah, they often want to pick candy or junk cereal. That's all right. They understand that for other kids, the kids in shelters, it is demeaning to have only the bare food essentials. They understand that, just as we are entitled to That Something Extra that makes life a little nicer, so, too, are others entitled; the fact that the candy is for poor people or homeless people is irrelevant.

Some adults, who should know better, sometimes miss the point. They stand there wondering what good it could possibly be to send shelters the leftover food from the local deluxe restaurants and finest catered affairs. Something bothers them about homeless and hungry people eating fancy appetizers and filet mignon. Their reactions are sometimes hostile, snide.

It is nice to note that one law firm or business concern in Washington recently had its Christmas party snowed out. They sent the few thousand dollars worth of food over to the shelters. *They* understood. I think I also heard that they decided next year either not to have a party, or not to have one quite as extravagant and to donate the difference in cost so that others would have a decent holiday celebration.

I happen to think that firms and businesses *should* have Christmas parties, but within reason, and that other money — for the unreasonable excess — could be used for Tzedakah.

The Obnoxiousness/Innocence Quotient

I. The Proposal

We need courses for adults called "Innocence in Jewish Tradition".

II. We Know Who They Are

1. If we dislike running into obnoxious people, and
2. If we enjoy the presence of, and interaction with, pleasant people, then
3. Should we not find ways to spend more time with pleasant people?

People who are obnoxious are more than a nuisance, more than just nood-niks who take your time, bore you, wear you down. Your cells don't get so worked up with people who are a mere nuisance as they do when some obnoxious person walks into your life, sits down opposite you, and proceeds to display Grand or Petit Obnoxiousness. Both syndromes have a good dose of malice in them, a lurking, troublesome, and destructive element that wounds.

I remain astounded by how many people keep at their jobs with obnoxious bosses (though I understand the need for making a living).

I am equally astounded by the others who have courageously made their move, switched to other endeavors, and surrounded themselves with pleasant people, a decent boss, and a palpable quality of niceness in the workplace.

If you work with little kids, one of your main pleasures is associating yourself with The Innocent Ones.

In your joking/cynical moments you might say to yourself, "Oh, Lord, in just a few years, they'll be so obnoxious," But that may not have to be an absolute principle in the flow of human years. It may not be totally avoided, since no doubt human beings do have obnoxiousness-fostering hormones and juices that seem to display themselves during the pre-pubescent and teen-age years. I leave a clear grasp of that phenomenon to the child psychologists, though I differ with them about the degree of obnoxiousness that may be considered normal.

At the moment, let it suffice to proclaim "Siegel's Obnoxiousness/Innocence Principle":

The ratio of Obnoxiousness to Innocence in any growing child is always potentially less than whatever the experts' findings have demonstrated in any scholarly or popular paper ever published in any journal or magazine.

III. Scanning for Innocence

My computer (it seems so effortless) can scan hundreds of pages for key words in a matter of a few seconds.

Since it takes so little time to scan the manuscripts, I checked for the words "innocent, innocence" to see where I had applied them to certain Mitzvah heroes. In "so little time" I found 5 individuals and 1 Mitzvah project. I have met more than those few, but I didn't scan for synonyms for innocence, and I am sure I avoided the word when describing other people, for fear of sounding repetitious. The easiest hero that comes to mind — with or without the computer — is Trevor Ferrell, the Kid in Philadelphia Who Takes Care of Homeless People. At age 11, he sees on TV that there are people living on the streets of his city, convinces his parents to take him down to see them, gives a homeless person a blanket, and the whole process begins.

Innocent as can be.

And *that* innocence seems to be what appeals the most about him to people who meet him or hear about him.

In a few hundred pages of writing about Mitzvah heroes, I have *never* considered any of them obnoxious.

Thus, Siegel's 1st and 2nd Rules of Innocence:

The 1st Rule of Innocence — If you want to learn about innocence, listen to and watch some people while they are doing their Mitzvah work.

The 2nd Rule of Innocence — If you want to attempt innocence, hang out with the Mitzvah people.

And thus, Siegel's 1st and 2nd Rules of the Avoidance of Obnoxiousness:

The 1st Rule — If you want to learn to avoid obnoxiousness, listen to and watch people in their Mitzvah work.

The 2nd Rule — If you want to attempt to avoid obnoxiousness, hang out with the Mitzvah people.

IV. Biblical Insight

I have asked a number of people who are fluent in both English and Hebrew what the Hebrew word for "obnoxious" is. There is always a long pause as their brain cells try (much less successfully than my computer) to come up with a good word. I just now opened Alcalay's 2135-paged[1] *The Complete English-Hebrew Dictionary*, and there — nestled between "obmutescent" and "obnubilated" — is "obnoxious" with a list of 5 words and 2 phrases, none of which really carry the weight and full lousy flavor of the English word.

On the other hand, "innocence" comes from the Latin *nocens*, and means not-hurtful, not-injurious, not-noxious, not-culpable, not-criminal, not-wicked.

In Biblical Hebrew, the words most commonly used for innocence are "Tam" and "Tamim", complete with a large number of variant grammatical forms from the same root. For example, "Temimut" is the abstract form, meaning

---

[1]There are 2 columns on each page. Total text: 4,270 columns of words and definitions.

"innocence". Mandelkern's Concordance to the Bible[1a] lists a number of definitions for this root, including *integritas* and *innocens*.

Noah is described as being "Tamim". Our ancestor Jacob is described as "Tam", which the Jewish Publication Society's edition of the Bible translates as "mild", as opposed to Esau the hunter.[1b]

This root is often associated with words like "Yashar" and "Tzaddik" meaning "upright", "good", "Menschlich", "just".

Abraham, one-half of our most all-encompassing common Jewish ancestor, is told by God (Genesis 17:1), "Walk in My ways and be Tamim."[1c]

Deuteronomy 18:13 states, "Be Tamim with the Lord your God." The Aramaic translation of Tamim in that verse is "Shelim", from the same root as "Shalom", meaning "complete", "whole."[1d]

Psalm 101:2 states, "I will study the ways of people who are Tamim, when shall I attain it?" Our Jewish tradition indicates that being Jewish includes seeking out those who are Tamim, learning all we can about them, and that, by doing so, we may hope to take on some of that quality in our own lives.

And Psalm 15:1-2 states, "....Lord, who may sojourn in Your tent, /who may dwell on Your holy mountain?/ One who lives Tamim/ and does what is right (Tzedek)...."

V. *Moments of Innocence*

The Mitzvah act sometimes floods the people involved in the act with a powerful feeling of innocence. At times, the feeling reminds them of moments of childhood, when they were unencumbered by so many experiences of life's heavy moments. It is good to feel innocent and childlike. It is only pathological when someone wants to stay stuck in childhood. Moments of innocence in times of adulthood remind us that innocence (1) does, in fact, exist in the world, (2) feels much better to the soul than sleaze, obnoxiousness, ugliness, or self-destruction, (3) is potentially achievable for many future moments in our lives.

There are people who are locked into depression or are too cynical to function without abrasiveness to others and sometimes even to themselves. There are

---

[1a] I.e., *Veteris Testementi Concordantiae Hebraicae Atque Chaldaicae.*

[1b] In my joking/cynical moments, I wonder (1) how the Temimut of a college applicant would be tested (like College Board scores for knowledge and intellectual prowess); (2) how much weight the Temimut Scores would have in relation to College Boards, and (3) where are the Temimut Scores to be positioned on the application in relation to College Boards?

[1c] In my joking/cynical/savage moments I wonder why the verse didn't include the phrase, "And do well on your College Boards".

[1d] In my cynical moments, I think of the pop psychologists who advocate "wholeness", but the starting point for many of them is too-egocentric. They begin with a self-search that sometimes never gets beyond the Self. Jewishly, wholeness begins with Mitzvah work, whose starting point is always personal involvement in the lives of other people. We "discover" our selves, refine our selves, complete our selves as we do Mitzvahs.

others who find innocence appealing, and still others who have an aura of innocence about them but would seek to refine this quality.

For all of those people — and anyone else even mildly curious — a real
course on "Innocence in Jewish Tradition" is a must. It would have 3 components:
(1) Jewish source material, (2) a study of the personalities of Mitzvah workers and
Mitzvah heroes, and (3) field work with the Mitzvah people.

The course would *not* be taught by one of the Mitzvah people. I would
surmise that they would be too shy and modest to do it.

But the course *would* stress the practical element: a very real desire to eliminate some of the grand quantity of obnoxiousness in the world around us, and the
similar grand increase in the quantity of innocence.

I suppose, then, that the title of the course should really be *"Practical* Innocence in Jewish Tradition."

An old, old joke illustrates the importance of such a course:

The rabbi is in the middle of a eulogy about a fine person who lies in the
coffin in front of the gathered mourners and friends. Suddenly, an old woman in
the back shouts out, "Give him some chicken soup."

The rabbi, somewhat taken aback, looks up and says, "Ma'am, it won't
help," to which the woman replies, "It wouldn't hurt!"

"Practical Innocence in Jewish Tradition" certainly wouldn't hurt, and it
might even help.

Yes, undoubtedly it would help.

Farflaysht
Or
Why We All Need A Training Course
At Nordstrom's

I. The General Problem

I get very uppity when I feel I am not being treated like a person. When someone doesn't seem to be relating to me entirely as a Me but as a Something Else, I get jumpy, angry.

It happens to everyone, all the time, when you go shopping. You just stand there at the counter being ignored. And when you re-tell the story, you almost always say, "It's as if I didn't exist!"

In department stores it's certainly true, independent of high season or not. "I could have had a coronary thrombosis," you tell your friends afterwards, "and they wouldn't have said, 'How may I help you?'"

There is an exception to this situation: Nordstrom's. The popularity of these stores is based on customer service. They'll do practically anything for you, which is precisely why Nordstrom's is the latest rave in shopping.

I am probably a special case, though, being the child of a doctor. When I was a kid, whenever I got sick, I always knew Daddy would take care of me, and he'd always do it lovingly, even if it hurt sometimes to get cured. But then, when I grew up and moved away from Daddy-the-Doctor's home turf, I needed other doctors now and again, and, while I always got good treatment, I didn't always get good "treatment". I was depersonalized. If there would be a Yiddish word for this kind of treatment, it would be "Farflaysht"[1], i.e., being treated like a piece of meat. Actually, that is a little strong: most of the time it was a matter of being depersonalized, being treated as "some problem that needed fixing", "a classic case of bee sting", "a simple outbreak of the hives", "a sebaceous cyst".

I didn't like it, and fortunately I've been spared the experience more than most people. The last time I was hospitalized was when I was 2 or 3, to have my tonsils removed. So there's never even been any long-term problem. But I hear it a lot from people, this feeling of being farflaysht.

II. The Sub-Problem: Terminology

On the one hand, "patient" is sometimes a useful term. On the other hand, it can be a killer if the person who is sick is exclusively treated only as a patient, is

---

[1]In Yiddish, "flaysh" is meat, as in "milchig" and "flayshig" — milk and meat products.

depersonalized, demoted from Human Being by the process of being Farflaysht, turned into a piece of meat.

The late Rabbi Abraham Joshua Heschel tried to change the emphasis when he titled a speech to the American Medical Association, "The Patient as a Person." That says it all.

Yes, "patient" is all right, sometimes. On occasion it serves its function meaningfully, but when it is inappropriate, "person" is the right term. And that is all I am saying in this article: when it is right to use it, use it; when it is hurtful, find other words. Usually, "person" works better.[1a]

Some terms are now definitely out of bounds: We no longer use "idiot", "imbecile", and "moron" to describe IQ levels, though I remember reading those exact terms in my father's medical books when I was much younger.[1b] "Crippled" is out, and "wheelchair-bound" is a misnomer. "Senior citizen", I think, has been a poor substitute for the straight term, "older person". It sounds a little patronizing to me, but I may just be oversensitive on that one.[1c]

Other terms and labels are in transition. People are struggling with the term "retarded". My British friends tell me that it is totally unacceptable. In other circles "developmentally delayed" is used, though that is cumbersome and I have always felt that the piling on of syllables is a cover-up, a depersonalization. ("Lymphoma" or "myeloma" will never have the raw force of the word "cancer".) Others substitute "people with special needs" for the word "retarded", though the former term covers many kinds of people. During the transition time, as we grope for a more appropriate term, we are entitled to some slip-ups, because we are trying our best to correct the situation, e.g., "disabled bathroom" which implies — at least to me — that the toilet or sink isn't working to full capacity, rather than the fact that it is a bathroom for individuals who may have some disabilities. But people are trying. For another example: Detroit's JARC used to stand for "Jewish Association of Retarded Citizens", but they are now just "JARC". The word "retarded" doesn't sit well with them.

Sometimes a little humor goes a long way in changing terminology. My good friend, Janet Marchese, was at a conference about individuals with Down Syndrome[1d]. Some of the people in attendance were individuals who themselves have Down Syndrome, and a number of them wore buttons that read, "Mildly

---

[1a]A useful exercise for medical professionals would be to take a certain stretch of time — say an hour — and substitute the word "person" for "patient" or the person's proper name for the entire time-frame. That should give a good sense of which is more appropriate and when. The same exercise is beneficial for use of the word "client", as we will see later on in this article.

[1b]Dad is a member of the 1940 graduating class, which should give you a good idea of when the terms were in use.

[1c]I am possibly also oversensitive on the "depersonalization" of Tzedakah money. I feel uncomfortable whenever someone says we raised "three six" when they mean "$3,600.000.00". The latter much more vividly expresses the amount of Mitzvah power the money can yield.

[1d]Nowadays, people who work in the area of special education tell me that the term "Down Syndrome" has replaced "Down's Syndrome".

Normal", "Moderately Normal", "Severely Normal", and "Profoundly Normal". It was such a simple twist, yet so very effective, turning completely around the all-too-common labels of "Mildly Retarded" all the way to "Profoundly Retarded". It was a rather brilliant stroke by whichever person thought of the idea.

All sorts of people are struggling during the transition time, offering "physically challenged" or "partially able" as replacements for "physically disabled". Someone even suggested "chronologically advantaged" for "senior citizen", though that one hasn't quite caught on yet. And in a heavier vein, my friend, Rabbi Steven Glazer, has pointed out to me that the term "day care" for elderly people is entirely inappropriate, harkening back to the Talmudic statement, "When we were young, we were told to act like adults. Now that we are old, they treat us like babies."[1e]

III. The Special Case: "Clients"

Throughout my years of seeking out Mitzvah heroes and learning about the way they function and carry out their Mitzvah work, I have never heard them use the term, "client".

Still, I see and hear the word used in other contexts, in articles, in conversations, so I began to tune in on "client" as a word. In particular, I became curious about its etymology. According to *Cassell's Latin-English and English-Latin Dictionary*, "cliens, clientis" means "In Rome, a client, dependant, one under the protection of a patronus". *Cassell's* continues, "In Gaul and Germany, a vassal." The way the etymology reads, "client" sets up and defines a helper/helpee situation.

In modern Hebrew, there is a more unfortunate streak: the term for "client" — which I learned only recently — is "Lakoach". I had known the same word for years, but with the meaning, "customer". The *Brown, Driver, and Briggs Hebrew and English Lexicon of the Old Testament* does not mention the noun form at all, neither as "customer" nor "client", and the Talmud only uses the term in the former sense.

Jewishly, the English word "client" and, even more so, the Hebrew "Lakoach" are problematic. The overall mode of operation of Mitzvah work can be understood by reference to three terms: "Tzedek", "Tzedakah", and "Kavod". "Kavod" is human dignity and always carries the weight of the person-in-need's being a person, with no possibility of depersonalization. "Tzedek" and "Tzedakah" both mean "setting something right which is out of kilter, off-balance, out of stride". In the Bible and Talmud, people who lack goods and services of various types are referred to as "Ish", "Isha", and "Adam" — a man, a woman, a person...nothing less.

The contrast between the two frames of reference — "client" and "Kavod/Tzedek/Tzedakah" is very strong. According to Jewish tradition, a re-

---

[1e]Bava Kamma 92b.

cently-arrived Soviet Jewish immigrant family, a poor person, a person without a roof over his or her head, a mentally ill person, a person with special needs, a person under incredible stress and out of his or her mind is *always* etymologically referred to as a person.

I do not wish to imply that people who use the word "client" are not being Menschlich towards the people with whom they work. Most certainly not. And, as I said before, certain terms function for good reasons. But, when a better term can be used, then — as Jews —perhaps we ought to start substituting, even when there is only the slightest risk of depersonalization. Somehow "helping others" seems to me to be a little weaker than "preserving/restoring someone's sense of Kavod" or "performing the Mitzvah of Tzedakah" or "bringing a little more Tzedek into the world". A marvellous contemporary example of good terminology is in a letter I just received from a shelter in Chicago called Rest (=Residents for Emergency Shelter.) People who come there are referred to as "our shelter guests". The term is accurate, works well, and is effective in restoring the sense of Kavod of the shelter guests. It works.

IV. Depersonalization, Burn Out, and Jewishness

In certain fields of endeavor, the professors teach their students about the need for depersonalization. They are right to teach it, because there is a need, at certain times, to depersonalize. For example, in order to carve up a human being to correct a damaged heart valve, a surgeon needs to concentrate on the mechanics of the operation. But what about the post-operative time? At what point should the surgeon switch back to seeing The Patient as a Person?

One of the points the professors make is that there are times you need to depersonalize for the sake of self-protection. Seeing too much pain and suffering can cause the helper to become dysfunctional and to burn out, and then no one benefits.[1f] Personally, I have never understood how a pediatric oncologist can continue to function after a few weeks in the wards, nor how intensive care nurses hold on for so long without being driven to the limits of emotional breakdown. Depersonalization helps control the stress level.

But Jewishly, there must be another solution to depersonalization, and that is where the Mitzvah heroes and our specific Jewish terminology both come into play. A certain Carol Watson, who founded Missing Children Minnesota, which tracks down lost kids, takes an interesting approach. An article describing her indicates that, "....She's available to parents 24 hours a day and says she gets emotionally involved in all the searches."[1g] How does she do it?

[1f]In his book, *Souls on Fire*, Elie Wiesel presents some interesting insights as to how the great Chassidic Rebbis held up under the constant pressure: day in and day out, hour after hour, the Rebbi's followers would lay their personal problems before the Master. One of the Rebbi's functions was to advise them, pray for them, soothe their aching souls.

[1g]*The Giraffe Gazette, III:3.*

Furthermore, as Jews, we are taught to be "Mitzta'er immo", i.e., to participate in the pain of the other person". It is such an opposite approach to depersonalization. "Jewish distance" would appear to be an oxymoron in the light of our system of Mitzvahs.

What might be concluded is this:

1. Vocabulary which depersonalizes — for whatever reason: professional-
ism, self-protection, whatever — should be avoided wherever possible.

2. Emotional involvement is to be preferred over detachment.

3. If there is danger of overstress and burnout, then we should bolster and
refine our stress management techniques. We ought to teach these techniques from
the very beginning of any endeavor involving work with people with human needs:
how to take relaxing vacations, how to leave work behind at the office, how to become gourmet cooks or play board games or look out the window and think of faraway beaches and sunsets. There are experts in the field of stress management.
Let us call them in and learn from them, rather than choose the other path, the way
of depersonalization by word and by act.

V. Calling the United Airlines Mileage Plus Premier Desk

If you are a Premier flyer in the United Airlines Mileage Plus program, you
are given a special 800 number to call.

That's good.

You feel important.

And you really *do* get fabulously special treatment...once you get to speak
to some human being at the other end of the line.

You see, first you get an electronic voice on the phone telling you what
button to push for what services. (Depersonalization #1.)

When you push the right button — if you aren't put on hold — they ask for
your Mileage Plus #. (Depersonalization #2, I have become a number.)[1h]

Finally, to prevent abuses and to protect you, they ask for your name, address, and phone number, and *then and only then* can you settle in on a one-to-one
basis to plan the flights to the South Pacific, Hong Kong, or Tokyo.

No one likes being made into a number.

No one likes being farflaysht.

No one likes being treated as anything less than a human being.

We, all of us, just need a little refining of our vocabulary and sensibilities to
take us further towards our goal of treating others with the utmost care and Kavod.
One way to begin is to substitute "he", "she", "they", "that individual", "this person" or whatever other term is appropriate whenever we are about to use any other

---

[1h]Which is just like depersonalization #3, your phone card ID #; which is just like
depersonalization #4, bank account ID # for automatic teller machines; which is just like
depersonalization #5, credit card ID with expiration date; which is just like depersonalization #6,
social security #; which is just like depersonalization #7, insurance claims ID #,...

term that hints at depersonalization. And there are other ways, of course, and we should study them as extensively as is necessary to reach our goal.

These are transitional times, but each of us can move forward, get over the hump, and settle into a more comfortable professional relationship with others.

All we have to do is remember the last time the salesperson ignored us down at the department store.[1i] And if that memory should make us bristle with anger, let's us recall those lovely, lovely people at Nordstrom's.

[1i]After completing this article, my friend, Vikki Bravo, a social worker, indicated to me that the issue of emotional distance is being mentioned more frequently at professional conferences she has attended. She gave me a few examples of speakers who advocated the position that it is all right — even preferable — to be more emotionally involved. It is healthy discussion, and, again, should be encouraged...with specific reference to burn-out.

A Priest and a Rabbi

There is a disease mentioned in the Book of Leviticus, *Tzara'at*, and whether or not it is leprosy or some other disease is not what concerns us. What is at issue is that it is contagious. How much that person with *Tzara'at* (the *Metzora*) was an outcast or an integral part of the ancient community is detailed in the text.

We are in pain nowadays in our modern Jewish communities because of other extended contagions, though I think we are not in sufficient pain. Among the "afflicted" are the Jewish alcoholic and chemical abuser, the battered spouse and child, the single parent and child, the Jewish poor person, hungry, and homeless individuals, the Jewish person who can not hear as well as we hear, or at all, and other Jewish disabled individuals (physical, mental, psychological, emotional, whatever). There must be some contagion, because so many of these individuals feel like outcasts, on the fringes, and, worse, as if they do not exist. In Leviticus it is clear that the community at least recognized that they existed. Actually, I cannot tell what today's fear is in the overall Jewish community, though I suspect it is more shame and embarrassment than fear of contagion. So, it is only a partial analogy.

In any event, it is clear that there are many (read: many, many) Jews who cannot even begin to be integrated into the Jewish community because they don't even exist as far as the community is concerned. Jewish prisoners, for example. And, most analogous of all: Jewish AIDS victims.

I found an interesting Talmudic text on this subject by way of a statue of a priest in Honolulu:

It seems that about 100 years ago a leper colony was founded on the Island of Molokai, the smallest of the 5 major Hawaiian islands.[1] Somewhere in the history of that colony, in the late 19th Century, a certain Dutch priest named Father Damien chose to go live with them, to minister to them. The inscription on the statue to Father Damien says it most clearly, something like, "so that they should know that they had not been abandoned by God nor by man."

Father Damien died of the leprosy he had contracted from his congregants. We would have wished otherwise, but the priest well knew the risks involved.

After returning from Hawaii I thought off and on of Father Damien and began to recall a story from the Talmud (Ketubot 77b), a story about Rabbi Yehoshua ben Levi. The context is a discussion of *Ra'atan*, a nasty, highly contagious disease. The passage mentions the precautions some people took to avoid *Ra'atan* sufferers, including those who entirely avoided the neighborhood where some of them lived. However, about Rabbi Yehoshua ben Levi the Talmud records the following

---

[1]You can still visit the few remaining residents of the colony on a supervised tour. Otherwise, the area is closed to outsiders since this is their home, and the remaining residents have chosen to stay because it is a fine, friendly place to be. The trip — either by small plane or 2-hour donkey ride down the mountain — is well worth it.

words: that he would "Michrach Beho" — stay with them, be with them, "hang out" with them, the people with Ra'atan, and engage in Torah study with them.

And his reward? He was blessed with being one of the few to enter Paradise alive.[1a] (Some texts say there were 7 such people in all of ancient Jewish history, other texts put the figure at 9, and few go higher than 11 at most who were granted such a wondrous blessing.)

The lesson? It is time to do as the Priest and the Rabbi did — whether with real or imagined contagions or some combination of both.

There *are* some Jewish AIDS projects. There *are* people in various communities caring for those who suffer those dreadful sufferings. Perhaps we will find more people — following the lead of our own Rabbi Yehoshua ben Levi centuries ago and the Catholic priest of more modern days — who will choose to do more of this difficult work. As with all Mitzvah work, both sides of the Mitzvahs need it: those who have been put at a distance by the Jewish community, and those who have, knowingly or unknowingly, kept them away. In the final analysis, neither can live at the level of full Jewish or human potential without the touch and the care of the other. When one hides from the other, both suffer.

And, by extension, we would do well to remember that the *Tzara'at* and the *Ra'atan* of our day includes many, many more people than just those who have AIDS. Whatever it is that they have that drives us away from them (call it "the shame of not being Middle Class", use the junior high school term "cooties", call it addiction, label it as you will), there must be a more active reaching out and response.

For the less courageous among us and for the more courageous of our people, for those who would risk real contagion or only imagined contagion, there is room for all to do this sacred Mitzvah work, now.

[1a]Some commentators understand the phrase "entered Paradise alive" to mean that he did not suffer the terror or pain sometimes associated with death. Others give it a more mystical interpretation.

The Noble Profession: Teaching the Good Life

I. Introduction

Some studies reported in some recent popular articles say that teaching is making a comeback.

Some rumors in the air carry messages like melodies in the breezes at dusk on some mythical beach in the South Pacific, little faintly heard melodies that say the breeding and training for greed is passing and people want something more out of their work beyond penny stocks and junk bonds and mergers and Dow Jones and trade balances.

I tend to doubt it.

I get sour over too much optimism like that. But I do recall something about colleges-that-train-teachers that spend lots of money on campaigns to draw students into the field of teaching. I even vaguely recall the near-mystical rewards being offered for such a move.

I like that.

Everyone should have some near-mystical rewards in his or her life.

II. Jumping the Gun: The Desired Results of This Article

I'd rather not wait.

What I would like to happen is that 27 people who read this essay will either (A) drop out of their present job and go into teaching, (B) keep their old jobs but start teaching on the side, or (C) if they are just setting out to select their lifelong occupation, will go into teaching.

As I said, we teachers offer near-mystical rewards, a sublime sense of fulfillment, or what our mother tongue, Hebrew would call, real Sippuk Nefesh-Satisfaction for the Soul.

III. Jumping the Gun II: The Rewards

1. You get to work with people rather than things, facts and figures, machines. You are in touch with live, breathing creatures.

2. You get to observe a unique kind of unpredictable growth, one that is unlike any Wall Street trend or any slump in the trade deficit or slowdown in the Gross National Product.

3. You never have to decipher a spreadsheet.

4. You share your vision of life with idealists, sensitizers, optimists, and value-oriented people.

5. You help create an environment, a society, a world that is more Menschlich, loving, warm, and caring, and as a result you don't have to worry if anyone will ever care for you if you are in need.[1]

6. You will automatically seek out authenticity and authentic people and enjoy the benefits of regular spiritual exchange with them.

7. This, in addition to what our ancient Jewish texts tell us:

A. Whoever teaches Torah to someone else's child — it's as if you have given birth to that child.[1a]

B. Whoever teaches Torah to someone else's child — has the privilege of sitting in the Grand Yeshiva in Heaven.[1b]

C. Whoever teachers his own child Torah — it's as if you have taught your child, your grandchild, and all the other generations to the end of time.[1c]

D. Whoever teaches another person even 1 verse of Torah or 1 law or 1 Rabbinic quote — it's as if he or she gave that other person Life itself.[1d]

IV. Four Ways to Teach JEWISH Jewish Values

I'd set it down as an axiom: Jewish Values, Human Values, Justice, Fairness, Decency, Kindness, Caring, Dignity, Love, Menschlichkeit, Edelkeit, Ehrlichkeit, Ziesskeit, Shaynkeit, Feinkeit and every other human quality we would like to see in ourselves and other *can* be taught.

Let those who think otherwise bolster their own position. I am tired of being on the defensive.

Four — but not the only 4 — ways of teaching Torah (=JEWISH Jewish values-teaching) are (in no particular order of importance):

1. By texts: Jewish texts — from the Bet of Beraysheet all the way down to today's texts hot off the press — Jewish texts are loaded with values. We are not teaching, geometry, witchcraft, astrophysics, or the manufacture of automobiles (though they are all in there, in the texts). Our focus is Good Things, Good People, Quality of Life[1e], the Good Life, the Jewish Good Life.

---

[1]To borrow some of the jargon of the wine-tasters of the world, Life will be fruitier, more well-rounded, full-bodied, enduring, barely acidic, more expressive, huskier, brisker, invigorating, unpretentious, pleasantly pungent, with a faint, distant sense of herbs and spices.

[1a]Sanhedrin 19b.

[1b]Bava Metzia 85a. This particular institution of higher learning beats Harvard, Yale, Princeton, and Brown, *and* has the Ultimate Professor on the faculty, *and* offers many more courses than any earthly university.

[1c]Kiddushin 30a.

[1d]Tanna DeVay Eliahu Rabba, 5.

[1e]A topic well worth pursuing is "Quality of Life: In the Medical Profession, In the Legal Profession, and in Judaism". While there are innumerable discussions of this term in medicine and the law, I am surprised that there is no comparable, extensive body of literature from the Jewish side. It is a much-needed piece of work that should be done, and I would invite scholars and front-line laypeople alike to embark on this all-important task. Suffice it to say that — at

2. By situational positioning: Putting the students (we, ourselves included) into places and situations where they will see the best of the human soul play itself out in the thick of life. In general, avoidance[1f] of such situations should be considered the 366th Negative Mitzvah, i.e., something never to be transgressed.

3. By action: Having the students (young and old, we, ourselves, included) *do* things that bring out the best of our human souls through our hands, feet, faces, all 248 Talmudic parts of the body. Sometimes the body remembers better than the circuitry in the brain. The body never forgets the feel of delivering a Passover food package to a lonely person too poor to buy Matzah. A year later, the body will tell the mind it's time to do it again. So, too, with the hand's memory when it takes money and puts it in a Tzedakah box. So, too, our fingers, eyes, arms and shoulders, remembering just how it felt to take clothes off the hangers in our closet, folding them, and taking them down to those who need them more than we do.

4. By example: Exposing the students (we, ourselves, included) to as many of the Good People of the Earth will inevitably attract us to imitate their acts and attitudes. Working with Jewish Family Service in San Francisco to provide for the needs of Jewish AIDS victims will demonstrate to all who partake of the act just exactly how fine human beings are. Hanging out with the women in Chicago (Sara Cohen) or Denver (Elizabeth Yanish) who gather thousands of overcoats for the unjustifiably freezing people of their cities will beckon the student (we, ourselves, included) to join.

Some say #4 is the strongest, most effective and long lasting, and overall best method to educate Jewishly. That may be true, but all 4 categories interplay so well that we should not ignore 1-3.

V. A Sour Note and A Story Which Is a Solution

I keep wondering why, all along in my secular education, no teacher ever thought I might have talent as a writer. No one, not in junior high or high school, not in college and certainly not in graduate school.

I had thought that's what teachers were for.

Then my cynical friends told me I was wrong, and I agreed with them.

Now I have returned to my original position: that *is* what teachers are for.

I'm no longer angry about it, but I am still very confused as to why it happened the way it did, and *very* disappointed. It would have been nice had it happened otherwise, and it might have saved me a number of years of wandering.

---

least in the popular literature — the assumption that Quality of Life (as in "What kind of quality of life could that person possibly have?") is essentially related to so-called "normal" brain function is very distant from the Jewish view. The practical consquences, often involving life-and-death decisions, demand a detailed Jewish examination in order to prevent abuses.

[1f]Calling a spade a spade in Jewish education would also help. We should have courses called, "Avoiding Jewish, Things to Avoid in Life If You Want to Be Very Jewish", etc. We would do well to sit down and review all the *real* problems in life, and use that as a point of departure for the curriculum.

And, furthermore, in my Jewish studies in college and graduate school, no one thought to suggest to me that I might be able to write about Jewish things.

No one.

Hushlachti LaZe'evim, as they would say. I was thrown to the wolves.

I had to fall into poetry by accident, and Jewish poetry at that, at age 24, by a mere fluke.

And it had to take my good friend, Bill Novak, to suggest to me when I was 30 years old that I might be capable of writing decent[1g] Jewish prose:

I wrote two bad novels while I was in Israel for a year.

He read them.

He found passages that he thought were excellent, and when the time came back in 1975 to summarize my first Tzedakah adventure in Israel, it was Bill who suggested I make it into an article and submit it to a magazine.

But where were my professors who should have been on the look-out for talents that would contribute to the welfare of the Jewish community?

So here is a story I read which we might want to recite to ourselves as teachers as frequently as necessary:

A certain rabbi is teaching Torah and one of his young students is moping somewhere in the back of the room, in a mind-haze, unconnected to the Torah teaching. He is "somewhere else".

When the class is over, the rabbi pulls the student aside and asks him to take out a pencil and paper. He asks him to make a list of 10 things he is good at. The student is a bit confused and reluctant. Still, he gropes around in his mind and pauses to ask, "Well, I climb trees well. Is that OK?" The rabbi tells him to write it down. "I doodle nicely. Is that one of them?" The rabbi tells him to write it down.

So the story goes: the student comes up with a list of 27 things he is good at. He feels much better about himself (naturally), and tunes in to class that much more avidly.

Not sour, not angry, just confused and disappointed, I ask, "Why didn't anyone try that little trick with me?" Or is it possible that they did, and I have buried it in my memory, indicating, perhaps, that there wasn't enough reinforcement?

All this is written fully realizing that I should stop whining and move on with my life.

All right.

I have said it, and now I can move on.

[1g] I am not implying any self-praise for my writing. I rather prefer Robert Benchley's line, "It took me fifteen years to discover I had no talent for writing, but I couldn't give it up because by that time I was too famous."

VI. A New Test, Based on an Old One

We all remember the test: all kinds of crazy questions, analyzed, factored, correlated, results presented to our parents with the utmost seriousness. "Your child will do best as a baker, a funeral director, professional sadist, carburetor adjuster, genetic engineer, airline pilot for Air Molokai, or coach for the U.S. Olympic Javelin Team."

I sure hope my Mom kept the results of that test and that they are sitting in some file drawer. She cleaned out a lot of those things a few years ago, so I doubt we'll find them.[1h]

The test I think we need to develop could be based on that infamous exam, but expanded, value-ized and Judaized. We really want to explore two areas: (1) what talents — even the most offbeat talents — the testee[1i] might have, and (2) how these talents might be put to work in the world of Mitzvahs.

Some of the questions might be:

1. Are you a good laugher? (Useful for work with latchkey kids, for people with no self-image, for entertaining in institutions, semi-institutions, quasi-institutions.)

2. Do you need less than 5 hours a night sleep to function well? (Good for long-haul pick-ups and deliveries of Mitzvah goods on the Good Lord's many highways.)

3. Do you kvetch a lot and enjoy that kvetching? (Excellent for beating down recalcitrant bureaucrats who refuse to see the light about the needs of people in need.)

4. How is your hugging? Is it gentle, strong, strong-yet-gentle, spontaneous, reserved, reserved-yet-spontaneous? (Good for hospital visits: pediatrics, geriatrics, newborns, any ward imaginable.)

5. How would you rate your ability to tell tall tales? Feh? Eh, i.e., a little better than Feh? So-So? Average? Above average? Astounding? Spellbinding? (Spellbinding tall tale tellers are needed in a variety of Mitzvah settings, with or without campfires.) We *definitely* and *desperately* need more astoundingly spellbinding tall tale tellers.

6. Are you a good, fair-to-middling, or inordinately fine climber? (Excellent for lonely kids, retrieving wild pets high up in the maple, gathering luxuriant branches for Sukkahs, selecting mountain goat horns for Shofarot.)

7. Are you argumentative? (Great for litigation brought against those who would unfairly evict elderly people from their homes. Bet Tzedek's people in Los Angeles do exactly that, among many other fine, fine Mitzvahs. We need a Bet

---

[1h]Some parents save absolutely everything. Others pick and choose over the years, but they sometimes err, using adult criteria instead of adults-looking-back criteria. I have never forgiven Mom for giving away, my 3rd-grade reader *More Streets and Roads*, my plane and solid geometry books and *El Camino Real, Book Two*.

[1i]Accent, second syllable.

Tzedek in every conceivable Jewish community. Now. *Absolutely definitely* and *very desperately*.)

8. The Kindness Quotient: How would you rate your abilities to be kind? Are you kind almost always, kind even under stress, capable of kindness even when you are depressed or have the flu, able to summon up your kindness even when surrounded by a savage, drooling pack of SOB's? (Very useful for far too many Mitzvah situations to list.)

9. Do you have unlimited stamina? (Much needed for packing hundreds of crates of donated food for Mitzvah projects, teaching the art of swimming, baseball, obstacle-course-running to unwanted kids who have been shuffled from foster home to foster home.)

10. Do you have an abundance of love for children? (Adoption of Jewish kids up for adoption, including kids with special needs.) Do you have an abundance of love for human beings, children and adults alike? (Highly recommended, a *sine qua non*, for Torah teachers.)

11. Do you have a talent for making money without even trying? (Funding any one of 1,035,621 Tzedakah projects.)

12. Do you dance? Do you dance poorly but enjoy it so much your partner loves dancing with you and says to you when the orchestra's last notes fade into memory, "It's so good to be alive!"? (We need many, many of these.)

13. Do you do make-up nicely? (For battered women's shelters, to help restore self-image; in nursing homes and old age homes, for painting lonely kids' faces for a night on the town for Purim.)

14. Does your cooking merit 3 Michelin forks, at least according to your own taste? (Needed for Mitzvah and non-Mitzvah work alike.)

15. Can you clean bathrooms sparkling clean? (For shelters, for places where people can no longer do the basic cleaning, and when they reach that point where they can no longer do it, begin to fold up and die.)

16. Do you *love* doing the laundry?[1j] (Same as #15, plus other Mitzvah locales, many other Mitzvah locales.)

Juvenal's line *mens sana in corpore sano* (a sound mind in a sound body) is too Roman. Jewishly it would be *Neshama sana in corpore sano* (a sound soul in a sound body).

I would be willing to let the experts in test-writing prepare the text of such an examination, and I would be happy if expert test analyzers and correlaters could work up the appropriate scales and measuring rods. I'd even partially fund the printing of the test and find people who would write up the results for various journals. I think it would be good for the test writers and analyzers and correlaters, and testers and the testees, the Jews, and the world.

[1j]This one is really a borderline case. Anyone who *loves* doing the laundry and gets his or her jollies from watching the TV ads for the new Tide and Fab and Duz products ought to be considered a psychopath and mercifully institutionalized. (See "The Classic Nut Case", *Journal of American Psychiatry*, Bernstein, Burnstein, and Burnstine, March, 1987, pp. 27-42.)

VII. A Present-Day Reality and the Uncertainty Principle

1. High percentages of my audiences are presently employed in occupations unrelated to what they either were trained for or expected to find themselves in 10 years ago. I know, because I ask them. I ask them what they do and what their degrees are. I ask them how many of them fell into what they are doing now. Some people answer with satisfaction, some with a distinct tinge of, "Damn, I am so sorry I am stuck in this rut" in their voices. There's a lot of free fall and floating out there until people settle into "what they do". The time is ripe to take advantage of this phenomenon and grab the floaters and free-fallers for teaching.

2. Siegel's Uncertainty Principle of Mitzvah Teaching: You never know just how the student is going to turn out, and *that's* the glory of teaching Torah-and-Mitzvahs. You never know. You just never know if the day you had them wrap Purim packages for poor Jews might not get them to take on part-time Mitzvahs as a more permanent part of their life patterns. You never know. You just never know whether or not the text, "Tzedakah saves from death" didn't just turn them into permanent, full-time life savers. You never know.

Well, that's not exactly true. So many of my friends tell me, "I got a call last Wednesday from someone I gave a Tzedakah box to who told me he's cranked up a Tzedakah collective in his community." Or, "Melissa, my student — the hot shot fiduciary specialist for Metropolitan Life — is now spearheading the campaign for resettling Soviet Jews in her community." Or "Jack chucked it all, the takeovers and retrenchments and leverages of his past....He's teaching Midrash at the day school."

You just never know.

And that's the glory of it all.

Reefer Madness

I. Retreats

At any given time on any given week-end at just about any retreat center anywhere in the country there are at least a dozen Jewish retreats taking place. There are low seasons and off-seasons, and holidays. (For example, if Yom Kippur falls over a Shabbat, there will be no retreat; on Super Bowl Sunday, there is *never* a retreat.) Retreats are where so much Jewish education is happening....We would do well as a Jewish community to have more and yet more of them.

Away from the troublesome worries of making a living, away from too-familiar surroundings, off in some lodge in the woods somewhere, there's nothing for people to do but spend Shabbat together and come face-to-face with the topic chosen for the week-end. For intensity and impact there is little that can compare to the week-end away to touch people's thinking and actions.

II. The Specific Retreat (Speakers Listed in No Particular Order of Importance)

It would be most unusual and certainly a bit risky.

The logistics, while difficult, would not be *too* difficult to manage.

The guest speakers, i.e., the teachers, would have to speak from behind screens or have their faces darkened. At all costs, the organizers of the retreat must prevent any possibility of a sense of voyeurism. In whatever way it could be worked out, the speakers' anonymity must be preserved, because the topic of the week-end would be "Jews Who Don't Really Exist in the Community". The participants would be Jewish community leaders, both professionals and lay people, the directors of agencies, the presidents of a broad spectrum of Jewish groups, and anyone else who wields power and can make things happen quickly and effectively. The speakers would be Jews Who Don't Really Exist in the Community.

One speaker might be a Jewish alcoholic. I am not speaking of a teen-age alcoholic, but if a teen-ager decided to participate, that would also be productive. Let the alcoholic person speak of the addiction and how it forces him or her to rotate all activities of life around the drink. If he or she is recovering from the disease, let him or her speak of where he or she went for the recovery process. If the facility was a Jewish place, such as an alcoholics' group in a synagogue, let the person say it, and let the leaders be justifiably proud that they came through. And if there was no place within the community for such a Jewish recovery process, let the leaders take note and consider what is to be done to solve the problem "within the family". *(Jews take care of their own.)*

And if the guest speaker is still in the thick of his or her addiction, that, too, will be instructive, and will perhaps lead to immediate action. The leaders might hear the desperation in the speaker's voice, the need to be recognized in the Jewish community, and by Sunday when people go back home, a solution may well be near reality. It would take great courage for the speaker to address the issue in such a forum, and it would take a different kind of courage for the audience to listen and respond, a courage to wake up to the need and to act.

Soon.

Now.

Other speakers might be other substance abusers, such as drug addicts.

And battered spouses could be guest speakers.

And a Jew who has to use the food bank (Jewish or otherwise) in order to make it through the month.

And a Jew who has lost his or her home.

Or a jobless Jew who is so close to abject poverty it is just a matter of time before he or she sinks into despair.

And it would be important to have a Jewish AIDS victim speak. Because for all we read about and hear about the disease and the people passing through the pain and the waste, few Jewish leaders have actually heard directly from one who is going through the agony. Non-Jewish groups in the general community have them speak in all kinds of settings. We ought to do the same.

And Jewish prisoners, either prisoners on work release programs or already finished serving their time.

And Jews who have had mental and emotional difficulties, who may have been in intensive psychiatric care. They, too, would be appropriate speakers, for they, too, are Jews Who Don't Really Exist in the Community.

And Jews with all kinds of other special needs. I am a great admirer of B'nai B'rith Youth Organization's summer camp. In the summer of 1989 they had as their guests for a few days 2 residents of Jewish group homes in Washington. I came to camp a few weeks after they had been there, and from all reports, the effect they had on the kids was tremendous. "A good time was had by all", and the formal and informal exchanges between the campers and the guests will have long-lasting effects we can never accurately estimate.

Without sounding patronizing, would it not be important, perhaps community-altering, if a Jew in a wheelchair took us through a typical week of trying to be active in the community? The speaker could tell us of barriers, isolation, failed and successful attempts at adjustment, whatever we need to know.

Or a Jew who cannot hear, or can only barely hear, or cannot see or can barely see....They would all be important speakers.[1]

---

[1]A number of years ago, United Synagogue Youth's annual International Convention was held in Tampa. The theme was, "....Who makes people different", i.e., individuals who have some physical limitations. The guest speakers enthralled the kids — and the staff — to the point where anyone who has attended 10 or 15 conventions and remembers them as a blur...always remembers

III. *The Results*

It is hard to say.

Each retreat would be different.

But I would suspect that some of the speakers would reveal their identities at some point during the week-end. Some of them that I have mentioned probably wouldn't need to be anonymous to begin with, but now I am thinking of some of them who would start out behind the screen.

Would the alcoholic Jew — very possibly someone well known to others at the retreat — step out to join the Friday night services and dinner. Will he or she join the students later on, say during the Shabbat afternoon break, to take a long walk with some of them, to exchange thoughts, to expose complex and painful emotions, to help plan a strategy and practical program for the community? That depends, of course, on the guest. But it may happen, and, while that is not a necessary end result of the retreat, it would probably get the process of new programs well on their way to a speedy reality.

Whether or not such a thing happens, by Sunday's lunch, there has to be some commitment on the part of the leaders to reshuffle their priorities and to get down — starting Monday morning — to doing whatever has to be done: establishing a Jewish battered women's shelter, a Jewish group for substance abusers, a Jewish food bank, an interest-free loan society to strengthen Jews in acute or chronic financial crises. Without the practical element, the danger of voyeurism will hang too strongly in the air. The closing session must clearly emphasize that the participants want results, real, *very* real results.

The logistics *are* difficult, and it *is* risky.

But the results....

The results are certainly worth the difficulties and risk. What may have been neglect or injustice in the community can be fixed, pain and loneliness for many can be eliminated, and we can honestly face ourselves and say, "Jews take care of their own".

---

the Tampa convention. The speakers spoke straight, and their words opened up many people to areas of Jewish life we had too-long ignored.

Bubbe, Zeyde, and Mac

I. The Movie

In this movie, see, there's this computer whiz kid who somehow taps into a Defense Department computer and sets the process rolling. All hell, i.e., World War III, almost breaks loose.

It was an OK movie, maybe 1 digit of 1 thumb up. It entertained, and, yes, contrived though it may have been, it was sufficiently tense at the end to satisfy the basic moviegoing thrill-seeker. I remember that I felt I had been entertained, so it served its purpose on some afternoon when I needed to get away for a couple of hours. I can't remember the name of the flick, nor the name of the main actor, the whiz kid, but I know from the teeny-boppers who saw it that he was considered cute, probably a 9 or 10 on a scale of 1 to 10.

And yet, now, I feel troubled by it. Not the content of the movie. The plot was just what the audience wanted to see. No — it's the main character that bothers me. I am wondering why it couldn't have been an old man or woman, preferably a resident of an old age home, who decided one day to potch around with the computer to see just how far he or she could go with a machine and a little human talent.

Why not? The producers may not have drawn in so many drooling teen-age girls, but they might have made up for it in ticket sales from other, more mature elements of the general population.[1]

II. Personal Computers (PC's) in Our Day and Age

I am a latecomer to computers. I started at 43. My nephews and nieces started when they were about 10. And my older niece, Debbie, has come over on a few occasions to show me new tricks. She works so quickly I have to repeatedly warn, "Wipe out the disk, and you are dead meat, kid!"

They're everywhere, these magic machines. Air lines, Wall Street, schools, dry cleaning establishments, gas stations, drugstores.

But I am not interested in "everywhere". I only have 2 special cases to discuss, the 1st easily disposed of:

1. Computers for people with special needs. Call 1-800-IBM-2133, and they'll tell you about their fabulous printed matter on the subject. I received 5 hefty

---

[1] I also want to know exactly why on the AT&T "Reach out and touch someone" commercial — why all the phone calls to elderly people were made to the Old Ones while they were at home. Why, O why, did they never call them at work? Are there no people over age 60 or 65 who work? Do they all sit at home and wait for their no-goodnik kids to call them to break up some enormous boredom? Maybe McDonald's and Wendy's watched enough of the AT&T commercials, figured too many old people were bored, and *then* started their campaign to hire the Old Ones?

pamphlet/booklets from them, all about their software and hardware for people who needed special accommodations to work on their machines. A few phone calls and you can find out the same resources Apple offers for their Apples and Macintoshes.

2. For elderly people.

III. *Elderly People and the Personal Computer (With Particular Reference to Elderly People in Old Age Homes)*

If it is as true, as many people believe, that American society tends to foster isolation and loneliness in elderly people, then, cutting them off from the world of personal computers compounds the isolation and loneliness. They feel more out of the main flow of life because their children, grandchildren, great-grandchildren, and anyone else not in any labelled category are doing all sorts of wonderful things on these machines, and they don't know the 1st thing about them.

Now, lots of kids have helped me think this one out.

They always go wild when I ask the question, "What do you think elderly people would like to do on a computer?"

Here's a quickie list of what some of the Old Ones might want to do with the help of a PC:

1. Start World War III (described above).

2. Write letters.

3. Record their life story.

4. Record the family history.

5. Make calendars.

6. Make holiday cards.

7. Keep track of their finances, possessions, recipes, items in their coin or stamp collections, accumulated airline miles, batting averages and ball scores, birthdays and anniversaries of relatives and friends, medications, and anything else anyone wants to keep track of.

8. Make a list for daily use, if they are list-makers.[1a]

9. Play games (and whup their children and grandchildren who think they're so smart and quick at those same games).

10. Doodle.

11. Design and publish newsletters.

12. Make banners.

13. Plug into computer bulletin boards.

14. Create petitions for important political issues (i.e., raise hell in the community, as they did when they were younger, or, if they didn't do it then, will do it

------

[1a]There are two kinds of people in this world: list-makers and non-list-makers. I am a list-maker, and one of the greatest joys of a PC owner is being able to whittle down the file called, "List".)

now because they have always wanted to do it, but never seemed to have the time to do it back then).

15. Plan trips.

16. Shop.

17. Tutor latchkey kids in spelling, math, any schoolwork.

18. Raise hell with the landlord, manager, or supervisor about food quality, noise from the leaf-blowing machines, or particularly silly or irksome rules of the residence.

19. Compose and play music.

20. Finally finish their master's thesis or doctoral dissertation.

21. Finally learn calculus, Shakespeare, Bible, Hebrew, Polynesian art, Jewish history, French, or whatever they always wanted to learn but never quite got down to doing it.

22. Produce a dazzling *curriculum vitae* to get a good job.

23. Create programs to suit their particular needs.

24. Break into their grandchildren's school records and change all the grades to A and A+.[1b]

25. Break into their children's bank accounts, remove $20,000, and disappear on a 6-month cruise to the Far East.

26. Do some insider trading on the stock market.

27. Break into SABRE or APOLLO, two of the airlines' most famous scheduling programs, and re-route all planes to Jerusalem.

28. Re-program the telephone company's computer to block all calls from noodniks, paskunyaks, noodgy people, survey-takers, and people trying to sell them things they most certainly do not want, particularly useless supplementary health insurance.

29. Do their taxes.

30. Learn tax programs well enough to do other people's taxes, either as a source of income or *pro bono*, as a Mitzvah project.

31. Co-ordinate the schedules of volunteers for any one of a number of Mitzvah projects.

32. Teach kids not to be afraid of old people or to ignore them. By inviting the kids to work with them on some computer project, new and exciting connections will be made.

33. Write novels, poetry, short stories, plays, essays, newspaper articles, letters to the editor.

34. In general, anything else anyone else might want to do on a PC, regardless of age.

[1b]Or, if they are particularly cranky or mean-spirited, and dislike their grandchildren because they are a bunch of noodniks, they can change the grades to D or F. Each according to his or her own particular style.

IV. *The Special Case: PC's in Jewish Old Age Homes*

It's already being done in Oakland, CA, at the Home for Jewish Parents. Call 415-536-4504.

Computer projects for the residents.

It makes a lot of sense, in light of the partial list, items 1-34, but the idea has not caught on. There is a lot of resistance, though the people I ask can't quite figure out why people in power object.

It can't be the added expense: kids offer to bring in their own computers to start the program going.

It can't be the question, "Who will teach them?" Kids are willing to do that, too. Any BBYO or USY or NFTY or NCSY or day school or afternoon school kid will easily come up with a group of friends who will come in and do it. They'd love it.

It can't be because the staff thinks the residents are too incapacitated to learn computers. No one *really* believes that anymore.

It may be that some administrators are not computer literate and cannot picture the benefits because they don't have a feel for the machine.[1c] I know that feeling. For years, I swore to my brother, the family computer expert, that I could do without it, and, anyway, I was sure I'd never be any good at working a PC. I was wrong. A few simple demonstrations and a little time playing around with the keys proved how easy it was. So a few demonstrations at the old-age residence may solve that one.

I am sure it's just a matter of time.

In fact, one of my fantasies goes something like this:

It is the middle of the night, no night in particular. One of the residents cannot sleep. She slips out of bed, goes into the computer room, switches on the Mac, opens up a the file called "Autobiography" and begins to fill in the chapter about growing up in a small town where there were only 15 other Jewish families. She works at it for about an hour, spends 10 minutes editing, saves and backs up the file, then, a little drowsy, shuts the Mac down, and goes back to bed.

I do things like that all the time.

I can't sleep because something's going on in my mind.

I need to get it down before I lose it.

Get it down, feel at ease, go back to sleep.

[1c]My friend, Reuven Lerner, just taught me how a staff member's computer illiteracy might — quite to the contrary — be a good starting point for launching the project. Some people who have not worked on PC's view them with fascination, a Magic Box, as it were. They are aware of the signs and wonders that computers can perform. Starting from there, you just say, "Just think of how the elderly people will be thrilled to have some of that magic at their fingertips."

It makes sense, and it's probably only a matter of time till these little machines spring up all over the place in residences for old people, just like they did in schools in the 1980's.

That's the irony of it (Jewishly): On the one hand, we're still doing it *far di kinder* (for the kids). On the other hand, we blow blaring trumpets of self-praise about how we take care of our elderly (which we are good at)....but no computers.

As the ancient and sublime Hebrew phrase goes, "Karov, Aval LeLo Sigar — Close, but no cigar."

We're almost there.

But not quite.

V. One More Thing Elderly People Would Want to Do on a PC

The man's ungrateful children never come to visit.

The man — let's say "Jacob"[1d] — opens up the Mac to the file called "Last Will and Testament".

He selects the entire document, meaning he wants to make changes that cover every relevant phrase and clause, top to bottom.

Jacob touches two keys, Control and H.

The Mac asks, "Find what?"

Jacob types in, "Children".

The Mac displays, "Change to:".

Jacob types in, "my dear pussycat, Whiskers", and then moves the mouse and clicks on the words, "Change All".

Zip, bing, jingle.

On the lower left-hand side of the screen, the Mac displays, "6 changes".

In no time flat what used to read, "*To my children* I leave all my possessions, my money, the house, and everything within it, the car, jewelry, absolutely everything I own..." now reads, "*To my dear pussycat, Whiskers,* I leave all my possessions, my money, the house and everything within it, the car, jewelry, absolutely everything I own..."

Jacob smiles, prints up 2 copies, signs both, and leaves them by the door to remind himself to take them to a notary later on in the day.

Total elapsed time, 47 seconds.

Whiskers, the heir, rubs against his ankle. Jacob picks her up and walks to the kitchen to give her some Nine Lives Chicken or Tuna.

He makes a mental note that he hasn't felt so good in months.

[1d]"Jacob", because Jacob wrestled and beat the angel, because he wouldn't take things lying down, because he knew how to fight back and fight back hard if something was wrong.

Synagogue Access
For Individuals With Disabilities

For My House Shall Be
A House of Prayer for All People
(Isaiah 56:7)

My synagogue has large print prayerbooks and Chumashim.

My synagogue has a special sound system — complete with earphones — for people with hearing impairments.

My own synagogue — B'nai Israel Congregation of Rockville, MD — is wheelchair-accessible, not only to the building itself and the bathrooms, but also to the place where the Torah is read.

And my synagogue has a TDD, a Telecommunications Device for the Deaf, one of those typewriters that connects to a phone so that deaf individuals at the other end can connect *their* TDD's to a telephone and the two sides can communicate on a display screen over the phone wires.

Does it sound like I am bragging? I *am*, and I *could* and *will* go on:

B'nai Israel is always open for the Sh'ma V'Ezer and JFGH crowd. Sh'ma V'Ezer is the Jewish special education program in Washington and the JFGH is the Jewish Foundation for Group Homes. On holidays, Shabbat, and special occasions, participants in special programs and residents of the group homes and independent-living apartments are in the congregation. In fact — just this past week there was an adult bar and bat mitzvah ceremony at B'nai Israel for Sh'ma V'Ezer and JFGH people (my sister, Leslye, among the celebrants). It was a most moving event.

That's my kind of synagogue!

Which is *exactly* the point....A synagogue should be a place where not only are all individuals welcome, but also *able* to be a part of the life of the synagogue.

As I travel extensively around North America, I see varying degrees of progress in this area, ranging from radical refurbishing and rebuilding to a state of not-yet-sufficiently-raised consciousness about the matter at hand.

On the plus side, for example, is the unique touch of Congregation Etz Chaim in Marietta, GA, where Rabbi Shalom Lewis had a special elongated Mezuzah designed, so that people in wheelchairs might be able to kiss it as they go in and out of the building. And on the plus side — I was recently at Congregation Beth Sholom in Anchorage, Alaska, to speak at the dedication of their new building and be a part of the celebration of the 30th anniversary of the congregation. When I arrived the Sunday before the anniversary week-end, they were still working 16-hour days to finish the building, but I could already see that in the almost-completed sanctuary, there was a ramp going up to the Bima.

And on the plus side, at Beth El of Birmingham, AL, a brand-strapping-new elevator, ready just in time for Rosh HaShana, 1989. The donors wanted to give some money to Tzedakah for (as they put it) a Living Mitzvah. It is a fine, apt phrase, and a wise selection for their Tzedakah money. And the elevator does not sit idle. It really makes the synagogue much more a "synagogue", from the Greek words meaning "a place where people may gather together". Now more people can gather at Beth El because they can get around the building.

On the down side is a story of a synagogue executive director whose mother had been previously deaf. She had used a TDD for years. When — due to the miracles of modern medicine — she became able to hear again and no longer needed her TDD, she offered to give it to the synagogue where her son had worked. The synagogue said they didn't need it, because they didn't have any deaf people! (This — in a Jewish community of a 500,000-600,000 Jews. Statistically, *just statistically*, how many Jewish deaf people must there be in numbers like that?)

And on the down side, I find it inordinately ironic that I can pick up any hotel-chain directory — Hyatt, Holiday Inn, Marriott, even the smaller chains — and know exactly which resorts, hotels, and motels in which towns and cities can accommodate me if I have specific disabilities....But it is impossible for me to open a national synagogue guide and determine the same facts. If I have to spend Shabbat or a holiday in Kansas City or Atlanta or Des Moines, I have to begin the laborious process of calling around (and that would be impossible if I were deaf and used a TDD.)

The United Synagogue of America is beginning to attack this problem nationally. A questionnaire has been sent out to all congregations asking them to fill out information about access. This is the first step in the process of publishing a directory, and will hopefully, in turn, encourage more and more synagogues to strive towards greater access for all Jews. We should urge all synagogues to fill out the forms as thoroughly as possible, in the hope that even the first edition of the directory will supply sufficient information to make a major contribution towards opening the synagogue's doors to so many more people who really do want to come in. (And it is hoped, following the lead of the United Synagogue of America, that the Union of American Hebrew Congregations and the Union of Orthodox Hebrew Congregations will do the same for their synagogues, so that individuals with disabilities will have the same choices as anyone else, which is what this is all about.)

I take particular note of the work of the National Council of Jewish Women, Cleveland Section's, Access Guide to Cleveland, a marvellous document which lays out, in detail not only the accessibility of houses of worship (Jewish and non-Jewish), but also of restaurants, libraries, places of entertainment, and so many other locations in the Cleveland area. I would also take special note of the efforts of United Synagogue Youth in this area: a few years back, their national theme was "...Who Makes People Different", a study of the needs of people with special needs. The International Convention where the theme was introduced was in Tampa that year, and many "old timers" who had been to a dozen or more conventions will most certainly agree that it was by far one of the most meaningful and intense events in USY history. At the back of the source book was a checklist for synagogues, an item which serves as the basis for the United Synagogue questionnaire on access, a fine, sensitizing document. One phrase, introducing the checklist is very powerful:

> "Occupancy in this building is limited to everyone.
> There are no barriers to belonging
> that God's people cannot overcome."

Where to begin in the home synagogue? The range and extent of the "accessibilization" process runs from easy-and-inexpensive to more-complex-and-costly. Each synagogue should design its own programs according to its specific needs, but the very simple beginnings include large print Siddurim, Chumashim, and Machzorim. (I always recommend that the religious schools get involved in contributing funds from their Tzedakah collections towards this part of the program.) Next — for larger towns, where the odds are better that there will be more deaf Jews — maybe a TDD. People are astounded that the least expensive one I have located at a store not 6 blocks from me is only $169.00. (My audiences usually guess $2,000, $5,000.)

Special sound systems — infrared, audio loops, whatever kind is best suited for your own synagogue — are more expensive, but manageable for most places. (Indeed, Rabbi Joel Soffin, a Rabbi from Succasunna, NJ, is involved in a special company, Aurionics, which assists synagogues in selecting, purchasing, and installing these systems. (Call 201-584-4458.)

Re-doing a bathroom is more expensive, ramps, chair systems for going up and down steps costs, re-designing a sanctuary for wheelchair access to the Bima can be either *very* inexpensive or *very* expensive or somewhere in between, but *always* worth the effort and money, if the money is available.

A wide-ranging and far-reaching publicity campaign in the Jewish and non-Jewish media is essential in all of these efforts concerning re-design and additional equipment and access accommodations. If the synagogue announces that it is accessible — ramps, large print, sound system, TDD, etc. — it is a near certainty that, in any Jewish population of reasonable size, individuals with special needs will come out of their homes, enter the doors of the synagogue, and become a more active part of the life of the congregation. (Indeed, I have often made a money-back guarantee to places that purchase a TDD that, after an appropriately extensive publicity campaign, if no one avails himself or herself of the services of the TDD within six months, I will buy it back from them. [No one has called me on a buy-back yet.])

As the world of access expands in your synagogue, we should remember additional access needs:

1. Food barrels as a permanent fixture in the synagogue lobby, so that people may bring in food for homeless and hungry people. *Every* town has a soup kitchen, food pantry, or shelter that needs the food.

2. Programs for alcoholics and drug-dependent individuals need to be synagogue-based. JACS (Jewish Alcoholics, Chemically Dependent Persons, and Significant Others Foundation — 212-473-4747 — is the national organization that can help set those up.) Access for that group of Jews is most critical. The situation is still scandalous, and Jews are all-too-often left to attend AA meetings in churches as an last refuge.

3. Services that are interpreted for the deaf: I believe there is a need in any Jewish community of 10,000 or more. There *are* people who know sign language everywhere. Many are most ready and eagerly waiting to be asked to do it. All we need to do is get the word around. The issue is willingness, and money.

And if money is short, let us consider a quote from our Jewish sources:

> We may sell a synagogue, and, similarly,
> all holy objects — even a Sefer Torah —
> in order to provide for Torah students and...orphans.
> *(Shulchan Aruch, Orach Chaim 153:6)*

Surely many of the individuals with disabilities we are speaking of feel as though they are orphans — lonely, cut off from the community, at a distance. If necessary, we should know that the Jewish tradition allows us to sell even a Torah to raise funds for such needs as orphans may have.

It is a glorious task. Let us set our minds to the projects — large and small — for the benefit not only of those who might feel orphaned, but for our own benefit as well. Everyone will surely gain by the Mitzvah work we undertake.

The only thing left to do is to do it.

The Strange
And As-Yet-Unsolved Case
Of the Missing TDD's

"I'd hate to be hearing-impaired
in many Jewish communities."
(Various Jews)

I. Just Exactly What a TDD Is

A TDD is a Telecommunications Device for the Deaf.

A similar item is called a TTY, or a Teletypewriter, and it is just exactly that, a little typewriter with a modem. They come in small portable varieties, or fancier models with printouts and large-letter displays and memories. The purpose of the TDD is simple: to allow deaf people to communicate with each other or with hearing individuals over the telephone wires by typing messages to one another.

The TDD is very simple to operate:

1. You plug the TDD into any wall socket, or operate it with batteries.

2. You turn the machine on.

3. You pick up the phone and put the earpiece into the modem and then dial the number you want.

4. The person at the other end picks up the phone, and puts it into his or her TDD's own modem. (If the person being called is not deaf, he or she will hear a distinct signal that indicates that it is a TDD on the other end and then know to put the earpiece into the modem.)

5. You type messages back and forth. Anyone who can type can use a TDD. (There's even a little ingrained patience in TDD users for people who (a) type slowly, (b) make spelling mistakes because they are typing so fast because they are so thrilled to tell the person at the other end of the line something exciting. There's the additional fun of filling in "the tone of voice", as with any written text, as you try to figure out whether the person is angry, questioning, impatient, exhausted.)

6. Installation time from opening the box to first phone call: less than two minutes. I have absolutely no mechanical abilities, so if I can learn to use one in a matter of a few minutes, then just about anyone else can, too.

II. Three Stories

1. The executive director of my synagogue in Rockville, MD, Glenn Easton, calls me to say he's on his way out to buy a TDD for B'nai Israel. He wanted to know if I would join him. I already knew a little about TDD's, because I knew he owned one because his own mother had been deaf for a number of years

until she had one of these miraculous implants and until then he needed one to stay in touch with her in Los Angeles. I had seen his TDD, which had been used at B'nai Israel, but now he wanted to get a more versatile model for the synagogue.

I was excited. I'd never been to a TDD store, and I wanted to be a part of my synagogue's "upgrading for access". B'nai Israel is loaded with access: ramps everywhere (including to the Torah-reading stand), a special sound system for the hearing-impaired individuals, members and non-members, who come for services or other events, large print prayerbooks and Chumashim for visually-limited individuals...all kinds of good things.

When I arrived at the parking lot, Glenn was waiting; he was standing with someone and finishing his conversation.

When he got in the car, I got the first glimpse of the uphill battle Jewish deaf people are fighting: the other person was the executive director of another synagogue with whom Glenn had had a meeting that morning, and out in the parking lot he had invited her to come along and consider getting a TDD for her synagogue. Her answer was that, since they didn't have any deaf members, they didn't need one.

[The anger builds: (1) Washington, DC, has close to 160,000 Jewish people. Statistically there are bound to be a number of deaf Jews in the area, whether in the suburbs or downtown. (2) The most famous school of higher learning for the hearing-impaired in all of America is located in Washington — Gallaudet. There are enough Jewish students there to warrant a part-time Jewish student advisor attached to the Chaplain's Office. (3) Saying they have no deaf Jewish members is like saying, "Because there are no Jewish drop-off places for clothes and food for Jews on limited incomes in most cities, it must mean there aren't Jews in that town who need food and clothes." (4) Glenn's mother decided to donate her TDD to the synagogue out in Los Angeles where Glenn used to work. They didn't accept the gift. They said that, since they didn't have any deaf members, they didn't need one.]

In any event, Glenn and I drove about 5 minutes up Rockville Pike to Potomac Telecom. I knew there was a Japanese restaurant in the shopping center. I knew there was a computer store, a furniture store, an eyeglass place, but I didn't know that down at the end of the strip, just up on the fourth floor was this TDD-and-other-equipment-for-the-hearing-impaired business. On display were a half-dozen kinds of TDD machines, light bulbs that light up when a phone or doorbell rings, telecaption machines for TV's, other devices, and all kinds of literature explaining how the various machines work and giving additional information about the needs of hearing-impaired individuals.

Glenn knew what he needed, told them which model, and in a few minutes we walked out of the store with the brand-strapping-new machine in a nice Potomac Telecom bag.

End of the story.

2. Louise Cohen runs the Boston Jewish Bookfair. In their 1988 publicity brochure, they advertised that some of the programs would be interpreted for deaf people, and that if there were other programs that hearing-impaired people wanted to come to, they would arrange for interpreters.

After the Book Fair, Louise and I spoke on the phone, and she felt compelled to spill out the wondrous atmosphere of one or two of the programs where this had taken place, this simple thing, this ever-so-simple gesture of providing interpreters. A wondrous moment not only for the deaf individuals who enjoyed programs they would have otherwise missed out on, but also for the rest of the other people in attendance, many of whom had never experienced such an event.

The plans for the 1989 Book Fair are the same; it is now standard practice for Boston. (And, in addition, there is a display of Braille materials, to educate the community even more on special needs.)

End of the story.

Well, not exactly the end.

On November 13, 1989, Louise added a note to a letter to me entitled "Honest-to-God verbatim phone call that just this minute happened":

We sent Book Fair press releases to several organizations for the hearing impaired. A woman just called to <u>make sure</u>[1] she was reading it right. She was so excited she was crying — just because we finally got an audio loop.[1a] She said she had gone to a lecture last night for single parents. Her friends were grumpy because there weren't any men. She said they didn't appreciate how lucky they were just to be able to hear the speaker — let alone meet people. They didn't know what isolated and lonely really could be.

She kept saying, "You mean now I can go to *any* lecture? Are you sure?"

She has an amplifier on her phone so she does well in phone conversations, but at one point there was a long pause. I asked her if she wanted me to repeat what I had just said, and she said, "No — I heard you fine. I'm just so excited I got a little choked up and couldn't talk! Now I can really become involved in the JCC. You can't imagine what that means to me!"

End of the story.

3. Rabbi Danny Grossman brought me into this silent world a number of years ago. He is hearing-impaired (a long story) and a marvellous interpreter. On many occasions he has interpreted as I have read my poetry in different communities.

Danny has fought for the production of a film on Jews who are hearing-impaired.

Danny Grossman has worked hard to introduce authentic Jewish signs into common parlance among the members of the deaf Jewish community. He has ex-

---

[1]Louise's double underlinings.

[1a]Audio loops are one kind of enhanced sound system that allows hearing-impaired people to hear better.

plained again and again that many of the standard American Sign Language signs are not-very-pleasant representations of what Jews and Jewish symbols and realities are.

Rabbi Danny Grossman has helped pull deaf Jews out of cults. He has had them say, "Rabbi, I know Jesus loves me." (Did we ever take note of how many televangelical programs have interpreters and that no Jewish programs I know of have that little corner of the screen cut out and someone doing the appropriate sign language?) He has worked with college students to keep up and intensify their Jewish contacts. He has explained time and again that the intermarriage rate among deaf Jews is higher than that of the population of hearing Jews.

He is a Rabbi, a forceful pusher for the rights-of-entry of deaf Jews into the day-to-day life of the Jewish community, a fighter and a *creative* fighter to set things right.

He is my Rebbi in this realm of Yiddishkeit.

If you want to find out how you locate hearing-impaired Jews, you are welcome to call him at his synagogue in Trenton, NJ. 609-599-2591.

III. TDD's Are (Almost) Everywhere in the Big World

Noticing TDD's is like when you learn a new word like "excoriate" or "exacerbate" or "execrable" or "exfoliate" — once you learn it, it keeps cropping up all over the place and you wondered how you missed it all along. There it is in the newspaper, Charles Kuralt or Dan Rather uses it in some news report, it's in a report you have to read at the office. Until then, you either ignored the word, or your eyes skipped over it while you read. And you are surprised to hear it finally pronounced, since you have always read it with your eyes, and didn't realize the full sound of it till someone said it, or until you yourself finally use it. "Extirpate", "exomorph", "endometriosis", "basal mesothelioma", "peritoneal"— words like that.

One day you are catching a plane and you see a sign with an arrow "TDD". On the return flight you stop by to see what it looks like. Or you have business at some corporate headquarters, and by the secretary's desk is a little typewriter with a modem, but it's not a Fax machine, nor a computer modem....You recognize the TDD. In the real estate office, at the car rental stand, in the hotel, in newspaper advertisements.

They are there, thousands of them, and, now seeing them, reading about them, you wonder about how many more there might be, and how many more might be needed beyond that.

You still hear stories of people struggling to get their police station or fire station to get one. In case of dire emergency, what is the hearing-impaired person supposed to do, in the terrifying presence of rape, mayhem, fire?

You still hear stories about getting City Hall to install one, the library, the local hospitals, doctors' offices.

IV. *How the Kids Can Help and Are Helping*

I once challenged a group of 13- or 14-year-old students in Baltimore, saying the school would contribute half the cost of a TDD from its Tzedakah money if one of the students would raise the other half and then present the TDD to the synagogue. Apparently unencumbered by preconceived notions of "no need to have one", one of the students took on the project. Jill Miron raised the money, and now Chizuk Amuno in Baltimore has its TDD.

Someone a few years back must have alerted the National Council of Synagogue Youth (NCSY) to the need for reaching out to hearing-impaired Jewish kids. They have had a full-blown program going already for a long time. It's not yet so in the other youth movements, but perhaps they will pick up on it. By now, it must seem the most natural thing in the world — which it is — to have hearing-impaired teen-agers as part of a program.

I guess that — after a brief introduction — the kids catch on faster, see the need, and without adult-like preconceived notions or overburdened senses of priorities, they just go do it.

Another example: I am talking to a 5th or 6th grade class at a Jewish day school in Toronto. I grope around to see which areas of Tzedakah strike their particular fancy. In some places they are particularly interested in working with hungry and homeless individuals — they have been to shelters, fed people, had canned food drives, brought blankets, sweaters, and coats. Other places take a particular interest in animals that work with lonely people or people in institutions. For some, it is parties and outings with residents of local Jewish group homes.

In this particular situation, I asked, "How many of you know sign language?" About 4 or 5 hands went up, out of a group of 35 or 40 kids. I asked, "How many of you know *a lot* of sign language?" One kid raises her hand, and I ask how it is she knows "a lot" of sign language. She explains that her younger brother is hearing-impaired, and they use it at home.

I ask, "Suppose I were hearing-impaired and needed to call the police. How would I do it?"

The same student raises her hand and says, "A TDD."

I am wowed that right there in some chance classroom I happened to visit, someone not only *knows* what a TDD is, but *has* one at home, and is willing to ask her parents if she can bring it in to demonstrate to her classmates how to use it, with the ultimate hope that the school will purchase one.

It all seemed so natural to this student and to her classmates that this might be the right thing to do.

Since I believe very strongly in Kid Power, maybe TDD's can be a special campaign of theirs.

The kids deserve it, this feeling of leadership. If they get it early on, perhaps they will be a source of even greater Mitzvah power when they are older.

V. The Price

The Minicom III, the least expensive model available in Rockville, sells for $169.00, and if you buy bunches, there are 5% and 10% discounts. Most people think they cost $1,000 up to $5,000, little suspecting that, as with VCR's, computers, calculators, disc players, cordless telephones and similar contraptions, little suspecting that technology has made this particular device, the TDD, much simpler, considerably more portable, and much more affordable than even 5 years ago.

We spend $500, $1,000, and often much more, to "send a kid to camp", and that is as it should be. We spend $500, $1,000, $2,000 and more on all kinds of tchatchkas for the synagogue or Jewish communal office. And we most certainly throw out more than $169 worth of food after some Jewish communal events.

$169 is an incredibly cheap price to pay to bring more Jews into the mainstream of the community.

There is one more expense: The International Telephone Directory for TDD Users. It costs about $10.00, and while it is not an exhaustive directory, it can help a community locate some of the Jewish deaf people.

Contact Alfred Sonnenstrahl, Telecommunications for the Deaf, Inc., 301-589-3786 (voice), 301-589-3006 (TDD).

VI. It's Good Business (=It's Good for the Jews)

For some reason I received in the mail a flyer from a real estate or insurance agent. It listed a TDD number. I have gotten a few of those over the past year, for different kinds of business. The smart business people know it's good business. There's a lot of hearing-impaired people out there who are consumers or who need services, and while they may not ultimately like the quality of the services or goods being offered, you have a much better chance of getting them into your office or store if you have a TDD. Without it, there's all their good money out there going to someone else.

The analogy to the Jewish community should be clear: we might spend just a little less time beating our breasts about assimilation in the North American Jewish community, and just a little more time getting in some TDD's (and interpreters), and we'd possibly have that much less assimilation. I well recognize that small towns with, say, 500 Jews might not need one (though they might), but certainly any Jewish community of 10,000 or more ought to start looking for TDD's to install. And if they cannot find a store that sells them, go to the local hearing-aid specialist, who will know how to get one.

The Union of American Hebrew Congregation's Religious Action Center received a classic letter about a year ago. It said essentially that the author of the letter would have called, but he is hearing-impaired, and the Center didn't have a TDD. (Now they do.)

Local Jewish agencies (particularly synagogues, Jewish community centers, Federations, and Jewish Family Service) need them, and national agencies need them. The United Synagogue of America is pursuing it now for its central office in New York.

It's good business, and it's good for the Jews. Progress goes slowly on this one, though it needn't go slowly. One person in the office makes a few phone calls to locate a TDD merchant, picks the machine up, installs it, someone reads the Directory, scanning for Jewish names and businesses that already have them, the organization advertises in Jewish and secular publications that they now have a TDD, and then things begin to happen.

We just can't afford to keep saying, "We don't need one....We don't have any hearing-impaired members."

We really can't afford to do that to ourselves any more.

It just doesn't make any sense.

Access Directories
(Another Idea
From the World Outside)

I. In a Nasty, Frustrated Tone

Radisson Hotels have it, that little symbol with the person in the wheelchair. So I know that, if I want to stay at their hotel in Burlington, VT, and I am somehow limited in my physical mobility, there is a place for me to stay. Or if I want to vacation in New Orleans at their lovely facility, the symbol tells me I can do it.

But I have no way of knowing about going to synagogue in Burlington or New Orleans (unless I call ahead).

Or let's say I have a conference in Charlottesville, VA, and I want to stay at the Omni. I just open the directory, and there's the little symbol, so I am safe. There's a nice Marriott in the Inner Harbor in Baltimore, and there's the symbol. But what synagogue do I pick? Can I go to a lecture at the JCC? Is the floor at the Associated Jewish Charities easy to get on to, and might there be a special sound system, if I were in town and a visiting dignitary was giving a talk in the Board Room — could I pick up my earphones at the door and tune in?

I can call Northwest Airlines on my TDD (Telecommunications Device for the Deaf) (indeed, I *have* called them on a TDD, and they are as pleasant by teletype as by phone), and Amtrak, but where do I look up to see if there is a TDD at Jewish Family Service in Denver or St. Louis, or the Religious Action Center of the UAHC?

God forbid, suppose my friend is a battered wife, and needs access to a battered women's shelter, a Jewish one, and she is hearing-impaired? How does she call?

II. In the Nicer, Less Whiny Tone of Voice

I recently spent a holiday at Beth Israel of Randallstown, MD. My friend, Mark Stadler, is the youth director there, and I like the synagogue. It's *haymisch*, and the rabbi always hits a number of particularly of fine points in his Torah teaching...things I can use in my talks on the road. But what I *really* like about the synagogue is that, when you walk into the sanctuary, the large print prayerbooks are easily accessible, well-displayed, ready to be used by anyone with visual impairment.

Call it "growing older" (I'm 45) and a parallel growing awareness of more frequent aches and pains, more soreness after less tennis, a moderate grumpiness, and a gnawing feeling that my mild dyslexia is getting worse.

Call it "growing up" — knowing my Mom has that special license plate with the figure in the wheelchair, so she can park closer, to accommodate my sister's special needs.

Call it "grand kvetchiness" when I saw a Rolls Royce parked right smack dab in the parking spot by my post office that is set aside for people with disabilities, and a totally disinterested response — no, it was a terribly nasty response — from the driver when I and another person railed against her insensitivity.[1] (It seems like such a small thing. I think if it had been a Chevy, we wouldn't have been so mad.)

Or, if you so wish, call it, "We-Should-Be-Tired-Of-Having-To-Learn-All-Of-This-From-The-Goyim Syndrome", from the Marriotts and American Airlines, even the ever-so-slow-to-move government agencies.

The government is doing it now, too, with a new law on access.

But, in this, the "nice Tone" section, this is about what we *have* done, not what we *haven't* managed to accomplish. This piece is *not* about access to our buildings and activities. It is about directories. National and local directories.

III. The Appeal

The United Synagogue of America published its first edition of "Directory of Accessible Congregations" about a year ago, and the second edition is due any week now. The first edition has about 60 (out of 800 or 900) congregations listed, detailing whatever special accommodations they have for individuals with particular special needs. It's a start.

Now we need the following:

1. All the other Conservative congregations to fill out their forms and send them in.

2. All the other movements to publish similar directories.

3. All local Jewish communities to publish similar directories.

They are long overdue.

And, as any business can tell you, it's good business. Think of all those un-accessed people who might just show up at community events, the blind Jews, the Jews who are visually-impaired to a lesser degree, the deaf Jews, the Jews who are hearing-impaired to a lesser degree, the Jews in wheelchairs, all those Jews who are hanging back.

---

[1]The Disabled American Veterans organization has a printed notice you might find useful. It says, "<u>Warning</u> You are parked in a space reserved for handicapped people....To most of us, finding a good parking place can be very difficult. To the handicapped, it can be almost impossible! [Then there is the well-known symbol of a person in a wheelchair.] This symbol identifies facilities that can be used by physically handicapped people. Unfortunately, many of us are too busy to notice these signs...we're in a hurry and besides...*we're just going to be a minute.* The minute you take might be the minute a handicapped person needs. Remember, a handicapped person has *limited access....*DON'T PUT YOURSELF IN THEIR PLACE." You can then place this notice under the windshield wipers of someone's car if they have parked in the wrong spot.

Call the United Synagogue of America office in New York (212-533-7800) and ask for Mildred Holtzman, to get a copy of the directory and the form they sent out to their synagogues. Modify the form as you wish, but get started.

As my two good friends, Malka Edelman and Beth Huppin, taught me this year:

Anything worth doing is worth doing poorly.

Let's do it as wrong as it might turn out, but let's do it *now*, rather than wait to do it just right a year or two or more down the road.

IV. A Little Irony

The National Council of Jewish Women in Detroit and Cleveland researched and created fabulous access directories for their cities. I would imagine NCJW has done it for other cities too, but I only have the directories for Detroit and Cleveland. Enormous effort went into it: restaurants, civic buildings, other points of interest, and religious institutions. They certainly have the expertise. I would imagine that the sheer number of hours they put in on those two towns would equal the amount of hours needed to do 30-40 Jewish communities.

If *they* can muster the volunteer forces to do Cleveland and Detroit, there must be resources that are musterable for the Jewish communities all around.

I remember a friend from San Francisco, a friend in a wheelchair, who was at a Federation meeting, and the meeting must have run very late. Someone had turned off the elevator, and his friends had to carry Tom down quite a few flights of stairs. In that case, it was just a simple error. Other circumstances might range from lack of funds to outright neglect.

I can't quite put my finger on what it is about this directory business — hints subtle and otherwise have been flying already for at least 18 months. It must be something else, something for Large Group Therapists to figure out. But until the therapists do it, consider this The Layperson's Attempt #43.

Only...this one will work.[1a]

[1a]After I had finished writing this article, my friend, Glenn Easton, sent me an article from *The Washingtonian* Magazine, December, 1989. It had a short article about "Novel Gifts for the Visually Impaired" and indicated that Waldenbooks in Montgomery Mall is carrying a stock of about 50 large-print titles, indicating that they are good presents for people with visual problems. I happened to be doing my morning walk at Montgomery Mall the morning I read the article, and passed by the store. It wasn't open yet, but someone was inside. We talked a little through the security grate, and, though I didn't get to see the display, I was happy to see it happening. For Waldenbooks, it's good business. For people who can't read small print, it's a blessing.

The Moratorium on Silver

I. Into my Dream World, A Confession

I am in an extremely high-risk category. If my insurance company reads this, my premiums will probably soar. I am a poet by nature and profession, and while poets may be destined sometimes for some kinds of greatness, longevity is a rarity. Read their biographies, as I do when I am in a masochistic mood, and you will read of "unusual" and often unpleasant personalities, depression, drugs, alcoholism, and sometimes worse.

Tzedakah work is a good antidote, but not a wonder-drug. While Tzedakah may be translated as "The Life Force", the side-effect is occasional emotional exhaustion, and a need to break away from heavy suffering to some escape in vacation dream lands and minor frivolous indulgences.

In an act of emotional self-defense, I have come to appreciate things, vacations, fineries and the like more and more. I have a custom of buying a new hat (the last was a Homberg) whenever I publish a new book. Sometimes I'll buy a few more clothes than I really need, because I took off 25 pounds, because my suit-seller sells me suits at a discount if I give the difference to Tzedakah.

I even traded in my last car with only 13,000 miles on it because my friends, Bob and Andy Kaplan, who sell Dodges, were giving me an honest price, a good price, and the new car was a tad nicer and larger and no doubt a tad more fun to drive. It was a new, harmless toy, and I even restrained my fun on that account by buying the least expensive of the three models The Dodge Boys of Salem, VA, had on the lot. And I joke about the Big Dodge. Now and again I'll go out in the parking lot of my building and, surveying the cars, ask myself out loud, "Now *who* owns that biiiig blue car over there? I do!" And I tell my friends, "Well, I either had to rotate the tires or buy a new car, and rotating tires is such a pain, and costs so much nowadays, and, besides, it takes 4 or 5 hours in some places to get it done, and it only took an hour and a half to buy the new one...."

And I make sure I play Kol Nidray on the tape deck at least once a week to remind me it's just a toy.

And ever since the airlines introduced their frequent flyer programs and I started earning enough miles for free tickets and discounts at 12-star hotels, I have come to appreciate the slight excesses of a luxury vacation. Call it therapy, but therapy and relief from the strain of poetry and Tzedakah work can come almost as easily by camping out in West Virginia an hour away from my home. There's really no need to fly 9 or 10 hours to get to Hawaii to bask by the Hyatt Regency pool. We have pools around here, too. (*Well*, I *am* stretching it a bit on that one.)

But it's harmless. And it is terrific therapy.

But....

II. The Faulty Comparison - #1

Follow me.

Trust me.

I should never compare a Dodge Dynasty or a Homberg or a week in Paradise on Maui to a Sefer Torah, but I feel I have to.

We should, I believe, differentiate between frivolousness-in-perspective and the more common variety of frivolousness, i.e., excesses beyond the acceptable standard of excess.

The issue is silver.

Even though I am not a rabbi, I have often conducted overflow services for synagogues on the holidays, in Florida and Minnesota, and New Jersey. This past High Holiday season, as I took the Torahs out of the Ark to hand to the congregants who would carry them around the synagogue, I noticed once again how heavy they were. It happens in whatever synagogue I find myself for Shabbat or holidays. Sometimes, if I am a guest in a synagogue, they'll let me carry the Torah around, and, again, they *are* heavy.

But when we take off the crown or the breastplate to lay the Torah on the reader's stand to read from the Torah, they are lighter — still heavy, for sure, but often much, much lighter. The essential difference, of course, is all that silver.

Now the silver on a Sefer Torah cannot be compared to a sun roof on a new car nor the higher-level stereo system. The silver is an adornment, an honoring of our most sacred Jewish object, the source of our wisdom as Jews, our guide in life. When we buy such silver objects, and when we ceremoniously dedicate them, we are doing it in good faith, and making real the traditional concept of *Hiddur Mitzvah*, making our Mitzvah objects that much more beautiful, like buying a fine Tallit, or building a Sukkah that is pretty, or using the finest-quality oil in our Menorah on Channukah. And perhaps, for all the beauty we have accumulated for our Mitzvah objects, perhaps it is time to take a short break, to allow us to step back and re-orient ourselves.

III. The Sources

Three traditions come to mind:

For centuries, traditional Jews have left a portion of some wall of their houses unpainted (or something else unfinished in the house), as a reminder of the Destruction of the Temples. It is an interesting practice, and I see it every time I visit The Rabbanit Kapach in Jerusalem, one of the Mitzvah people I like to spend time with. A nice apartment, a nice wall over the couch in the living room, but with a blue rectangle in the middle of the design, an unfinished part of the wall, a constant reminder that there is something not quite right with the world.

Then there is the text (Shulchan Aruch, Orach Chaim 153:6) that instructs us that we may sell the synagogue itself, all holy objects, even a Sefer Torah, in order to provide for orphans and Torah students.

And, finally, on the issue of *Hiddur Mitzvah*, i.e., making Mitzvah-objects beautiful, a Talmudic source (Shabbat 133b) does indeed indicate that one way to glorify God is to get beautiful Sukkot, Lulavim, Shofarot, Tzitziot, Torah scrolls made with the finest ink, written by the best scribes. But in that same text, one of the sages, Abba Shaul, gives an alternate interpretation of the verse under discussion (Exodus 15:2), "This is my God, and I will glorify Him." He interprets it to mean, "Be like Him....Just as He is gracious and compassionate, so, too, should we be gracious and compassionate." Abba Shaul takes the verse out of the realm of objects and things and places it squarely into the context of human qualities, of just precisely who and how we are as people. To him, that is the true *Hiddur*, a more appropriate Jewish beautification project. It is People compared to Things...even Holy Things, even the Holiest of Things.

IV. The Proposal Itself

For a year, let us have all congregational rabbis and the leaders of any groups that have Torahs (including museum directors) gently and politely — but firmly — encourage their congregants and followers *not* to purchase silver for the Torahs. If someone approaches the leader and proposes to purchase such objects, let the suggestion be made that, instead, for a year, the money might be put into a congregational Tzedakah fund, to be used for immediate needs. Further, let them announce the policy publicly and extensively.

I am not asking synagogues and others groups that own Torahs to sell their Torahs or silver. I have tried that, but there were no takers, though I am convinced some will want to do that. (I was never suggesting they sell the silver to art dealers....I meant, and mean, they could perhaps sell the items to other synagogues or groups that might need at least a bare semblance of adornments for the Torah.)

When burglars break into synagogues, they often take Torahs, but more often than not — not knowing where to fence a Torah — they go for the silver. Alarm systems abound in congregations around the country, and some synagogues even put the silver down in the safe after services are over, not trusting the alarm system. If we cut back on the silver, we could almost hang signs outside the synagogue saying, "There's not much here to steal"...like buses and taxis and convenience stores that have signs, "Driver/Cashier has only $20.00 in cash".

After a year, we could begin to amass data about how much money was then used for Tzedakah, and for what kind of Tzedakah.

I don't think there is any question about the fact that we need more Tzedakah money: the amount needed for providing for resettlement of newly-arrived Soviet Jewish immigrants in America and Israel at present is the big item; day school scholarships, camp scholarships, feeding hungry Jews and non-Jews, buying the critical car that someone who is on the economic edge needs to get to work, interest-free loans for all kinds of things, rent subsidies for those who have lost their homes, Passover food packages, diapers for families who can't afford even diapers, meals on wheels, publicity campaigns to free Ethiopian Jews, and additional Jewish Family Service workers to take care of troubled families are a few of the others. There are so many possibilities that finding appropriate use for the additional Tzedakah money is hardly a problem.

I am out of my dream world now. I know that some contributors and good-willed people will still insist on purchasing silver for the Torahs. They wish to honor their parents, or their son or daughter who is getting married, or they want to mark some other good turn of fortune. That is why I suggest "gently and politely — but firmly". And if the contributor still insists, then we should graciously accept, on behalf of the congregation, their open-hearted contribution of silver. There is nothing wrong with what they are doing, and we appreciate it, but let us at least, first, offer the alternative.

V. The Faulty Comparison - #2

It is traditional for Jews to say "Lehavdil" or "Lehavdil Elef Alfay Havdalot" when making an outrageous comparison to make a point. The phrases mean "Recognizing that there is really no comparison" or "A thousand, thousand differences exist between the two things being compared, but I must compare...."

So, then, "Lehavdil Elef Alfay Havdalot" — years ago there was a book and a movie, "The Shoes of the Fisherman". It was about a Pope (played by Anthony Quinn in the movie) who sold off the Church's riches to provide for the needy. The movie did up the big scene in its usual corny fashion, but, leaving the theater, you felt good, sympathetic. For Jews, and Jewish travellers overseas particularly, we feel offended at times by the enormous expenditure of gold and jewels and other precious items we see adorning church buildings and church accouterments, when all around the peasants are living in poverty. Whether or not this is an accurate picture is not the point; at least to the untrained èye, that's the way it appears.

So, "Lehavdil Elef Alfay Havdalot", to some degree this is our situation in America. We are short of money, good, solid hard-nosed Tzedakah dollars. But we are not short of money, discretionary Mitzvah money that may be, at least for now, misplaced. The moratorium on silver may help free some of that money, and as a result — while our Torahs will be less elaborately adorned — our Jewish lives will be that much more beautiful because our community's life will be that much richer.

A Place to Live

I. In Ancient Days

Where to live?

Where is the good town, the nice place to raise a family?

Nearly 2,000 years ago, the Talmud[1] provided a list that mentions 10 criteria for such a decision, saying, "A Talmid Chacham[1a] is not permitted to live in a city that does not have the following 10 things:

1. A court that is empowered to punish, and is capable of, punishing guilty parties,
2. A communal Tzedakah fund, monies for which are collected by 2 people and distributed by 3 people,
3. A synagogue,
4. A bath house,
5. Sufficient bathroom facilities,
6. A doctor,
7. A bloodletter[1b]
8. A Sofer [scribe],
9. A butcher,
10. A Torah teacher for children."

The same text adds one more comment, "It was stated in Rabbi Akiva's name, 'Also a variety of fruits, because a variety of fruits brightens the eyes.'"

It is an interesting list, and this particular passage in the Talmud yields many good moments of discussion when I teach it to my students and talk it over with my friends. In the minds of the Talmudic teachers, it was a list of 10 essential ingredients for a good Jewish life, though one wonders what was so absolutely critical about a good bath house [a *schvitz*][1c] to merit its making "The Top 10" chart. Obviously, they were interested in more than just the spiritual life. Indeed, Rabbi Akiva's addendum about fruits appears to lighten the tone. I think he was remind-

---

[1]Sanhedrin 17b.

[1a]The term "Talmid Chacham" is usually applied to one who is a sage, someone well versed in Torah wisdom. However, in the extended sense, as in this case, it is reasonable to extend the meaning to anyone who makes wise decisions and acts wisely.

[1b]Bloodletters were a type of ancient and medieval medical personnel. Actually bloodletting was still practiced until the last century, and you can see the bloodletter's tools in any good historical museum. The theory was that, by draining the body of the bad blood that was present in the sick person, the disease would be cured. Often, the barber served as bloodletter. "Uman", meaning "artist" is the Talmudic term for bloodletter.

[1c]American-born that I am, I was unfamiliar with the enormous fondness for a good *schvitz* until I started hearing family stories. It seems that, in certain Jewish circles, the pre-Shabbas or pre-holiday visit to the *schvitz* had a near-holy aura to it, almost as if Moses had included a commandment "to sweat thoroughly in a steam bath" when he descended from Sinai with the 2 Tablets of Stone. Clearly, the Talmudic Sages saw it as preparation for Shabbas or the holidays, to put the person in an appropriately refreshed frame of mind.

ing the list-makers that too much high-sounding stuff isn't good, and that it was time to come down from the clouds and remember that people have physical needs that must be satisfied in order to partake fully of the spiritual life.

What is clear is that most of the Talmudic list is certainly applicable to the Jewish community today. However, other items need to be added, and some of the original listings might need to be contemporized for 20th-Century Jews living in America.

II. In Modern Times

I have always found it interesting to ask people, "Well, just exactly how did your Grandfather and Grandmother wind up with a drygoods store in Fargo, ND?" (They came off the boat in NY, they had relatives in Minneapolis with a similar store, they worked there for a while, then moved on to a smaller town to strike out on their own....) "How did you end up being raised in Sioux City?" (Grandpa was a Shochet[1d]. Sioux City was a Kosher meat center for the Midwest and beyond. Mom stayed, met Dad when he came to town to visit his cousin[1e] for the summer, and they decided to settle down right there. It was a nice, clean place to raise a family....) "Los Angeles?! Your ancestors were in Los Angeles? No one lived in Los Angeles before The War!" (Showing the inquisitive questioner a picture of a rather dapper young man....That's my Zeyde, Dov Berel Sosnowiecer[1f]. Dad says he was the adventuresome one[1g] in the family. He just went Wester and Wester till he hit the Coast, knocked around for a few years, and started one of the first grocery stores in the Valley, when the Valley was almost empty and you could still buy a house for less than $500,000[1h].)

Switch down 2 more generations into the future, and the answers might be "for jobs" (Grumman transferred him in 1967 to the Kansas City office; Orlando was booming and Mom was brand-strapping-new out of Med School, a kidney specialist, and it was a good place to set up practice; or "for health" (my Grandmother swore she'd never go through another Winter in Boston, so when a professorship opened up at the University of Arizona, she grabbed it),...each move with a story of its own.

The following is a crude, preliminary list of possible things to look for when considering what kind of Jewish community we would consider for ourselves when it comes time to locate in our own day. The list is presented in no particular order of importance:

[1d]A ritual slaughterer who slaughtered the animals to provide kosher meat for the Jewish community.

[1e]Whose father was the Shochet in that town, of course.

[1f]Who later became D.B.Smith.

[1g]I.e., the weird one, the one who was out of sync, the black sheep.

[1h]Nowadays, houses in the San Fernando Valley that sell for less than $500,000 do not include indoor plumbing.

1. Jewish communal buildings that offer complete access to individuals with limitations and disabilities,

2. A Mitzvah-hero, to learn from and to work with,

3. A *Mitzvah-Chevrah*, i.e., a group of friends who share the enjoyment and enthusiasm for doing Mitzvahs for the benefit of other people,

4. An interest-free loan society,

5. A Jewish day school that — besides teaching Torah and secular academic subjects on a high level — also makes special accommodations for slower students, and pays its teachers at least as much as it pays its administrators,

6. A reasonably-priced *Chevrah Kaddishah*-Burial Society that buries with dignity and without pressure to violate the rules of basic Jewish burial, e.g., not offering fancy coffins at all,

7. A Jewish substance abusers' group that meets in a Jewish building,

8. A safe house and/or shelter for Jewish battered spouses,

9. A *Bet Din*-Jewish Court that is universally respected and empowered to adjudicate grievances such as unethical firings of Jewish communal employees, character assassinations, and power-plays that ruin lives,

10. Effective and respected communal sumptuary laws that clearly define limits on how much money community members may spend on bar/bat mitzvahs, weddings, and other significant life-cycle events[1i] .

And to get our heads out of the clouds, I would throw in, Talmudically, "Rabbi Stuart K. and Jack G state, "Don't forget a 1st-class *schvitz*, where you can eat fruits after your pores have had a good work-out,....It can brighten the eyes."

III. The Exercise

It might be beneficial to our communities if we circulate questionnaires. First we quote the passage from the Talmud. Then we ask, "What 10 things are essential for you, your family, the welfare of the Jews? What do you look for and want in a Jewish community?"

It is amusing when people move from parts of the Northeast to some town far away and jokingly lament, "You know what I miss most? You just can't get a good corned beef sandwich down here."

It is sad when they say it with ultimate seriousness, as if the most meaningful Jewish deprivation they can think of is 2nd-class delicatessen.

[1i]These restrictions might also be applied to ritual objects and other religious items. A good friend of mine made his position on this matter respectfully but clearly to his teacher. When it came time for him to get a *shtreimel* — the traditional fur hat accepted as standard Shabbas and holiday clothing in his particular community — he indicated that he did not feel he could buy a new one. New ones cost a few hundred dollars. With all of the other pressing expenses he had, it did not seem right to him to spend that much on a *shtreimel*. So he asked his friends to keep their eyes out for a used one, and when it became available, he purchased it for considerably less money. He was not being hard-nosed, nor did he wish to be defiant. He just felt that it would be crossing the line of reasonable expectations to spend that kind of money for that particular Jewish item.]

I'll start. Here's 10 blank spaces.

1.

2.

3.

4.

5.

6.

7.

8.

9.

10.

Fill them in and send them in to the local Jewish community leaders. Find some way to make it anonymous.

Maybe it will take us and the next generation of Jews beyond "a good corned beef sandwich".

The Good News
And the Bad News

I. Introduction

"An expert is anyone who comes from more than 50 miles away."
So goes the joke about guest speakers in the Jewish community.

My family's joke is a little different...."Why don't you go out and get a job." I tell my audiences that is Dad's lament about me, now going on two and a half decades.

I suppose I am one of those you read about in the synagogue bulletin or Federation invitations or flyers on the JCC bulletin board, The Guest Speaker, the one who has finicky eating habits, whose room arrangements always include some idiosyncrasy like a certain kind of microphone (flexible neck) or seat arrangement (theater style, first row no more than 4 feet from the podium, 27-degree curve), or speaking time (no less than an hour and a half, with questions).

Still, despite the communal joke about expertise, and My Father's Complaint, from where I stand, it's a good life. Whether or not I might be a greater expert than the locals is debatable, and whether or not I would go crazy in a 9:00-to-5:00 job is not of any immediate importance to me. I am a Speaker on the Circuit, and the best part of it all is I am always meeting great Jews, and picking up little snatches of hints about the Jewish community by being one day in Tucson and two days later in New London.

The third joke goes that I was funded by an august Jewish Foundation to the tune of $30,000 to discover what the most common words in Jewish communal life are nowadays. (It used to be "Entenmann's"; now it's "cholesterol". I guess with my hundreds of thousands of frequent flyer miles and my ear for poetry, I am uniquely suited for that study.) The fact is, though, by listening and watching while on the road, I have managed to piece together a few positive and negative trends and emphases — nothing formal or scientific — which might be worth noting. Here are three of the juiciest plusses and three of the worrisome minuses:

II. The Good News

1. The Plethora of Fine Jews: It makes no difference if the audience or seminar attendees number 350 or 25, everywhere I go — *everywhere* — there are so many fine Yiddn, unsung, unpublicized, sustaining the Jewish community. They are all ages, both sexes, in every shape and height and weight. They are the sellers of JNF trees on a one-to-one basis, they are the finders of the fine quality couch for recently-arrived Soviet Jewish immigrants, they are the ones who tutor the special-education adult who wants to be part of a Confirmation class in a synagogue. They are the minyan-makers for the Shivas of people who otherwise would

not have a minyan (and the ones who call, day and night, to gather friends and strangers to assure a quorum of 10 people.) And they are the ones who pick up the flowers the day after a bar mitzvah or right after a Jewish community dinner and take them to the old age home or hospital. And they are the ones who make sure the rabbi's discretionary fund has enough money to bury with dignity a Jew who dies without enough of an estate to afford a decent funeral.

I cannot think of a town I have been in in the last few [read: 27] years where I haven't met at least one or two of them, if not more. They are the Builders and Sustainers, the Quiet Ones, and they are everywhere.

2. The Adult Bar and Bat Mitzvah People: No question about it: the single most powerful and long-lasting Jewish educational program in America is the adult bar and bat mitzvah program. All I need to do at one of my programs is ask, "Have any of you ever had an adult bar or bat mitzvah, and, if so, what was it like?" — Boom! Hands go up, faces light up, the flow of words begins: the excitement for many of learning Hebrew at long last, of being able to follow in the prayerbook, to stand before family, friends, and the congregation and announce, "I have begun my journey. I feel good." One such, a certain Barbara Bermack of Pomona, NY, began by secretly learning Hebrew to surprise her son on his bar mitzvah, then celebrated her own bat mitzvah, then became president of the synagogue. Another — a great-grandmother — joined her great-granddaughter and became a bat mitzvah on the same day. Courageous people, and glorious benefits for them, their circle of friends and relatives, and the entire Jewish community. No longer will they whine and complain, "I got a lousy Jewish education as a kid. I am doing something about it." Universally, they recommend the experience to others, no matter how many hours, weeks, months, it takes to prepare.

They take seriously Maimonides' ruling and the ruling of everyone from the Talmud up to modern-day Jewish law codes: If a parent wished to study Torah, and a child also wants to learn, the adult takes precedence. Adult Jewish education is not a side issue, an adjunct tacked on to other budgets. It's *the* issue.

3. While Standing on One Foot — How to Learn How to Read Hebrew in One Day: I would say that by now it's been done in over 25 different cities, this Hebrew Literacy Marathon. I think that more than 1,000 people have been through the program. I'd say the satisfaction/dissatisfaction ratio is about 997/3. Rabbi Noah Golinkin, my childhood Rabbi from Arlington, storms into town with his wife, Dvora, and the class settles in for a long day of Alef-Bet, complete with calisthenics, *nosherei*, and lots of humor. After years in congregations, Golinkin is "retired" and living in Columbia, MD, and doing what he has wanted to do for years (if he only had had more time). After first developing a 13-week course called the National Hebrew Literacy Program which taught 60,000 or more people how to read Hebrew, he boiled it down to a one-day marathon event, while at the same time not denying the need for the longer course.

Does the one-day Marathon work? It works. On the Shabbat afterwards, can people follow what is going on in synagogue? Yes. Do faces light up and words begin to flow after I ask how it went? Faces light up and words begin to gush. (I admit, Golinkin admits, a follow-up session is also good. But they are over the hump, all those people who said, "I'll just never learn to read Hebrew.") Call 301-964-ALEF and see for yourself. The Hebrew readers benefit, their families benefit, the community will benefit beyond our wildest expectations.

III. The Bad News

So much for the good news.

Three items of bad news:

1. The Russians are Coming: These are exciting times, and they should be reminiscent for many of us of the immigration of our own grandparents and great-grandparents. But something is awry when it comes to the settling of the new wave of Soviet Jewish immigrants. For years we kvetched that the Russians wouldn't let the rest of the Refuseniks out. Now big numbers are coming and we are, at best, sluggishly raising funds to help pay for the settling-in process.

But I hear the rumblings, the grumbling, the undertones that communal leaders pass on to me: some people don't want to give for the local campaign for re-settlement. They say, "The last ones — look what we did for them, and now that they are here for a few years, they're not involved. They stay to themselves, they don't want to integrate into the community." (Some even sling the ugly whisper about, "It's not really so bad over there what with *glasnost* and all".)

To that, my only response is, that, as I understand the Mitzvah of Pidyon Shevuyim-Redeeming Captives, it is up to *us* to help bring them to freedom and get them started in the new life, and up to *them* to decide what to do with that freedom and that new life. We owe them everything and they don't owe us anything, though everyone would be delighted if more of them did get more involved. The Mitzvah is *our* obligation.

How soon we forget.

How sad that so many of us Russian descendants do not call to mind the boats, the steerage, the ancestors with their pushcarts, their drygoods stores, their junkyards, to put us through college and medical school.

How soon we forget.

2. The Still Slower-Than-Desired Response to Growing Problems in Special Segments of the Community: That means battered spouses, Jewish adult alcoholics and drug abusers, runaway Jewish kids, poor and hungry Jews, and Jews with disabilities.

I didn't say we are doing nothing.

I just said "Slower-Than-Desired".

For all the battered women's shelters in North America, I can still count in 30 seconds how many are for Jews and run by Jews: Los Angeles, New York, Montreal, Toronto, Baltimore, Chicago, and maybe one or two more. And two or three of those began in the last 18 months. Anyone involved in the Outside

World's (Yiddish: *Goyishe Velt's*) battered women's projects will tell us there are many (more than we admit to ourselves) Jews among them. And Jews have special needs in this area.

For all the AA chapters around and all the statistics on cocaine, crack, Valium, and other abused drugs, the number of JACS (Jewish Alcoholics, Chemically Dependent Persons, and Significant Others Foundation) and similar endeavors lags far behind the need.

For all our demographic studies on Jewish poor people (37,000 in Chicago, 65,000 in Los Angeles, 15% of San Francisco's Jewish community, 15,000 in Toronto, and New York: possibly the third most populous ethnic group of poor people in the city, etc.), we're still not reaching nearly as many as we need to reach. Note the number of Jewish food banks (many serving non-Jews as well as Jews): Los Angeles, New York, Philadelphia, Dallas, Baltimore, Milwaukee, Chicago, Seattle, and maybe a half-dozen or dozen more.

The runaway kids — New York's Covenant House now has some rabbis working with the runaways there. There must be a need. Some of the kids who wind up selling their bodies and dealing drugs on Times Square or 8th Avenue are Jewish, enough to need some rabbis. And in other large metropolitan areas?

Access: Still a struggle, despite great strides. Not enough interpreters for the deaf, not enough TDD machines so the deaf can call in by typewriter over the phone wires to connect with the Jewish community, not enough ramps to the Bima to the synagogue itself, bathrooms, lecture halls, Jewish group homes for adults with special needs, involvement of the special needs community in Super Sunday, Yom HaShoah, Yom HaAtzma'ut, not even a national directory of Jewish communal buildings that are wheelchair accessible or have special sound systems for the hearing-impaired, though the United Synagogue of America has already published its first preliminary listing with 60 or so synagogues.

3. No Significant Progress with the Big Numbers: I've been warned and fail to heed the warning — what about the thousands and thousands of others who remain uninvolved, assimilated to the nth or the nth-minus-one degree.

The Israelis have a point about that: you can be *very* secular and still *very* Jewish in Israel. In America, you can be very secular and *absolutely nowhere* Jewishly in the Diaspora. You don't give to Jewish causes, you don't affiliate with Jewish organizations (check Orange County, California's numbers, check Suffolk County, NY), you don't have to care in any way about the destiny of the Jewish People.

You read about the masses in the Monday society page of the *New York Times*, the mixed marriages.

You hear about them when you ask Federations how many are givers out of how many in the Giving Pool.

You know about them when you announce the adult education courses in a 1,750-member synagogue and 79 people sign up.

The Sage Traveller and Expert, D. Siegel, has no panacea. I am just being descriptive. I have only seen a little progress in the area of The Big Numbers since I hit the road 25 years ago.

Some progress, but not much.

Not much at all.

IV. Conclusion

No conclusions, just a report.

Well, maybe one: a meeting of (a) the experts, (b) the leaders lay and professional, (c) the wealthy movers-and-shakers, and (d) the red-eye-back-from-LA-to-the-East-Shleppers who are on the circuit — in order to list them all, i.e., as many good news and bad news items as we can possibly list, and then a re-ordering of the agenda, a kind of catching up on where the Jewish community *in toto* is at.

If the good news is so good in certain areas, let's beef these programs up on a massive scale. If the bad news is so bad in certain areas, let us set our minds and resources to stemming the flow with new and different insight.

To quote our Holy Text, "Though your beginnings be small, the end result will be exquisite." (Job 8:7)

Mitzvahs, Mitzvahs Everywhere

I was worried.

No, I was *very* worried.

When I stepped into the room at Congregation Har Shalom in Potomac, MD, I saw they had set up too many tables for the breakfast. We were going to be embarrassed; I just knew we were going to come up short.

This was the very first meeting of the synagogue's Mitzvah/Tzedakah Committee, the first follow-up since they had given cards on the High Holidays to everyone in synagogue. The printed cards explained that they should turn down a particular tab if they wanted to be involved in certain types of Mitzvah projects — more specifically: working with aging Jews, with people with disabilities, with hungry and homeless people, or with individuals in the congregation who are going through a crisis.

I estimated that 200 seats had been set up, and I figured that — at most — 75 people would show up for a congregation that size.

I was worried...until the streams of people began coming in. And until they had to set up more tables. (I think there were around 230 people who finally took part.)

My initial reaction was "Wow!" then, "Let's see if this thing keeps going. Let's wait till 6 months from now."

Now it is a little more than "six months from now", and the Mitzvah/Tzedakah Committee is still in full swing, and people are being fed, visited, taken care of, loneliness is broken, Mitzvahs are happening all the time.

And besides the ongoing Mitzvah work, whenever I spot a much-needed-to-be-solved Mitzvah, I just pick up the phone and call Bob Sunshine, the chairman of the committee, or drop him a note, and I can be certain it will be taken care of.

No curb cut outside the new Chinese Kosher restaurant for easier access for people in wheelchairs? Call Sunshine.

Refuseniks recently-arrived in the neighborhood who need X or Y or Z, call the Committee. (Call Bob at 301-340-2787.)

And the same holds true at the Marlboro Jewish Center in New Jersey, with their committee. (Call 201-536-3358; ask for Anita Bogus.)

And the same for Ohr Kodesh in Chevy Chase, MD, with their committee. (Call Zelda Segal at 301-530-9492.)

I.e., their committee, which is composed of individual members who are enamored of and committed to doing their large-or-small part in Tikun Olam, Fixing Up the World.

And the same for a certain Women's Coalition of the Worcester Jewish Federation, with their Rachel's Table, which picks up leftover food at synagogues and communal functions and delivers it to shelters. One call and it's done. We need more Rachel's Tables. (Call 508-799-7600.) And please note: *every state and the District of Columbia — all of them — have laws that explicitly state that the good-faith donor to a non-profit program feeding hungry people cannot be sued in the event someone gets sick from the food.* Call a lawyer and get a copy of the law.

And the same for the network around North America of people who expect a phone call: we need 6 pairs of new jeans, we need a typewriter, a couch, a bed, a dining room table, a minyan for a shiva, a ride for someone unable to drive to the evening program, fourteen cakes for a Simcha...whatever is needed. One call and that's it. Done.

It's exciting to watch, and, of course, those who benefit from the Mitzvah work are many. And, as best as I can tell, the Mitzvah committees, and the Mitzvah people who make up those committees who carry out those projects aren't sitting around waiting for thank-you's; they are not saying, "I quit because I don't get any ego-strokes."

Nice, pure Mitzvah work.

Let me give one more example: I was at Har Shalom for a Shabbat (my brother and his family belong there), and there was a bar mitzvah. A nice bar mitzvah, and a tasteful and tasty Kiddush that would satisfy low and high cholesterol Jews alike. At the Kiddush I was standing with Bob Sunshine and the president of the sisterhood and asked about leftover food. They explained that people will often leave some or all of it behind, to be delivered to shelters and soup kitchens. I asked about this specific Kiddush food. So the sisterhood president walked over to one of the BMK's (=Bar/Bat Mitzvah Kid's) parents and asked if it was all right to take some of the leftovers to a shelter. "Take all of it," was the unhesitating reply.

The Extended Rule #1: Set a policy in the synagogue that any food-sponsoring family be asked the same question. No pressure, just make it a policy to ask. If the answer is no, then the answer is no. If yes, lots of hungry people will benefit. Simple. Lots of synagogues are doing it already.

And Corollary to Extended Rule #1: Make a point of asking if the family would want to participate in MAZON-A Jewish Response to Hunger. For 3% of the cost of the food, yet more people will be fed through MAZON's international network. (I should know. I am privileged to be on the board. Nice, honest, devoted people.) Simple. Lots of synagogues are doing it already.

Switch to Israel: David Morris.

David Morris, former USY Regional President from St. Petersburg, FL, son of Dr. Leonard and Adele Morris, both former presidents of Congregation B'nai Israel of St. Pete.

David Morris, maybe 34 years old, Oleh 10-12 years ago, part-time tour guide, part-time Mitzvah man. Some of the readers already know him as a tour guide. He "worked" the Women's League Conference in Israel in 1987, among other tours. But he's also my Mitzvah Man in Israel. I have a small Tzedakah fund called Ziv (which means "Radiance"). He is in charge, over there in Israel, of staying in contact with our projects, showing the projects to others, working for the projects (like helping distribute Passover food, loading up the car with students and friends to take flowers to hospitals Friday afternoons), teaching about them, encouraging others there to get involved, and getting the tourists to think more about such work when they go back home.

I'm only 45 years old, and I don't want to sound like The Grand Old Man of Jewish Education, but I get real Nachas from having known him since he was a teen-ager. I've seen him flourish and become my teacher-in-Mitzvahs. Life in Israel is hard: hard work to make ends meet, Reserve Duty, bureaucracies to kill an ox (dead oxen are a terrible thing to behold), the everyday and day-to-day struggles. But my friend, my teacher, David Morris knows where the relief and perspective come from: a morning at Life Line for the Old, a round of irises and roses at Shaare Zedek or Hadassah hospitals, an evening of coffee with one of the Mitzvah heroes. (Call 011-972-2-767-894.)

Rule #2: If you want to see your kinderlach grow up to be *shayna yiddishe kinder,* get them started on Mitzvahs early. Then just sit back and kvell. Better yet, watch them in action, and join them. You'll be role models for each other.

Just think of the kid at B'nai Israel in Rockville, MD, (my synagogue) that asked people to bring a piece of warm clothing to his bar mitzvah party, so he could distribute the items to people who don't have enough clothing. Or a young woman who asked the same at her wedding. (She, too, is a former Regional President of USY.)

Corollary to Rule #2: You don't have to be an "adult" to make big things happen. And if you didn't get an early start, don't be discouraged. Sylvia Orzoff is still sitting in front of Cantor's Deli in Los Angeles with her JNF Tzedakah Box. She's on her 24th or 25th year now, 6 days a week, with more than $2,000,000 to her credit. And she's in her late 70's.

Simple.

And not too far from where Sylvia Orzoff sits in her baseball cap is Bet Tzedek, i.e., The House of Justice. A few years back a small group of Jewish lawyers decided to do some *pro bono* work for other Jews who couldn't afford legal services. Bet Tzedek grew, then grew some more, expanded to non-Jewish as well as Jewish lawyers, took on non-Jewish cases, too, and grew some more. How do we quantify the amount of relief Bet Tzedek has provided, the numbers of elderly borderline-poor Jews who might have lost their homes, the unfairly-fired younger Jews who were reinstated in their jobs?

Tzedakah and Tzedek are the same word. We could all use more Justice in this world. Want to find out how to do it, to start a Bet Tzedek? Call 213-939-0506. They're already getting started in San Diego.

Rule #3: Just do it.

Simple.

There's a woman out near Seattle named Ann Medlock. She and her gang search the United States for Giraffes. Giraffes are Mitzvah heroes, bringing Tzedek and Tzedakah into this world, with an added element: they take a risk when they set out on their work. I get their newsletter and flyers that describe Jim Walsh, who forfeited his high-school football team's entire season because that year's crop of kids was too small, and the league refused to switch them to play against smaller teams, and his kids might get hurt. And Ranya Kelly, who, after finding 500 pairs of shoes tossed in a dumpster, started looking in other dumpsters, and finally took on the entire shoe store chain, until they gave in and let her take the shoes that were being thrown out — 12,000 pairs in a year....all for poor and homeless individuals. (Call her, 303-431-0904, in Arvada, CO, near Denver. She expects calls.) And so many others Ann and her people have discovered.

Rule #4: Find some local Giraffes. Decide to be one. Call Ann Medlock to find out where they are and how to do it. 1-800-344-TALL.

Simple.

In sum, The All-Encompassing Rule: There's just about an infinite number of Mitzvah possibilities out there, waiting to be done.

If you alone or you and your friends or you and some group you belong to want to be the motivating factor in starting a Jewish battered women's shelter in your city, do it, or a group for Jewish substance abusers, or a Big Brother/Big Sister program, or a sign-language-in-order-to-bring-deaf-Jewish-members-into-the-synagogue group (call Rabbi Danny Grossman, 609-883-7394), or a Bet Tzedek, or a Rachel's Table, or a bookbindery where the books are bound by elderly people on the order of Life Line for the Old in Jerusalem, (call 609-822-7116, ask for Rabbi Lucas), or a city-wide access-for-disabled-individuals project, or a furniture-for-newly-arrived-Soviet-Jewish-immigrants committee, go to it.

We need it.

We, the Jews.

We, the world.

It's now almost a year since 230 people packed into the Har Shalom social hall in Potomac. There's no longer any need to doubt that Thinking Big is all right. Thinking Big for individuals, for groups, for entire synagogues.

The only thing left to do is to do it.

Christmas

I. Boston

It is Wintertime, and there is little leeway between being picked up at the airport and getting to the synagogue. Shabbas is in a few hours, and I have to set things up for my talks.

There is no time to go exploring with my friend, Louise, but we stop at the hospital, anyway, even for a few minutes. It is important. My friend, Amnon, is in from Israel with his teen-age son, Yosef, who needs chemotherapy. Besides the bitterness of the weather, I have to brace myself because I have never been in the cancer wards to visit someone I knew.

All is well.

Amnon's son is responding to the treatment. He is young; his body sucks in the good fluids from the tubes and syringes and mixes them in his system in a manner which pleases the doctors. The chemicals are fighting hard, and the cancer cells are retreating like so many cowardly infantry soldiers in the face of forces too powerful to resist.

There is hope.

There is more than hope. Amnon's and his son's strong faith in God, deep study of Torah, and basic human courage — coupled with encouraging prognoses from the specialists — allow them some ease-of-soul in the midst of the potential horror. We talk, little things and big things. Little things: are you throwing up from the chemo? Big things...."What page of Talmud are you studying today, Amnon?" "Temura 21." (Amnon has done the daily Page of Talmud for more than 20 years. A once-through of the more than 5,000 pages takes 7 years. He's done it 3 times. My question, "What page, today?" is natural enough.)

I ask what all hospital visitors ask, "Do you need anything?"...ready to volunteer Louise for errands and purchases after I leave town. No, he doesn't seem to need anything. ROFEH (the Bostoner Rebbi's Mitzvah Network for hospital patients who come from out of town for treatment) is working smoothly. An apartment is put at their disposal, all the Kosher food they need is stocked — fish, chicken, vegetables, challah (fine challah, Amnon says), wine — people visit, people support them, call them, worry about every little, medium-sized, and big need. Amnon even points out an electric Shabbas candlestick on the counter, provided by the hospital. They can't use real candles, of course, because of the oxygen all over the place.

Louise and I find some way to fit in, a niche of some sort, anyway. Amnon mentions a visit to the Aquarium, how much they enjoyed it. So Louise, and Louise's friends, and other friends of mine in Boston will do some chauffeuring in between the stints in the hospital. The therapy runs in cycles: a few days in, some other days or a week or two away from Pediatric Oncology, back in the apartment. When the time is right and it is once again safe and comfortable for Yosef to venture into the city, they will go sightseeing.

It is December 8th, but it is Christmastime already in the hospital, particularly in this ward. Right outside Yosef's door, all the kids are gathered around in chairs or beds, and some nuns are singing carols, someone is in a Rudolf the Red Nosed Reindeer suit, a magician is off to the side, ready to do his tricks. Plates of cookies and other goodies are piled high on a table, waiting to be consumed as only children can consume cookies.

The nuns sing fairly well on-key, and their hearts are full, which perhaps yields just a little finer harmony in the music. The kids are having a grand time. It is a lovely sight, and, as I recall, much more happy than sad. Not a single adult — not the nuns, not the magician, not the hospital staff, not the parents — lets despair override the joy of it all. I remembered Rabbi Yehoshua ben Korcha's words, "In times when one should be joyous — be joyous. When it is time to mourn — then mourn." (Genesis Rabba 27:7) This was the right time to be joyous, and a time of faith for the Christians, and since there was no necessary reason to assume these children were destined to die so young — it was certainly a time of pure, simple joy.

It was very, very moving.

I stepped back into Amnon's and Yosef's room and filled them in on what was going on outside. Caroling in their neighborhood in Jerusalem is not a common thing, as you can imagine. They understood, and continued to praise the hospital for all the sensitive care they have been giving, the sensitive care and caring sensitivity. I informed Shmuel that this singing and entertaining and the waves and splashes of red and green colors would continue through the 25th of the month, then said we had to go. I wished them a good Shabbas and told them I would call before I left town on Sunday.

II. Carols

Like many of my Jewish friends who grew up in an overwhelmingly non-Jewish town, we had heard the tunes of this season since earliest childhood. Quietly, among ourselves, we come clean, admitting to each other which melodies are our favorites...without the words, of course. Most of us agree that there are some tunes we like, have always liked. (A few of us who are Jewish educators even admit that we'd like to get our Jewish students to sing in synagogue with as much feeling as the carolers do their carols in December.)

And while we friends are on the subject, we lament the commercialism that has taken over the Christmas season. We feel bad for the Christians who have been sucked into buying presents and more presents and going into debt and making lists so as not to forget anyone and starting the buying way before Thanksgiving. They should know better.

We feel very bad that the few carol tunes we might like have become a burden to them, and to us, because they are so much background music for commercials selling everything from perfume to Black and Decker utility work tables. We are sad that things have been so watered down. They shouldn't have let it happen, and we hope that they will refuse more and more to fall for the commercialism of their holy season, taking their hard-earned money instead and giving good dinners for hungry and homeless people instead of one more present for the boss and partners and elevator operators and car mechanics who grease and oil their cars, their children, their parents, their aunts, uncles, and cousins, first degree, second degree, by marriage, and beyond.

In the true Christmas spirit.

Louise and I think it would be good if they would come to a cancer ward next mid-December to listen to the carols as they should be sung by good Christians for good children caught in a terrible squeeze who need the words and melodies more than any toy train or the newest game on the market.

III. *Washington*

My father is cured. The infection is gone, and the surgery was relatively easy. But he is taking a little more time to recover than expected.

Fairfax Hospital is a good place. The staff realizes he is a physician who has been curing and fixing and speaking good words in nearby Falls Church since before the hospital was built.

It is December, and we have had an unusual cold spell. Every long distance call anyone has made the last few days compares temperatures. The Miami people gloat about the water shortage (they are not allowed to water the lawn) because it has been so hot. "Gotkas" — the Yiddish word for long underwear — crops up more and more in conversation. ("I bought gotkas today." "I haven't worn gotkas for years, but I sure needed them tonight." "Any particular brand of gotkas you recommend?" "Did *Consumer Reports* do an evaluation of gotkas, which ones are better, more flame resistant?")

It is dark already, and cold, and it is December, and after the rush hour, I go out to visit. Driving in the dark, I think about late Spring and early Summer in Washington, the glorious trees, the lengthening days, the days my brother and I would play ball till dusk at 7:00 or 7:30, batting and fielding until we couldn't see the ball in the air any more.

It is bitter cold.

Once I am in the building, I begin to warm up, and by the time I am in Dad's room, things are back to normal. We sit and talk and I ask him medical questions, just as I did since as far back as I can remember. Diabetes and candy bars, chest pains and nitroglycerin, kidney stones and morphine. Now and again I get up and break into his stash of Godiva chocolates that a visitor had brought him. He's not allowed to eat them yet, and when he is, I'll replace them. I'm not sure he'd want them in reindeer shapes, anyway, so I'll switch to the more conventional shapes when the right time comes.

As we are talking, I hear caroling in the halls. At first I think it is piped in over the PA system, but then I realize it isn't commercial-quality singing. I step out into the hallway and ask what's happening and a nurse tells me it's a group of kids coming to sing for the patients. A little while later they come by my Dad's room, passing by (the staff must have told them he was Jewish), and a few feet down the hall, this group of 20 kids with one or two adults including one with a guitar, sings the standard favorites. On one of the high notes, the melody rises a little too high and squeaky and they laugh and then go right on singing.

Some of the kids are goofing around with others. Just a little bit. But that's OK; it's natural. They're entitled since they're teen-agers, and since they pick up the tune and join in once it gets rolling. I ask one of them where they're from and he says, "A local church" and adds, "Whoops, I hope you're not Jewish." I tell him I am not bothered by it at all, that it is beautiful to watch and to listen to. He wishes me a happy Channukah, finishes the song with the group, and then moves with them down the hall to the next room.

It *is* beautiful to watch and listen to. I was so moved by their innocence and, yes, their moments of purity (knowing full well they are teen-agers and what teen-agers do when they are not singing carols in the hospitals), I almost followed them down the halls on their rounds.

In particular, I was watching an elderly woman on a bed out in the hall. Her husband was wheeling her around to get some air and openness. While the children sang, she waved her hand in time to the music. She perked up. No, she more than perked up....She was suddenly animated. ("Animus", Latin for "soul", "animatus"="alive".) She was more alive than she had been when the ward was quiet, without the voices of the kids. She felt good, though you would have thought she would be feeling low-of-spirit, worried about all the things surgical patients worry about: infection, will the stitches hold? did they take out everything they were supposed to? will I be my old self again, soon?

Long after the kids have moved on to the other side of the corridor, too far to be heard by anyone in our area, the woman was still keeping time to the music.

I don't believe I had seen anything quite like it before. She looked better now than she had looked 10 minutes ago, before the kids came singing. So much better, it warmed your own heart as it surely must have warmed hers.

She looked like angels had just come by to visit her.

Channnukah

I. Channukah

Channukah is about the fight against assimilation.

Mattathias the Priest, his son, Judah Maccabbee and Judah's brothers, struggled against the Greek-Syrians so they could be Jews, *Jewish* Jews, not some make-over from the pagan culture around them. That oil burned in the Temple for 8 days instead of just a single day is secondary, though it has become one of our most powerful symbols.

This is one story about how we are losing the battle nowadays.

II. Donnie Dreidel

My friend, Cheryl Magen, sent me a newspaper advertisement which I hope is unique this December season (though I suspect it is not).

In what appears to be about 72-point bold print — 72-point is *very* big — this sad, sad ad screams out, "Meet Donnie Dreidel. Every Saturday 12-4pm at Valley Centre."

Next to the headline is a picture of a child who appears to be 5 or 6 years old. He is standing beside a man who is seated on a chair. This grown man has a rather grotesque facial expression, and one wonders what he will tell his family about this job he has for the holidays. He is dressed like a dreidel, if that is possible, which includes a band running from the top of his head to under his chin, and from the top of this band is a long, pointy object which is supposed to represent the handle of the dreidel.

The text continues (in approximately 24- or 32-point print), "Bring your child to Valley Centre for a photograph with Donnie Dreidel, their favorite Hanukah character. Every Saturday from 12 noon to 4 pm, between Thanksgiving and Hanukah at the Holiday Headquarters in Valley Centre. And make sure they bring their 'wish list' of gifts for Hanukah. Donnie will be taking notes."

Oh, well. Just when you think you've seen everything, along comes something else that reminds you there is a lot more to life than you'll ever know.

III. Commentary

The headline:

...*Donnie Dreidel* — Vey'z mir, vey iz unz. (That's good, old-time Yiddish for, "Woe", "Help, Jewish people are in pain!", "My O my!", "Is there no sense of decency left in this world?" and "Can you be held criminally liable for garroting the person who thought this up?") We should be thankful, at least, that they didn't substitute "Moshe" or Yitzchak" or some real Jewish name for "Donnie". (Maybe there is some shred of decency left.)

....*Every Saturday* — Shabbas! Shabbas! (Maybe there is no shred of decency left.) We have enough difficulty teaching the Wonders of the Sabbath without outside hindrances like these. Not nice.

The picture:

The setting — There's no big fancy chair, no throne-like presence, no lush foliage, no prettily-wrapped presents scattered at his feet. It's a bare setting and a cheap plastic chair peeking out from under the dreidel costume. If *I* were a self-respecting kid, I would run to where the action is, over by the man in the red-and-white suit.

The man playing Donnie Dreidel — Is there no shred of human dignity left? Maybe that's unfair. Maybe he's been unemployed for a long time and really needs the money.

The look on Donnie's face — If I were a normal kid, I would be frightened by his face and go running to the grandfatherly ho-ho-hoing man in the red-and-white suit who seems a lot less scary and a lot more *haymisch*.

The costume — There's no way to sit on Donnie's lap. If I were a kid starved for affection and hugs, I'd go running to where the man in the red-and-white outfit is sitting with a rather enormous lap. You-know-who *has* to be overweight — and probably packed with cholesterol-sluggish arteries — as we all know. But what does a kid know about low-fat diets, exercise, and high density lipids? All he cares about is the welcoming lap. The Valley Centre people are going to have to get their act together for next year. This is no way to sell gobs of merchandise to the *yiddn*.

The text of the ad:

...*Donnie Dreidel, their favorite Hanukah character* — Vey's mir, vey iz unz. We are in deep, unfathomably deep trouble if Donnie Dreidel is the favorite Hanukah character of our Jewish kids. I have reviewed the extensive literature on Hanukah, and beyond Mattathias, Judah Maccabbee, his brothers, and a few others, I have found no reference to Donnie Dreidel in our Sacred Texts. Do *they* know something we don't know? Have new scrolls been discovered near the Dead Sea or in Baltimore that I haven't heard about?

And make sure they bring their "wish list" of gifts — Subtle. *Very* subtle. This is directed at Eema and Abba, a reminder that any decent parent would not deprive his or her child of presents on Channukah. I am surprised they didn't phrase it like this, "Their Biblically-and-Talmudically-commanded wish list of gifts". Next year Valley Centre will have to remember to put that in.

Donnie will be taking notes — Returning to the picture, I just can't see how Donnie can pull this one off. The costume is so poorly laid out, Donnie would have to be Plastic Man or Rubber Man to bend his arms to jot down notes. Any self-respecting kid can see it's impossible for dear Donnie to write, bound as he is by the limits of his silly costume. And besides, the kid knows that just-over-there you-know-who has much more freedom of movement and probably takes down enough notes to fool any-and-all kids who want and/or need to be fooled.

IV. An Invitation

I invite anyone to beat this advertisement. If I am not wrong, this one is the Grand Prize Winner of 1989.

Der Ziesser Yid

I am not yet certain whether this story is about the disease or the man.

I am not even certain whether or not I know more people than others do, and as a result hear of more people dying of this or that disease every week.

And I am not even sure if I have any better understanding of miracles or the human condition or the essence of life — even after living through and reliving this story.

Where to begin?

Let it be with a high point. Then there will be a slump, but the slump will be followed by another high point, a place so high and lush, new human vistas will be seen, and despite the altitude, there will be warmth.

Shmuel Munk must be about 50 years old. He has a beard, wears a traditional black head covering, and is a resident of a religious neighborhood in B'nai B'rak. I know him because he works in Jerusalem at a place called Chazon F'taya, a series of workshops that employs people who have gone through serious personal crises and who are beginning to put their lives in order once again.

There are times in life when you reflect on what blessings you may have had over the years. You think of good health, good friends, a warm family. Sometimes you realize this at the immediate moment, and sometimes it comes only in retrospect. With Shmuel, it is both: the moments with Shmuel have an aura of life and liveliness and they are doubly enriched because you know — even as you live those moments with him — you know you will have other moments far away in Exile when recalling these same moments will bring you home, home to yourself, to goodness and to peace.

Though he will most certainly deny it, Shmuel may well be a Tzaddik, a righteous person, one of those put on this earth to exemplify the best of humanity, whose touch is so full of care, whose naturalness of love is so smooth and unblemished that all those who come to know them understand that here is a rare human being.

Shmuel is what you would call in Yiddish *An Edeler Yid*, a gentle Jew, a noble Jew, though he would most certainly deny it.

He is *A Ziesser*, one of the Sweet Ones. Sweetness radiates from his every move, from his speech, from those eyes that will not allow you ever to doubt the greatness of life and the glories of God as he understands life and God and the interrelationship of the two.

And he is an *Anav*, modest, humble.

I. A Brief Diversion

In some societies there seem to be levels of pariahhood. Some cultures dissociated themselves more harshly from selected sub-groups than others, and the harsher the out-selection, the greater the greatness of those who then plunge in to break the isolation of the outcast.

I do not wish to imply that I am being critical. I am simply trying to be descriptive, to get a grip on this situation.

One such breakdown, by class, might read something like this (starting with least severe ostracism):

1. Elderly people: many, fearing weakness, disease, and death, stay away from the old people, but more often than not, larger numbers of society will stay with them, because at least they can identify in some way with people who are old. Everyone is bound to get old sooner or later.

2. Physically disabled individuals: fear — "There but for the grace of God go I" — often drives people away. It is harder for able-bodied people to picture themselves with physical disabilities than it is to imagine themselves as old people.

3. Those who are mentally limited: it is a long, old, too-involved story to describe at this point. Accept it as an axiom.

4. Those who have suffered personal crises (that is how the Chazon F'taya supervisors refer to people who are otherwise called "mentally ill"): ignorance and the haziness about so many mental disorders unsettles those who have not had these crises. Plus, there is an added element: the fear of uncertainty....Will they be violent? Will they do something "crazy"? Will they embarrass us or terrify us?

As sketchy and undeveloped as points 1-4 are, category 4 is the most important. They seem to be at the end of the line in society, perhaps understandably so. They are on the fringes for the reasons stated, and many more reasons I leave to the psychologists, psychiatrists, social workers, other health care workers, and sociologists. What is important, though, is that these are the people Chazon F'taya and Shmuel, and Simcha Ovadia (founder of Chazon) work with day in and day out. They work with them with respect and care, and a most profound understanding of their human dignity, though to all external appearances, they are only shreds of human beings.

II. The Disease

Shmuel, Der Ziesser Yid, The Sweet, Sweet Jew, called me before I left for Israel in June of 1989. He was in Canada and the United States raising money for Chazon. We talked, and he expressed the hope that we would see each other later on in the summer. He was due to return to Israel a couple of weeks after I arrived.

I left Washington to catch the plane at Kennedy. When I was about to board, I was caught somewhat off guard because Shmuel was there in the waiting room, also ready to board. We talked a little, and I said we'd talk some more on the plane.

Part way through the flight, I sat down next to Shmuel and asked why it was he was returning to Israel earlier than expected. He said his wife had called him the day before and told him one of their children was in the hospital and that he should come right away. Beyond that he couldn't give me any more details.

He just packed and left.

That was the last I heard for about 10 days or two weeks, until I finally visited Chazon. Simcha, the director, told me Shmuel's son had cancer, and there was a dismal prognosis.

So it went — an old story, ugly every time you hear it, disgusting and striking at any optimism a person might have about the lyrical and wondrous elements of life. Ugly, sickening.

But that was all Simcha could tell me.

A few weeks later, I went on my dawn walk around Jerusalem, this time stopping by Simcha's home, just to catch up on some talk. I asked about Shmuel's son. Simcha said, "Haven't you heard? It's a miracle. Four or five weeks he was in the hospital. 'Cancer,' they said. 'Cancer,' they told Shmuel and his wife. They kept running tests, and finally they discovered it was only an abscess on his leg. They operated, he's home, he's almost up and around. A miracle!"

III. Shmuel's Torah Lesson

Sometime after my conversation with Simcha, I saw Shmuel. Why attempt to put into words how we felt, how this gentlest-of-gentle human beings felt? Cynics would say a misdiagnosis or a missed diagnosis caused unspeakable anguish to the Munk family, but as far as they were concerned, the only thing that mattered was that their son was safe and well into his full recovery.

Now it was my turn to move. I asked Shmuel and Simcha to come to my class the following week. Every summer I hold a class on Tzedakah up at whatever apartment I happen to be renting. The students are my friends, my Tzedakah apprentices, and usually some rabbinical, cantorial, and education students from Hebrew Union College who are over for the summer of their freshman year. There are always anywhere from a half dozen to 15 or 20 students who come, and I wanted them to learn about Chazon and to meet Shmuel and Simcha, hoping that during the course of the year's studies they would make a point of visiting Chazon to see how people treat people — "treat" not in the medical sense of the term, but rather in human terms.

It was a packed living room. I think it was the last class of the summer, and the regulars and some newcomers gathered on chairs, sofas, and the floor. I told Shmuel and Simcha they would have about 20-30 minutes to talk about Chazon.

When the time came to introduce Shmuel, I began by telling the story of his son, because I wanted him to know how much we, the gathered students, wanted to share his joy.

And that was the Torah-theme Shmuel taught that day, because for Shmuel and Simcha, the Torah they study, the Torah they teach, and the work they do, all overlap, each interweaving with the other most intricately and most profoundly, yet very simply.

Shmuel began by explaining how thankful he was to God for his son's miraculous recovery. He reminded us that traditionally, when someone survives great danger, that person goes to the synagogue, is called to the Torah, and then recites the *Birkat HaGomel*, the special blessing of thanks. Then he turned back the Jewish clock, centuries, millennia, as he explained what the procedure was in the time of the Second Temple. He had taken his text from the *Ha'amek Davar*, the commentary to the Torah written by Rabbi Naftali Tzvi Yehuda Berlin ("The Netziv"), the head of the great Yeshiva in Volozhin, Poland.

Shmuel explained:

In the time of the Temple, the grateful person brought a Korban Todah, a Thanksgiving Offering, which was made up of two parts: an animal sacrifice (a sheep or a goat), and some grain products, varieties of bread and matzahs. The problem was that — with the help of his Torah teacher — Shmuel calculated that the total amount of bread/matzah came to more than 100 pounds worth of baked goods.

Some things made sense, some didn't. The Priest took a portion of the sacrifice, but the rest was for the one bringing the offering. It was his to eat, but there was a time limit: till morning of the next day, though preferably to be finished by midnight.

Shmuel, portly Shmuel, Der Ziesser Yid, said, "Ah, Rebono Shel Olam-Master of the Universe, how could I possibly eat so much bread?" It was a touching moment, an amusing, lighter break from the heaviness of the background story of cancer and despair. We felt some relief as Shmuel prepared us for the insight of the Great Netziv of Volozhin.

Shmuel continued, saying that the Torah must mean, it has to mean, that the Thanksgiving meal must be shared with friends, with family, with strangers, with those who are hungry, so the joy will be shared, so the story of God's wonders can be proclaimed. A Jew's good fortunes, the joyous moments are not private ones. They are communal events. Just as a person should not lie alone and unvisited in a hospital, just as one who has suffered a loss need not mourn without comforters present, so, too, the good times the happiness of human happiness, brief and passing or sustained and abiding — is to be a moment of togetherness. *That* is what makes a community a community and a society a society.

IV. How It All Fits Together

The story began with a man, human, yet the best of the human, a Jew, but the very finest of Jews.

Passing through near-tragedy, the tale wound its own natural way through references to shattered people, people slow to overcome overbearing crises, people often treated as refuse.

And then, to words of Torah.

But they all came together: the person, the human experience, the Torah. So rarely are we privileged to sense these interconnections, and — even more — to recognize that they are happening as they actually occur. There was a certain magic in the air that day in Jerusalem, a feeling of some great event, though it was not spectacular like a rainbow or a bolt of lightning splitting a tree trunk down the middle. And yet, it was spectacular: Shmuel's eyes, his ever-so-softspoken words, who he was and how he fit into the long, long chain of our tradition.

Things made sense that day, a certain strength was given to the students, a touch of authenticity, security, a profundity.

And now I cannot even show this to Shmuel. He would say that I exaggerate, that his lesson was no more than a simple word of Torah, that he is merely another Jew being Jewish as best as he possibly can be. That is all.

I shouldn't exaggerate.

That's what Shmuel, Der Ziesser Yid, would say, no doubt.

Free Money
Or
The Real High Society Is
The Hebrew Free Loan Society

I. The Statistics

On any given day, every single Hebrew free loan society in America, Israel, or anyplace else, has a lower default rate on their loans than any bank you'll find.

Banks wonder about that. They've even been known to call free loan societies to see how they do it.

Hebrew free loan societies also have an overwhelmingly better track record than government student loan funds, though I am not sure the government has ever called the San Francisco Hebrew Free Loan society or the one in Los Angeles or Pittsburgh or Detroit to see just how they do it.

Usually the default rate for Hebrew free loan societies is less than 1%.

Just like some banks, some free loan societies give out high-risk as well as low-risk loans.

And just like some banks, some free loan societies expect to write off some loans, though I suspect the free loan people do it with greater equanimity.

But I don't recall any regulators ever coming into free loan societies, confiscating the records, handcuffing the president or director and hauling him or her off to jail for embezzlement and other so-euphemistically-labelled "white collar crimes".

I admit, though, that there are some free loan society people who think that if you're not losing more money, you're not doing your job. Some of their loans are most certainly gifts-in-disguise. They say they are lending the money, because they know the borrower really needs it as pure-and-simple Tzedakah but is too embarrassed to ask straight out for money. So the free loan society offers it as a loan, and the borrower accepts it as a loan.[1] But to tell the truth, even some of those loans-which-are-gifts get paid back. Maybe years later, but still paid back, and often the former borrower adds a nice contribution of his or her own as a gesture of gratitude for the good faith of the past.

On the extreme other hand, take the case not so long ago in Tucson, Arizona, of The Bank That Wanted To Take Over Another Bank. The regulations for such a procedure require that the bank prove they had not been discriminatory in their loan policies. The Bank That Wanted To Take Over Another Bank claimed, of course, that they were perfectly fair in their practices, but Nancy Bissell and her friends at the Primavera Foundation suspected that that might not be exactly true.[1a]

---

[1]This is the traditional Jewish approach. See the Talmud, Ketubot 67b.

[1a]The Primavera Foundation covers many areas of Mitzvah work in Tucson, providing shelter for homeless people, a stable living environment for former residents of mental

So the Primavera people got someone to check the bank's books, and, as was to be expected, found blatant discrimination against local Hispanic residents. The end result: in order for the bank to take over the other bank, they had to set up a $100,000,000 loan fund for low-income borrowers.

I would suppose the results in Tucson are essentially the same as with the free loan societies, i.e., people in need get the loans they need. The only difference is that free loan societies do it as a matter of course, whereas some banks need — let's put it delicately — a little outside help to see the wonders and glories of coming through for other people.

That's why I think the real Jewish High Society is the Hebrew Free Loan Society.

They've got real class.

II. The Secret

Trust.

That is the secret to success of the Hebrew free loan societies. Borrowers see that someone really cares for them and trusts them. In turn, they feel a greater sense of obligation to repay the loan. They feel more of a moral responsibility to make good because they have seen others fulfill their own moral responsibility to offer the loan.

Banks, whether private or government-based, are impersonal; they're in this business as a business. There's really no close personal relationship, and the fun of bank advertising nowadays seems to include showing how easy it is to get a loan at certain banks. When I am in the car, the Voice from the Radio has a ball trying to convince me how "the other banks" make you wait so very long to be approved, how tough they are on the borrower, whereas, of course, the bank that is advertising is just like your own Mom or Pop giving you a few bucks to play with...which you can pay back anytime you feel like it. It's really amusing to listen to; it brightens my day when I am crawling through Beltway traffic. They make it sound like you can just call in, say, "I need 1500 clams", and all you have to do is just stop in to pick it up without even signing any forms.

Ha!

And add to that the ever-more-greatly-spreading American moral principle that It's OK to Rip Off the Government Because They Have So Much Money Anyway They'll Never Miss It, and you'll understand better why so many people just can't seem to understand how or why Hebrew free loan societies do it.

And some of these societies have been doing it for more than 100 years.

And, no, the High Society People are not some kind of freaks. At the annual meetings of the Association of Hebrew Free Loan (AHFL), we always wait to

---

institutions, and other far-reaching and sensitive projects. This particular bank story caught their attention, and they took it on because something was wrong in Tucson and needed to be set right.

see if the San Antonio gang will come in in their cowboy boots and string neckties, looking exactly as you would expect citizens of San Antonio to look like.

For the banks, it's (of course) a business.

For the High Society people, it's a Mitzvah.

Of course.

I like it best the way Harold Lande, founder and director of the Rocky Mountain Hebrew Free Loan Society of Denver, explains it. "If we have $2,000, and someone needs a loan for $3,000, we lend it." Lande will have to find that other $1,000 somewhere, but it's a pleasure *and a privilege* for him to do so, because it's a Mitzvah. It's High Society's way of doing their double-entry book-keeping. And it's an incredibly refreshing way to re-learn all the rules of mathematics we ever learned in school. It's sort of another kind of New Math.

III. How Jewish It Is — Some Texts

There are many principles in Jewish tradition that explain the underpinnings of this Mitzvah of Jews lending money to other Jews without taking interest. Some of these principles are general, others more specific.

The most fundamental prescription is God's 1st definition of what a Jew ought to be, i.e., a person who "does Tzedakah and Mishpat"[1a], what is right and just in this world.

To the free loan people, it is only right that, if a person is in need of a loan, funds should be made available, and at that vulnerable and critical moment in a person's life, he or she should not have the added burden of paying interest.

In Exodus 22:25 is one of the specific laws of free loans: "If you lend money to My people, to the poor people among you, do not act like a creditor towards them. Take no interest from them."

In Leviticus 25:35-37, the text is more descriptive and detailed: "If your kinsperson, being in financial difficulty, comes into the range of your authority,...let him live by your side: do not take advance or accrued interest, but fear your God....I, the Lord, am your God Who brought you out of the land of Egypt to give you the land of Canaan, to be your God."

Deuteronomy 15:7-11 supplies the human element, instructing the lender about the lender's attitude: "If...there be a person in need among you,...do not harden your heart and shut your hand against this needy kinsperson. To the contrary, you must open your hand and lend that person sufficient money for whatever is needed. Beware lest you think mean-spiritedly, 'The seventh year, when debts are cancelled, is approaching,' so that you are mean to that needy kinsperson and you give nothing. The person will cry out to the Lord against you for this, and you will be considered guilty. Give to the person readily and have no regrets when you do it, for, in return, the Lord your God, will bless you in all your efforts and un-

---

[1a]Genesis 18:19.

dertakings. There will never cease to be people in your land who are in need, which is the reason why I command you, 'Open your hand to the poor and needy kinsperson in your land.'"

Furthermore, underlying this Mitzvah is a very real sense that everything we own belongs to God, and we are merely sharing it according to certain rules of decency and fairness.[1b]

Leviticus 25:23 states, "...for the land is Mine; you are but temporary residents with me." The "land" is the Land of Israel, but by fair extension, we are reminded that this world in its entirety belongs to God, and everything in this world is on loan to us while we are alive.

Centuries later, Rabbi Elazar of Bartota states it succinctly, "Give back to Him that which belongs to Him, for you and all you own is His."[1c]

And in a slightly different context, another text[1d] teaches us that not giving appropriately to poor people is tantamount to stealing from them. That particular text speaks of the portions of a farmer's field that are supposed to be set aside by the farmer for the local poor people. The passage has a very telling phrase. The texts states, "The Holy One, issued a warning that a person should not rob the poor person of these gifts *which are rightfully his* [1e]." So it's not like we are giving away anything or giving anything up. Not at all. Some of the money and other resources that we have in our possession don't really belong to us. Rather, we are trustees, and we are warned to be reliable, fair, trustworthy distributors of those funds and resources. This may not sit well with the modern flow of greed and possessiveness, but it *is* most certainly a vital part of Jewish tradition. We may choose to ignore it, but we cannot deny that it is there.

In fact, the well-known phrase, "Kol Yisrael Arayvim Zeh BaZeh"[1f], usually translated as "Every Jew is responsible for every other Jew", literally means, "Every Jew is a guarantor for every other Jew." "Arayv" is a legal term, meaning "someone who guarantees a loan". Each of us has to make good for the other's needs.

And that is one of the glories of free loan societies: they afford us the opportunity to loosen our grip on the concept of ownership and free ourselves of the craving to call things our own. Free loan societies give us freedom, a very real opportunity to catch the flavor of the sublime phrase, "I only own what I give away." I hear variations on that theme frequently, from unpretentious people who are most definitely *not* bragging. They really believe it and live by it.

[1b]The word "Tzedakah most definitely includes these "decency" and "fairness" in its many meanings.

[1c]Pirkay Avot, Chapter 3.

[1d]Numbers Rabb, 5:2.

[1e]My italics.

[1f]Shevu'ot 39a.

IV. More Texts

In the early centuries of the Common Era, Rabbi Abba said in the name of Rabbi Shimon ben Lakish, "One who lends money [to the poor] is greater than one who just gives it. And one who forms a partnership is yet greatest."[1g]

A millennium later, Rashi comments on "VeHechezakta Bo-Give the poor person strength"[1h] as follows: "Don't allow the person to go into decline and fall flat, making it that much more difficult to get back on his or her feet again. Rather, give that person strength from the very time the person begins to falter. An appropriate analogy would be — if a donkey has a heavy cargo on its back, while the cargo is still up there, one person can grab hold of it, steady it, and help the animal get back up. But if the cargo falls off, even 5 people can't lift it back up." Even worse would be if the donkey sags to its knees with the burden still on its back. It could possibly break the animal's legs, rendering the creature forever useless. It would be as good as dead. This principle is, of course, reiterated in Maimonides' highest level of Tzedakah, providing opportunities that allow others to stand on their own feet, without the ultimate support of others.[1i]

In a much-quoted text[1j], one of the Mitzvahs for which there is a double reward (i.e., benefits both in This World and the Next World), is Gemillut Chassadim, acts of caring, lovingkindness. These acts are usually understood to include providing for poor couples about to be married, visiting the sick, comforting mourners and the like. However, over the centuries, the practice of extending interest-free loans has come to be called Gemillut Chassadim, and free loan societies are called Gemillut Chassadim Societies, or in abbreviated form, a Gemach.[1k] The reward for the Gemachim in This World is obvious: this life of ours becomes so much more decent and pleasant because more and more people have the opportunity to realize their full potential. They are not strapped or bound or tied to scrounging for their basic necessities and they have a greater opportunity to be self-sufficient. The reward in the Next World, i.e., the higher spiritual goodness of it all, is obvious: another great Mitzvah has been actualized, brought alive, and given a chance to play itself out in the grand scheme of things.

An interesting insight is furnished by Maimonides in his law code, the Mishnah Torah. In the context of the treatment of widows and orphans[1l], he states, "People are required to be particularly careful in relation to orphans and widows because they are very, very much beaten down in spirit and emotionally drained — even if they have money. We are even warned about [being careful] with the widow and orphans of royalty....And up to what point are people consid-

---

[1g]Shabbat 63a.
[1h]Leviticus 25:35.
[1i]Mishnah Torah, Hilchot Matnot Ani'im, 10:7-14.
[1j]Mishnah Pe'ah 1:1.
[1k]The plural form of the abbreviation is "Gemachim".
[1l]Hilchot De'ot, end of Chapter 6.

ered orphans? Until they no longer need others to support them, educate and train them, and take care of them." I think it is fair to say that many people applying for interest-free loans feel orphaned: lonely, isolated, their self-image sinking lower and lower. Maimonides reminds us not only of the extent of our requisite involvement, but also of our attitude: we are not to be patronizing or nasty, lecturing them about how they most surely are the cause of their poverty.

Maimonides further speaks to this issue in a passage relating to Tzedakah in general[1m]: "If you give Tzedakah to the poor with a scowling face, avoiding eye contact — even if you gave that person 1,000 gold coins, you have lost out on the real merit of the Mitzvah. Rather, give pleasantly, joyously, identifying sympathetically with the poor person's pain,...and speaking with the utmost comforting words." What applies for the Mitzvah of plain Tzedakah, also applies to free loans. Our attitudes, our humanity and Menschlichkeit, must be an essential pact of the act.

And Maimonides continues in the next passage, "If the poor person asks for money and you have nothing to give, be soothing in your reply to the person. We are prohibited to scold the person or put the person down or to scream at the person, because, as it is, his heart is broken and crushed....Woe to the person who humiliates a poor person! Woe to him! Be rather like a parent to that person, both in your sympathetic feelings and in your words."

This is strong stuff for a law code. Not only does Maimonides say, "Woe to the person who...", but he also repeats it. Maimonides, considered by all as an intellectual genius, and by some a bit of a philosophical elitist — Maimonides really seems to be letting his emotions go at this point. There are wrongdoings in life and there are wrongdoings. But, as far as Maimonides is concerned, it would be hard to sink lower than taking someone already in a precarious human condition, and then tearing away at him or her, blasting any last shred of dignity they may have left in their souls.

Strong stuff!

And all of this philosophy of Mitzvahs, and all of these practical and psychological guidelines on doing it right, can be summarized by the Biblical injunction, "VeChay Achicha Immach-Let your kinsperson live with you."[1n] Our Talmudic literature applies this as the ultimate principle that everyone is *entitled* to a decent chance in life, and we are obligated to take part in making that happen. Letting others "live with you" is not simply an abstract ideal. In Jewish tradition it is very much a practical rule of life. We must preserve the others' rights, and those rights include a chance to live decently, comfortably, without grovelling or physical or emotional exhaustion to have shelter, pleasant furnishings, warmth, clothing, food, meaningful work, and yes, life, liberty, and the pursuit of some form of personal happiness.

[1m]Mishnah Torah, Hilchot Matnot Ani'im, 10:4.
[1n]Leviticus 25:36.

V. Today in Jewish North America

Until recently, the art of Hebrew free loaning was almost lost in many Jewish communities in the United States and Canada.[10] Nowadays, though, once a year the Association of Hebrew Free Loans gathers to review the previous year's activities in each city, to study Torah together, and to exchange ideas about how to operate more meaningfully and efficiently. And each year, representatives from a few more communities come to the meetings, including those representing newly-established groups or recently-revived groups. Observers are welcomed, and professionals and lay leaders from other parts of the Jewish community come to some of the sessions.

But we all remain astounded at how many people don't even know of the existence of Hebrew free loan societies, or even that it is a Mitzvah to lend money to other Jews at an interest rate of 0%.

A recent eye-opening moment brought this home to us: A few months ago there was a large conference about the resettlement of Soviet Jewish immigrants. Jewish professionals from all parts of the community spectrum attended. One of the sessions was a panel with representatives from Jewish leadership in 3 different communities. The panelists included 2 non-AHFL people, while the 3rd person was Devorah Danziger from the Toronto Jewish Assistance Services, which arranges the free loans in their community.

One of the panelists mentioned that their community had made arrangements with banks to extend loans to the immigrants. There was kind of a low, understanding "hmmmm" from the AHFL people in the room. Mark Meltzer from the Los Angeles group was reacting particularly knowingly (to himself, but we saw it), since his gang has a tremendously successful free loan program for the Soviet Jews. Devorah then indicated that her community extended free loans through the Toronto Jewish Assistance Services....And she explained that it was part of "keeping it in the family".

I noticed a number of non-AHFL people jotting down notes, their eyes lighting up, as if to say, "What great ideas! No interest on the loans. And 'keeping it in the family'!" It was like a revelation to them.

The AHFL people weren't being smug. I believe, however, that they felt frustrated that free loans have not become the common rule. I believe they were sad that the heyday of free loans — just a few decades ago — has not yet returned when it is so much needed in our own day. And I think they were troubled by the foolishness of having to pay out all that interest when that good Tzedakah money could just as well be poured back into a free loan arrangement.

---

[10]In highly-concentrated Jewish populations, the practice of Jewish free loans seems to have been thriving all along, but many of us were simply not being exposed to it. I have heard from different sources that there are 150 or more free-loan societies in Boro Park, Brooklyn,...and more than 300 in Jerusalem.

No one doubts that there are more Jewish poor people nowadays than in the recent past. More Jews struggle to make ends meet, more Jews live on the edge than we can recall since the days of the great Eastern European immigration at the turn of the century and the Great Depression. The demands on free loan societies are very great. But aside from all the "normal, everyday" demands for interest-free loans: car loans, rent, education, business, personal bail-outs, whatever, the needs for the next few years will be so enormous — because of Gorbachev's new policies — it is now prime time for stepping up our efforts to expand existing free loan societies, reviving dormant ones, and establishing new ones wherever needed. It will just make the entire process of resettlement that much easier. It is just waiting to happen.

VI. *Two Final Jewish Principles*

The Midrash[1p] tells us that "there are seven different terms for poor people". The text then proceeds to explain each term. But we know them already, with our own modern variations: people who used to be doing well or just OK but are now down on their luck, people who feel crushed, people who see all the things others have and just can't seem to get a hold on even a few of the basics, people treated like dirt by others because they are poor, people who are walked on like a doorstep because they are poor, all kinds of poor people.

This Midrash is a reminder to all of us that people in need are people, each with his or her own story, which they are either free to tell us or not to tell us. What they have in common is their poverty, and what *we* have in common with them is our Jewish sense of responsibility for their well-being and our fundamental obligation to be fully human and decent when working with them. The text is also a warning against the practice of labelling and the facile condemnation of the poor we hear all too often today. "Bums" (sub-categories: "druggies", "drunks", "crazies", "thieves", "bums" again and again), "parasites", "they take advantage of you", "they take advantage of the system", "why don't they go out and get a job?", "if they got a job and worked hard they'd do as well as I do" and all the rest of the claptrap that is bandied about in conversations at the dinner table. It sounds just one step removed from the practice of Debtor's Prison which used to be in fashion in enlightened societies not too long ago.

These condemnations are disheartening in general — and disheartening in particular to hear from Jews — when we see how much Jewish tradition stands so strongly against such attitudes.

Perhaps a little free-form interpretation will give an overall perspective to this situation. A Talmudic passage[1q] may be helpful at this point: "Rabbi Simla'i

---

[1p]Leviticus Rabba 34:6.
[1q]Sotah 14a.

explained, 'The Torah begins and ends with Gemillut Chassadim-Acts of caring, lovingkindness.'"

Now, I realize that Rabbi Simla'i is referring to all kinds of caring acts, particularly providing clothes for those in need such as visiting the sick, comforting mourners, burying the dead with appropriate dignity. But in our specialized use of the term "Gemillut Chassadim", i.e., interest-free loans, we could say that the ultimate meaning of Torah can be found in the practice of this specific Mitzvah. By extending interest-free loans, we are reminded of our principles of Jewishness-means-giving, of our essential humanity, of our common connection with *all* people, regardless of their financial circumstances. And we are allowed to rise to the occasion of being fully Jewish and human by responding to the needs of others in a sensitive and dignified manner.

That is what is meant, after all, by Torah, and by the 1st text that I mentioned — that Jews are put on this earth to do Tzedakah and Mishpat, the right thing, the just thing.

Final Exams:
Pavlov's Dogs, Father Guido,
Pinball Machines, and the Jews

I. A Reminder

Everything I mention in this article about schools and teachers applies to parents. Just substitute "Mother" or "Father" for "teacher" or "educator".

The same goes for youth directors and camp directors and whoever else is involved in any aspects of Jewish education, formal or informal.

II. Father Guido Sarducci and the Jews

One of the comedians on *Saturday Night Live* plays the character of Father Guido Sarducci, a rather hip, off-beat priest. One of his best comedy bits is lampooning college education. It's something like a review of every course you ever took in college — *all* of it reviewed by catch-phrases in under a minute. Physics? $E=mc^2$. Biology? DNA and RNA. English and American Lit? Shakespeare, Wordsworth, Hemingway. American History? "Give me liberty, or give me death", the Louisiana Purchase, the Emancipation Proclamation.

The Good Father rattles them off 1 after another, Subject, then 1 or 2 Facts meant to be memorized; then another Subject, another Fact Memorized. Then another round of the same. On and on, hollow and meaningless to the ex-student in his or her life at the present. From the response by the audience, Father Guido is striking some very deep chords. There is laughter and un-ease, because he is right, of course. He is right because it reduces us to nothing more than Pavlov's famous canines (though I cannot remember anything about Professor Pavlov, other than the fact that he had a Russian-sounding name, so he must have been from Russia, but *when* exactly or *where* exactly or *why* exactly he was playing with dogs is unclear to me. There's something about ringing a bell and saliva and food or lack of food and conditioned responses, but that's all I remember.) But I *do* sometimes use a borrowed throwaway line to loosen up my audiences, "Does the name Pavlov ring a bell?" (And, if they laugh, I also toss in, "Does the name Quasimodo ring a bell?")

The end result of the Sarducci-Pavlov approach is that bells ring, our adrenalin gets hyped up, and the blood flow changes slightly in the tubes and chambers and passageways of the side of the brain that remembers things...but not much more.

We have paid the price of being told to "do our homework" when we were kids, i.e., to memorize everything they told us to, plus more for extra credit.

III. The Contemporary Debate in the Field of Philosophy of Education

It was a hot issue, but not necessarily a new one.

Someone[1] published a book not too long ago advocating the theory of education that no one should graduate such-and-such a level of education without knowing certain basic, hard facts. The battle raged, rivers, oceans of ink were spilled, as the critics of philosophers of education had their field day, for and against. (They had to — it's how they make a living, filling their own self-imposed publish-or-perish quotas as they must.)

The Fact Man was right, of course, though I can't remember his name or the name of his book. (I don't have much of a head for facts.)

He was right, the ink-spilling supporters responded, pointing to studies that show X% of American high school graduates couldn't locate Chicago on a map, another Y% thought Thomas Jefferson was the CEO of a food conglomerate, and Gorbachev a kind of vodka.

The Fact Man is right that we are turning out ignoramuses of the basic facts of a functioning human being in society....They have even given us the term "functionally illiterate", a good term, indicating that graduates can't even do simple math to keep track of their finances, don't know the 1st thing about reading want ads in the paper, don't understand the process of registering to vote.

The nay-sayers said, "Nay". They said that the Fact Man is limited, that there has to be more to education than just the facts, and they are right, too, but the crux of the problem really is, "In a limited amount of school time, how much of which kind of education does a student get?"

IV. The Pinball Machine

I think a more useful image than Pavlov's Hounds is the pinball machine.[1a]

When a word or concept is thrown out at the student, we, the educators, have to consider whether or not it will register anything at all. If it doesn't, it is as if a pinball just rolls down to the bottom because the bumpers and lights and whistles of the machine are getting no juice.

When a word or concept is thrown out at the student, we, the educators, have to consider whether or not it will hit a bumper, bounce off once with plenty of

---

[1] I consulted my mentor in Jewish education who remembers neither the name of the book nor the author, though he narrowed the latter down to either "Bloom" or "Hirsch" (and he wasn't sure of the spelling, either). He said something to the effect that the book is "another peg in the casket of creativity in education". Recognizing that he had let me down, I dropped the subject and went on to ask him about his family.

[1a] The image of the pinball machine is my own, but the idea of associational and responsive thinking comes from the late Professor Max Kadushin, one of my teachers at the Seminary. We learned his profound idea of Organic Thinking in Rabbinic Literature from the thinker himself, as we worked line-by-line through his book *The Rabbinic Mind*.

zip, then roll down a little, softly hit another light (i.e., another word, another concept), slide to the flipper, and then be flipped back up to the 1st bumper, where it bounces again and again off the side as the score racks up higher and higher.

The pinball machine takes into account (a) the interaction of different words and concepts, (b) the intensity of the response, and (c) the active participation of the player who uses the flippers to bring himself or herself back again to the 1st concept or the 2nd concept for further reinforcement.

It's a little hard to picture, so I recommend that we take the school faculty out to the arcade for an afternoon to play the machines. After about 3 or 4 games, they should begin thinking of the analogies to education, and I think they'll understand better...and probably get higher scores and more free games as a result. In addition, everyone should have a grand old time of it and remember happier childhood days when they played the machines for hours on end. Even if they don't manage to make any pedagogical breakthroughs, it would be a nice afternoon out with the Gang.

V. Pavlov's Poor, Tortured Puppies, the Pinball Machines, And Jewish Education

We certainly don't want to produce Pavlov-Sarducci products. But we most certainly *do* want the shining graduates of our schools to react — and react deeply — when certain key words and ideas strike them in later life. And even more, we want them to *act* on their responses, to *do* certain things as a result of what they have responded to.

We would want the results to be something like this:

Sometime later on in life, when they hear the word "parent" they will think, "My mother used to drive homebound individuals to chemotherapy. I ought to do the same." When they scan the calendar and see that Passover is coming, they should think, "Passover....We had fine Seders when I was a child, and when I was in Hebrew school, we used to deliver food packages to people who wouldn't have had such a fine Seder unless we did the packaging and delivering. I ought to find out how to do it here in my new community." When they read the word "justice" in the newspaper, bumpers and buzzers and bells should start going wild in their heads, and they should say, "I remember when I was in confirmation class, the rabbi brought in a lawyer who used to do *pro bono* work for members of the community. I should support similar endeavors." When they hear the word "Torah", they should flip the flippers and get "Torah-Mitzvahs-Torah-Mitzvahs" bouncing back and forth in their minds, flashing lights, buzzers, leaping scores, and go out and *do* something.

Each school [read: *and* every household, camp, youth group, adult education class, etc.] should set up a basic list of priorities to develop a strategic plan for time allotments that can work in that specific framework. My own bias is towards Mitzvah work and human personality development, of course, or what I would call

"Jewish life skills", so I think there are universal categories of bumpers and bells we ought to set up:

1. Words: Mensch/Menschlichkeit, Torah, Kavod, Mitzvah, Tzedakah, Tzedek, Mishpat, Gemillut Chassadim, Chessed, Chevrah, perhaps 25 or 30 of the most basic functional words.[1b]

2. Mitzvahs and The Names of Mitzvahs: Tzedakah/Gemillut Chassadim, Ma'ot Chittin, Matanot La'Evyonim, Hachnassat Kallah, Hachnassat Orchim, Bikkur Cholim, Halvayat HaMet, Nichum Avaylim, Hava'at Shalom Bayn Adam LeChavayro, and as many more as might be needed for basic, functional Jewish vocabulary.

3. Stories: Abraham breaking his father's idols (explaining what idols are really like in modern society), Moses's speech impediment, Isaac's blindness, Jacob's limp, and Rabbi Prayda's reviewing a text 400 times for a slow student[1c] (and what these mean concerning individuals with disabilities nowadays), Binyamin HaTzaddik's feeding a starving woman with his own money when the community Tzedakah Fund is out of money,[1d] and more. And they should know these stories at least as well as they know Goldilocks and the 3 Bears or Snow White and the 7 Dwarfs.

4. Quotes: Genesis 18:19 (Jews do what is right and just), Second Samuel 8:15 (King David did what is just and right), Ben Azzai's quote that everyone is created in God's image is the most important Torah principle of all,[1e] "Even a poor person who is kept alive by Tzedakah must give Tzedakah".[1f] The teacher [read: parent, youth director, camp director] should select as many of these quotes as the student {read: child, member of youth group, camper] can handle. They should know them as well as they know any of the catchy phrases they hear on TV commercials. You know, "You deserve a break today...at McDonald's" or "The Great American Road belongs to Buick".

5. People: Hadassah Levi, raising almost 40 kids with Down Syndrome; Janet Marchese; finding homes for hundreds of infants with Down Syndrome, Myriam Mendilow, founder of Life Line for the Old, the Jewish Family Service workers who go way beyond their job description in helping Soviet Jewish immigrants in the re-settlement process, friends who are always quietly there to get the local Mitzvah work done. They should read about these people in books, *our* books, our *Jewish* books, in newspapers, and watch and listen for them on TV and radio. Most importantly, they should be *personally* exposed to these Mitzvah heroes in real life. As best as I can tell, there's nothing more effective than face-to-

---

[1b] Note: compare on a spot check test with a sampling of Jewish adults, asking them to list 25 Hebrew, Yiddish, or Ladino words that come to mind. It would be troubling if some of them include the first 8 words of their Bar or Bat Mitzvah Haftarah among The Biggies.

[1c] Eruvin 54b.

[1d] Bava Batra 11a.

[1e] Sifra, Kedoshim, on Leviticus 19:18.

[1f] Shulchan Aruch, Yoreh De'ah 248:1.

face encounters with people who personify all the values we are advocating. The Mitzvah people should be brought into the classroom [read: home, camp, youth group meetings] and then the students should go out and join those Mitzvah people in their work. And they have to know at least a dozen of them, to somehow counteract the commonly-held heroes of our society: the movie stars, rock stars, sports stars, the wealthy and famous who are heroes because they are wealthy and famous.

VI. The Plan of Attack

Exam time is now. Let's get cracking.

Tuesday Night in the ER

I. The ER

It is Tuesday night, 9:30 p.m, the paramedics have just come barreling through the door. On the cart is someone who can only be described as a mess: blood, severed muscles, nerves, crazy fluctuations in the vital signs, fluids gushing where they shouldn't, blood everywhere.

Blood.

Hours later, the ER staff will wonder whether little David had to think so fast when he first saw Goliath. The second hand sweeps around and the blood flows out. It is a gory, familiar picture.

Tuesday night, 11:45.

The rescue squad comes barreling through the door. On the cart is someone fading, unable to catch her breath. Attendants jump. All kinds of orders (with ex-clamation marks at the end of each order) start flying. Asthma? Heart attack? It is not such a gory picture, but the clock's hands move smoothly, while the vital signs go haywire. Seconds and minutes — time that would otherwise drag while you wait for a train or plane — now pick up speed, more speed, still more speed. How much time do they have to save a life? Is 10 seconds enough? 1 minute? 5?

I just don't understand why someone somewhere along the way in his or her medical training decides to specialize in Emergency Room Medicine. Yes, I *do* understand that they can see real lives being saved right there in front of their own eyes, and I would suppose that the ER doctor early on in med school figured the negative odds would be higher than in other specialties. They are ready, I am sure, to lose more patients than other doctors would. They have come to expect it. They wouldn't have chosen the ER if they didn't figure the grisly odds. It's probably like people who work for organizations like the Red Cross who go out at the 1st hint of a disaster to pull people from floods and tornadoes and plane crashes.

I am sure it is hard on them — the ER doctors and other house staff, the disaster relief people — and I wonder what percentage of losses/saves is acceptable to them before they switch out...to something safer, easier on the emotions, per-haps some other specialty that doesn't wear away at their vital energies so much.

I know someone out there has to do it, and I admire whoever they are, the ER people. I admire their reflexes, their guts, their wisdom and skill, their stamina.

But I just can't put myself into their shoes. Even in my imagination I can't picture being so close to life-oozing-away, even surrounded by all the instruments and bottles and and needles and bags of blood they have in the blood bank. There has to be a limit to how much failure someone can take.

And don't think I am building this up just from watching too many flashy TV shows. I talk to a lot of doctors; all the time I seem to be talking to doctors. I listen to ER doctors, and ER-doctors-in-training, grilling them on what it takes to do it. I already know it's not all gunshot wounds and knifings and car accidents. I already know that there are the usual scrapes and bruises and simple stitchings, but still, when it happens — the car accident, the industrial accident, the falls, the gun battles on the streets — it takes so much to fix, to make it right, I really can't understand why someone would *want* to do it. How many mangled or cut up human bodies do you have to see before you need a long, long vacation? Just exactly how many chests do you have to cut open, stick your hands right on a human heart and start massaging before you say, "I need a rest"?

And even more incomprehensible is how — in the midst of Time-the-Enemy and in the thick of incredibly ugly sights — how do they preserve a sense of calm? After all, what good is a doctor who loses his or her good sense and knowledge and rational powers when those qualities are exactly what the situation demands? How do they do it?

II. Nahum Ish Gamzu

It once happened that a certain Nahum Ish Gamzu was going to visit his in-laws. He had 3 donkeys trailing behind him, their packs loaded with food and other gifts. As he went on his way, a poor person came up to him and said, "Rabbi, feed me."

Nahum Ish Gamzu replied, "Wait until I take the food out of the animal's pack."

And, ever so sadly, while the rabbi was in the process of taking out the food, the hungry man died.

The Talmudic story[1] goes on for another few lines, picking up on other details, teaching more insights. It is a well-known story, and it deals with Nahum's reaction to this catastrophe and his students' reaction to the tale he tells. It is a difficult story, too painful to review too often in one's studies. As I said, the story is well known to students of Talmud, but it is often merely studied, maybe memorized, and then tucked away somewhere in the student's memory for future reference. The full, slamming power of the tale is rarely allowed to penetrate the consciousness. There's just too much raw reality to handle.

I find that — for the story of Nahum — this method of study is understandable, but inadequate. I think the story is one of a handful of ancient tales that is so shattering, it should be a basis for a way of thinking and action for a broader spectrum of human situations. And what is shattering is not the aftermath of Nahum's encounter with the hungry man, but the death itself: the man approaches, says just 2 words, "Rebbi, Parnesayni!-Rabbi, feed me!" and a short time afterwards he is dead. Was it 10 seconds later? A minute and a half? 4 minutes? It is so stark, so irreversible. The man is dead, and whether or not Nahum Ish Gamzu believed it or not, we, who read the text, must believe he moved as quickly as he possibly could.

---

[1]Ta'anit 21a.

Nahum was a well-known Tzaddik, a righteous person, and there is no reason whatsoever to suspect that he moved too slowly as he unloaded the food.

The man died.

Nahum did his human best, but the man still died.

III. Nahum Ish Gamzu and the ER Doctors, Reviewed

The only way I can deal with these issues is 1-2-3:

1. The doctors who go into ER medicine make a choice to be in the thick of this high-stakes' action. Nahum did not choose it. It just happened. I could only hope it would never happen to me. And mere "fear of failure" is too abstract an explanation. To fail an exam, to do a poor job on some project, even the costliest ones, cannot possibly be compared to the death of another human being. So mine is a kind of silent prayer, "Please let me save lives, yes. But please let me do the easy ones, not the ones that take squash time so much that a split-second delay or the most insignificant slip costs a human life." Since no human being can possibly say, "Tomorrow, exactly at noon, this person will die", that moment between life and death should be left to more qualified experts, the ones who are capable of saving lives whenever it is possible.

2. In the broader world of Tzedakah, we need to find and train experts who are like the ER doctors. When true life-and-death crises confront us, let us have experts who can guide us. On the one hand, we are tired of people screaming, "Crisis! Crisis!" when the situation may be only "serious". This is no good, because if they cry wolf too often, it makes us lose faith in their expertise. They — the Jewish leaders — were right, for example, in the days before and during the Yom Kippur War. They knew just how much World Jewry needed to respond and how quickly. They knew how much the noose was tightening around Israel, and how quickly we had to get people to cut the rope and give the gasping body some air. They helped save Israel and save us, back in those days of Yom Kippur, 1973. We needed the experts in life-and-death then, and we still very much need them, leaders-who-are-life-and-death-experts who can sort through all the possible needs in the Jewish community and in the world at large, who can say, "Now!" on one issue because it really *is* life-and-death, and "Later" for other programs, projects, and issues which can wait a little or a lot.

3. Perhaps it is a little far-fetched, but we might want to arrange seminars conducted by ER doctors. They could address our Jewish leadership and tell about the ins and outs of Tuesday nights in the ER, the incredibly fine lines between life and death, the methods they themselves use to overcome physical and emotional exhaustion so they can keep functioning at their best. Maybe our leadership is good at what it does, but just needs some higher-level training. And maybe, just maybe, a select few of the attendees will decide to specialize in this branch of Tzedakah work. They *are* only a select few, just as there are only a few ER doctors. We certainly need more of them in the field of community Mitzvah work.

I return to Nahum Ish Gamzu.

We should pray that such a horrible life-event — such a face-to-face encounter with life-and-death — should never happen. But it *will* happen, if not to us, then to someone else. Someone has to be there to confront the trauma, cut open the chest and massage the heart if necessary, to order the right shot before it is too late, to make the exact incision that will save the human life.[1a]

And if, as with the Rabbi from centuries past, we have done all that we possibly could, then we will have done all that we possibly could. There will be time and room for sadness, but at least we did *everything* humanly possible.

IV. An Additional Insight Into the Story of Nahum Ish Gamzu

My friend, Louise Cohen, believes that the real key to the story is different than the comments I have made. She says that the moment Nahum said, "Wait until..." — instead of saying, "Yes, I will feed you" — the man died in despair. According to this interpretation, the man could have survived physically for at least as long as it would have taken Nahum to take the food out of the animal's pack, but the fact that he said "Wait" crushed any last resistance he had to the Angel of Death. He died, not because his body shut down, but because his body *and his mind* gave up.

Nahum moved quickly, as quickly as humanly possible. The seconds it took to unload the food from the animal's pack was not the issue, though. The *real* issue was the human response, the words. Nahum was willing to help; of that there is no question. It is just that he didn't grasp as completely as possible that his words, his tone, the expression of his face had to be so absolutely reassuring, that the starving man would summon that much more stamina to survive.

This is a story of extremes. It is excruciatingly demanding, asking, perhaps, too much of another human being. And yet, Louise's interpretation is instructive and useful, a reminder that doing everything humanly possible means responding to *all* the needs of the other person, because the person is a whole being, not just something physical in need of nutrition for the cells.

People who work on hot lines — physical abuse hotlines, suicide hotlines, police hotlines — know this well. Since there are such experts in this related field, then it would be important to have them also teach this course, as well as the ER staff. All of them could help us refine our sense of life-and-death, and perhaps more people will live their full lives as a result. And saving however many human lives that may yet be saved is no small thing. As our tradition tells us, "Whoever saves a human life, saves the entire universe."

[1a]As my friend, Naomi Teperow, has pointed out to me, life-and-death issues are only a part of the broad spectrum of the world of Mitzvahs, as they are only a particular portion of the field of medicine. How much time, effort, and other resources should be devoted to life-and-death problems (both in Tzedakah and in medicine) would be a worthy subject for further study, though it is outside the realm of this particular article.

Cholesterol
And the Jews

I. Cholesterol

Sit any 3 or 4 of us down together for lunch or dinner and sooner or later someone will mention cholesterol. It's the latest rage in my age group. I secretly set my stopwatch as soon as we are at the table, and when the word first comes up in conversation, I note the time. Average time for people in their late 30's to early 40's is 4 minutes, 27 seconds, though it is usually sooner if the meal is Italian.

There's always 1 person there who's a classic Cholesterol Basher, who's read the latest article saying, "Well, you know, they're beginning to say it's not really *that* critical a factor."

There's always at least 1 who really plays dirty and hits hard, who, with gloating in his voice spouts all the details of the latest study on decaffeinated coffee (the last bastion of my physical enjoyment), how the scientists have proven you're dead meat if you have more than 1 cup a year.

And there's always 1 success story at the table, who, with gloating in his voice, says, "I brought mine down from 303 to 186 in a year. Carbs (=carbohydrates to the un-initiates), lots of pasta, rice, millet, and cous-cous.

There's always 1 person there who tells you the deadly tale of the development of his or her oatbran muffins from rock-solid bowling balls to fluffy and almost-tasty, complete with variations: raisins, crushed pineapple, blueberries.

And there's always someone who eats everything: a half-dozen eggs a week, at least 10 doughnuts, chocolate (white, dark, milk, semisweet, bittersweet, everything), and still stays well below the line. (The danger zone runs anywhere from 200 to 240 depending on which Yuppie reads what studies.)

There's always someone who pooh-pooh's it, but, when you ask what his or her "numbers" are, he or she will say something absurdly low like 140. (Few human beings, no gibbons, and not a single Malayan jungle lemur has *ever* had numbers that low.) I even dined with someone with a cholesterol count of 102. (He looked like he could barely lift his fork, his face was ashen-tending-towards-pallid, he slurred his words...but his numbers were low, for sure.)

By then the host or hostess has brought out the chopped liver, and that's when you *really* get to see:
who is honest and who a hypocrite,
who shall live and who shall die,
who by fire and who by water,
who by sword and who by pestilence,
who will say, "I'll pass on the liver" and who will be the True Snarfer.

It is hard to get any words of Torah into the conversation because they haven't discussed "The Ratio" yet, i.e., the ratio of high density something-or-others to something else, which shouldn't be more than 4.5.

II. *Gingivitis*

Gingivitis is the new rage, Beyond Cholesterol.

Now that advanced tartar-control toothpastes, fluoridation, and new-fangled electric toothbrushes whose bristles whirl differently than ever before are beating back Demon Tooth Decay, the dentists — tired of having to read their own old, outdated magazines in the waiting room for lack of patients — try scare tactics with gingivitis.

So, if it is a long lunch or dinner, we turn to that obsession, as Diner #1 sadly notes, "Joe's in Mass General, been there for a week."

Diner #2, "Oh, no! Lordy, Lordy! Is he OK? Heart attack? Stroke?"

Diner #1, "No, gingivitis."

Silence, dead silence.

We don't even know where the best gingiva transplants are being done. We don't know if our insurance covers it. We don't know if there's a cure. It spreads a pall on the meal. We don't even know whether or not low-impact aerobics could have prevented it.

Poor Joe...gingivitis done him in. It is all so sad.

We all make a mental note to visit him during the week, and to brush more carefully next time.

III. *Torah and Mitzvahs*

Bingo!

Proverbs, Chapter 3:

> Child, do not forget my Torah-teaching,
> Let your mind take note of my Mitzvahs;
> They will give you many days,
> Years of life, Shalom....
> It will be a cure for your body,
> Good medicine for your bones.

Torah and Mitzvah work are good for the body. (You were thinking "cure for the soul". As Tonto used to say to the Lone Ranger — when they would study Torah — "Atta To'eh, Ish Lavan-Wrong White Man!")

Here are three quick examples from Jewish tradition:

1. Binyamin HaTzaddik feeds a woman and her children who are on the verge of starvation. He is the director of the local community Tzedakah fund and,

seeing that there is nothing left in the fund, he buys the food with his own money. Heaven gives him an additional 22 years of life. (Bava Batra 11a)

2. Rabbi Prayda has a learned-disabled student. He reviews the material 400 times, and at one point, when the student loses his train of thought, he goes over it yet another 400 times. Heaven gives him another 400 years of life, *and* his entire generation merits life in the Next World. (Eruvin 54b)

3. Pharaoh's daughter bathes in the Nile. One Jewish text says it was because she had leprosy or some similar horrible disease. When she rescues the infant Moses from the river — the minute she touches the little boat his mother put him in, she is cured. (Exodus Rabba, Exodus 23)

And there are many, many more examples in Rabbinic literature.

IV. Head in the Books, Head in the Clouds

I am often accused of being "somewhere out there". They — the all-purpose "they", i.e., the scoffers and the wags, the armchair critics, street corner faultfinders and Monday morning kvetches — say I spend too much time inside the Talmud and other faraway books and don't really have a grasp of Real Life. The accusation is compounded by other catch-all accusations of "Poet!", which I am, but by which they mean, "How can you expect a poet to know anything really real or recommend anything practical?"

Well, all right.

But here's something from *American Health* magazine, March, 1989:

"Helping other people brings real physical benefits as well as psychological ones, according to epidemiologist James House and his colleagues at the University of Michigan's Survey Research Center....They studied 2,700 people in Tecumseh, MI, for more than a decade, to see how their social relationships affected their health....The article reported that, in this study, doing regular volunteer work, more than any other activity, *dramatically* [italics mine] increased life expectancy."

Note the word "dramatically".

And furthermore, good news for us males:

"Men who did not do volunteer work were 2 1/2 times more likely to die during the study as men who volunteered at least once a week."

So much for the pooh-poohers and all followers of the principle that, when you really get down to it, when Torah comes up short, turn to science. Well, we turned to science, and it looks like, if you want to live a long life — barring encounters with an 18-wheeler in the wrong lane or incredibly lousy genes — tutoring learning-disabled kids once a week or building houses for homeless people or wrapping and delivering Passover food packages for people who can't afford a Passover meal, might just get you all those Senior Citizens Goodies that are waiting for you down the road. Discounts at the movies, passes on the buses, cheaper midweek fares on the airlines.

Well, all right then! Let's get down to it!

V. A Few Things I Am *Not* Saying

I am *not* saying, "Substitute rescuing Ethiopian Jews for dialysis."

I am not recommending *pro bono* legal work in place of chemotherapy.

I am only pointing out that the All Holy Scientists substantiate what Mitzvah workers already knew, namely, that you can live longer if you make this kind of work part of your life. The front-line Mitzvah people didn't need a more-than-a-decade study to prove it; they could see it...lots of lowered blood pressure, peace-of-mind yielding a different-paced, less depression and loneliness, less eating their kishkas out over little things, more perspective on what counts and, consequently, nicer EKG readings. They knew it all along, University of Michigan Survey Research Center or no University of Michigan Survey Research Center.

I am also *not* saying that people should do Mitzvahs because it's good for your health. People should do Mitzvahs because they are Mitzvahs. *If* it turns out that there are many side benefits, that's fine and good. There are lots of benefits besides good health and long life — good feelings, self-dignity, tax benefits, etc. But above and beyond all that are the benefits for the beneficiary, the one who needs the ride to a community program and who would have otherwise stayed home alone were it not for the volunteer driver; the loving touch the visitor gives the resident of the old age home; the special attention a slow-to-learn child needs to make it through to bar or bat mitzvah, the *pro bono* time and effort to prevent a senseless eviction of a poor person. For sure there are benefits for the one doing the Mitzvah deed, but most important — I stress *most* — is that *they* need it.

It's nice, existentially speaking, that things work out this way: the one in need has the need satisfied, and, in addition, all kinds of other benefits accrue. But even if the Mitzvah doer didn't have all those supplementary goodies, Mitzvahs are still Mitzvahs and should be done, willingly, wholeheartedly.

VI. Violin Music in the Background

(Violin music in the background, soft voice), "Are you feeling a little draggy? Lost your pep? You may have Iron Deficiency Anemia."

[Author's note, "God forbid!"]

"Well, take Geritol...."

[Author's note, "Gezunterhayt — go ahead, take Geritol. But don't forget to buy an extra item of food for Tzedakah when you grocery shop, and buy cough drops for people in shelters when you pick up your Geritol, and make a point to go down to the demonstration at City Hall to free Jews in Arab Lands, and, while you're at it — don't forget to write a healthy check for Tzedakah."]

A Master List
Of All Tzedakah Projects
Mentioned in this Book

AACI-Jerusalem Scholarship Fund, 6 Mane St., Jerusalem, ATTN: Michael
    Bargteil, 660-772.
Access Directories for People with Disabilities (i.e., National Synagogue Listing),
    United Synagogue of America, 155 5th Ave., NY, NY 10010,
    212-533-7800.
ALYN Orthopaedic Hospital, POB 9117, Kiryat Hayovel, Jerusalem, 412-251,
    (Corner Olsvenger and Shmaryahu Levin Sts.), American Friends of
    ALYN, 19 W. 44th St., #1418, NY, NY 10036, 212-869-0369.
American Friends of Life Line for the Old — see "Life Line for the Old.
American Friends of Yad Sara — see "Yad Sarah"
American Jewish Joint Distribution Committee, 711 3rd Ave., NY, NY 10017,
    212-687-6200.
The Ark, 2341 W. Devon Ave., Chicago, IL 60659, 312-973-1000.
Arnson, Curt, c/o AKIM/Jerusalem, 42 Gaza St., Jerusalem, 631-728.
Association of Hebrew Free Loans, c/o Julius Blackman, 703 Market St., #445,
    San Frnancisco, CA 94103, 415-982-3177.
Atlas, Allison: See "Bone Marrow Testing".

Baltimore Jewish Times, 2104 N. Charles St., Baltimore, MD 21218,
    301-752-3504.
Bar/Bat Mitzvah Tzedakah Projects, Ranan or Ari Engelhart, 312-588-5024,
    6328 N. Central Park, Chi 60659
Bar/Bat Miyzvahs, Adults with Special Needs, Hyla Shapiro, c/o JCC 333
    Nahanton St., Newton, MA 02159, 617-965-7410.
Battered Women's Shelters (Jewish):
    Baltimore — Rebbetzin Chana Weinberg, 401 Yeshiva Lane, #2D,
        Baltimore, MD 21208, 301-521-3600 or 486-0322.
    Chicago — Shalva, Box 53, Chicago, IL 60660, ATTN: Sherry Berliner,
        312-583-HOPE.
    Essex County, NJ, Ellyn Stele, 201-439-3830.
    Jerusalem — Bet Tzipporah-Isha L'isha, POB 10403, Jerusalem.
    Los Angeles — Ellen Ledley, 818-908-5007, 213-652-0914.
    National Hotline — 1-800-533-8TSA (within Maryland).
    National Hotline — 1-800-622-8TSA (outside of Maryland).
Beged Kefet, c/o Les Bronstein, 80 Cranberry St., #9G, Broolyn, NY 11201,
    718-624-2925.
Ben and Jerry's Ice Cream, Rte. 100, Box 240, Waterbury, VT 05676,
    802-244-5641.

Bermack, Barbara, c/o Pomona Jewish Center, 106 Pomona Rd., Pomona, NY 10901.
Bet Gil, Emile Zola St. 15, Kiryat Aryeh, Petach Tikvah, ATTN: Israel Herzl, 03-923-2663.
Bet Tzedek, c/o Michael Feuer or Ralph Gottlieb, 145 S. Fairfax Ave., #200, Los Angeles, CA 90036, 213-939-0506.
Birds in old age homes, Carol Hutton, 317-251-9467.
Birds of Prey Rehabilitation Foundation, c/o Sigrid Ueblacker, POB 251145, Lakewood, CO 80226, 303-460-0674.
B'nai Israel Congregation (Rockville, MD), 6301 Montrose Rd., Rockville, MD 20852, 301-881-6550.
Bone Marrow Testing, Fern Ingber, 301-229-5037.
    or Life Savers Foundation of America, 800-999-8822.
Braille Haggadot: Jewish Heritage for the Blind, POB 336, Brooklyn, NY 11229, 718-228-4999
Braunhut, Sheda: see "Computer for Disabled Children".
Bread for the City, 1305 14th St., NW, Washington, DC 20005, 202-332-0440.

CAJE-Coalition for the Advancement of Jewish Education, 261 W. 35th St., #12A, NY, NY 10001, 212-268-4210.
    CAJE Tzedakah Network: see "Kinser, Kate".
Canine Companions for Independence (CCI) (all phones also TDD):
    National Office — c/o Bonnie Bergin, 4350 Occidental Rd., POB 446, Santa Rosa, CA 95402, 707-528-0830.
    Northwest Regional Center — c/o Katheryn Horton, 1215 Sebastopol Rd., Santa Rosa, CA 95407, 707-579-1985.
    North Central Office — 6901 Harrisburg Pike, Orient, OH 43146, 614-871-2554.
    Northeast Center — POB 205, Farmingdale, NY 11735, 516-694-6938.
    Southeast Center — POB 546511, Orlando, FL 32854, 407-682-2535.
    Southwest Center — 6461 El Apajo, POB 8247, Rancho Santa Fe, CA 92067, 619-756-1012.
Charleston, SC, Hurricane Relief: Charleston Jewish Federation, c/o Michael Wise, Director, 1645 Raoul Wallenberg Blvd., Charleston, SC 29407.
Chazon F'taya, c/o Simcha Ovadia-F'taya, POB 6070, 6 Shimon Chacham St., Jerusalem, 814-454.
Cheung, Susanna: See "Helemano Plantation".
Christian Service Program, POB 21, Shreveport, LA 71161, ATTN: Sister Margaret McCaffrey, 318-221-4539.
City Harvest, 11 John St., #503, NY, NY 10038, 212-349-4004.
Coat Drive for Homeless People: Sara Cohen, 312-539-3347
Computers for Disabled Children: Sheda Braunhut, Yerushalmi St. 6/10, Tel Aviv, 03-546-1989.

Computers for old age homes:
>   Ben Wood, 2002 Rockwood Rd., Silver Spring, MD 20910
>   Home for Jewish Parents (Oakland, CA), 415-536-4504.

Council of Jewish Federations Task Force on Jewish Individuals with Disabilities,
>   730 Broadway, NY, NY 10003, 212-475-5000.

Cribs in synagogue (for diaper collection for homeless babies): Jeannie Jaybush,
>   1929 42nd St., SW, Seattle, WA 98116,206-938-2364.

Daddy Bruce's Barbecue, 1629 E. Bruce Randolph Ave., Denver, CO 80205,
>   303-295-9115.

Detroit Jewish News, Stanley Horwitz, Editor, 20300 Civic Center Dr.,
>   Southfield, MI 48076, 313-354-6060

Dorot, 262 W. 91st St., NY, NY 10024, 212-769-2850 (Judy Ribnick)

Down Syndrome: See "Janet Marchese".

Elevator in Synagogue for People with Disabilities, Joseph Resnick, Birmingham,
>   AL 205-871-6357.

ELWYN: See "Hadassah Levi".

Ethiopian Jews:
>   Association of Ethiopian Immigrants, 23 Hillel St., Jerusalem, 248-722.
>   North American Conference on Ethiopian Jews, 165 E. 56th St., NY, NY
>   10022, ATTN: Barbara Ribakove Gordon, 212-752-6340.

John Fling, POB 5491, 2916 River Dr., Cayce, W. Columbia, SC 29171, 803-
>   256-7195.

Food banks (Jewish):
>   Dallas — Jewish Family Service, 7800 Northaven Rd., #B,
>   Dallas, TX 75230, Attn: Arnold Marks, 214-696-6400.
>   Los Angeles — Sova, 3007 Santa Monica Blvd., Santa Monica, CA
>   90404, 213-453-4604.

Fort Apache Youth Center, George Hankins, 1111 Fox St., Bronx, NY 10459,
>   212-328-2723.

Giraffe Project: Ann Medlock, POB 759, Langley, WA 98260, 1-800-344-TALL.

Gleaners, 500 E. Sahara Ave., Las Vegas, NV 89104, ATTN: Celeste McKinley,
>   702-731-FOOD.

Gomel L'Ish Chessed Interest Free Loan Society, c/o Dr. David Weiss, 56 Ben
>   Maimon St., Jerusalem, 669-363.

Group Homes (Jewish):
>   Dallas — CHAI, ATTN: Sandra Sundel, 10830 N. Central Expressway,
>   #171, Dallas, TX, 75231, 214-373-8600.
>   Detroit — JARC, ATTN: Joyce Keller, 28366 Franklin Rd., Southfield, MI
>   48034, 313-352-5272.

Washington, DC — Jewish Foundation for Group Homes,
        6101 Montrose Rd., #200, Rockville, MD 20852,
        ATTN: Barry Fierst, 301-984-3839.

HaAguda LeEzra Ve'Iddud VeShikum Keshishim VeCholim Birushalayim, POB
        7843, Ibn Ezra St. 24 Jerusalem, ATTN: Dr. Martin Kieselstein, 633-805.
Hadassah Levi, c/o Elwyn, POB 9090, 8 Grunwald St., Kiryat HaYovel,
        Jerusalem, 431-051, 052, or 053.
        Tax-deductible contributions: made out to "The JEI Foundation",
            c/o David Marcu, 111 Elwyn Rd., Elwyn, PA 19063.
            215-891-2007.
        Canadian Contributions, "Canadian Friends of ELWYN",
            161 Eglinton Ave. E., #604, Toronto, Ontario M4P 1J5.
Hatzilu, c/o Al Cohen, 38 Gainsville Dr., Plainview, NY 11803,
        516-349-7063 or 536-0290.
Hearing-Impaired Jews:
        Rabbi Danny Grossman, 609-599-2591 (General information).
        Used Hearing-Aid Project: Prof. Mark Ross, 9 Thomas Dr., Storrs, CT
            06268, 203-429-6688.
        Interpreters:
            Toby Marx, 210-272-2549
            Laura Rubin, 201-276-2649.
        Special Sound Systems:
            Louise Cohen, 9 Gibbs St., Brookline, MA 02146, 617-965-7410.
            Rabbi Sheldon Lewis, 415-948-7498.
            Rabbi Joel Soffin, 201-584-5666.
        Synagogue for the Deaf, Bene Shalom, 4435 Oakton St., Skokie, IL
            60076, ATTN: Rabbi Douglas Goldhamer, 312-677-3330.
Hebrew Reading Marathons, Rabbi Noah Golinkin, 301-982-1121.
Helemano Plantation, c/o Opportunities for the Retarded, Inc., 64-1510
        Kamehameha Hwy., Wahiawa, HI 96786, ATTN: Susanna Cheung,
        808-622-3929.
Homeless Jews (Also see "Synagogue Shelters"):
        Homelessness Prevention Project (HPP) of Dorot,, 316 W. 59th St., NY,
            NY 10025, ATTN: Sarah Peller, 212-666-2000.
        HUC Shelter, 3101 Clifton Ave., Cincinnati, OH 45220, ATTN:
            Matthew Eisenberg.
        Project ORE, c/o Educational Alliance, 197 E. Broadway, NY, NY 10002.
            ATTN: Peter Fine, 212-420-1150.
Hospice:
        National Institute for Jewish Hospice, 6363 Wilshire Blvd., #126,
            Los Angeles, CA 90048, 213-653-0795.
        Synagogue Council of America Task Force on Jewish Hospice,

327 Lexington Ave., NY, NY 10016, 212-686-8670.

IBM materials on equipment for people with disabilities, 1-800-
IBM-2133, (=426-2133), Marlene Garrigues.
Interpreters for the Deaf: See "Hearing-Impaired Jews"

JACS (Jewish Alcoholics, Chemically Dependent Persons, and Significant Others
Foundation, 197 E. Broadway, NY, NY 10002, 212-473-4747.
Jaffe, Dr. Eliezer: See "Zahavi".
Janet Marchese, Down Syndrome Adoption Exchange, 56 Midchester Ave., White
Plains, NY 10606, 914-428-1236.
Jaybush, Jeannie: See "cribs".
Jewish Braille Institute (JBI), 110 E. 20th St., NY, NY 10016, 212-889-2525.
Jewish Guild for the Blind, 15 W. 65th St., NY, NY NY, NY 212-595-2000.
Jewish Referral Service, Washington, DC, 301-770-4848.
Joint: See "American Jewish Joint Distribution Committee".

Kavod Caterers, Debbie Findling, c/o JCC, 4800 E. Alameda Ave., Denver, CO
80206, 303-399-2660.
Kapach, Rabbanit: See "Rabbanit"
Kelly, Ranya: see "Shoes".
Keshet, Milton Wakschlag, 312-902-5200.
Kids on the Block Puppets, Barbara Aeillo, 9385 C Gerwig Lane,
Columbia, MD 21046, 800-368-KIDS or 301-290-9095.
Kieselstein, Dr. Martin: See "Ha'Aguda Lema'an..."
Kinser, Kate: 1323 W. Albion, Chicago, IL 60626, 312-764-6955.

Large Print Prayerbooks (Conservative), United Synagogue Book Service,
212-533-7800.
Large Print Haggada: Nathan Goldberg, KTAV Publishers.
Life Line for the Old, 14 Shivtei Yisrael St., Jerusalem, 287-831 or 287-829.
Benefit Concerts: see "Beged Kefet".
Bookbindery in U.S. based on Life Line in Jerusalem, Rabbi Alan Lucas,
609-822-7116 (Ventnor, NJ).
Contributions: American Friends of Life Line for the Old, c/o Florence
Schiffman, Treasurer, 1500 Palisade Ave., Fort Lee, NJ 07024.
General information: Linda Kantor, President, American Friends, 203-795-
4580.
Information for organizing synagogue or group tours: Rabbi Ron Hoffberg,
201-276-9231.
Life Line products available in the United States, Helen Goren, 11 Ashford
Rd., Newton, MA 02159, 617-965-0691.
Lordi, Joseph: see "Youngstown".

Luther Place: See "Steinbruck".
LZ Birmingham, 24 Richmar Dr., POB 130444, Birmingham, AL 53213, 205-870-7706, Computer number : 205-870-7770.

Marchese: see "Janet Marchese".
MAZON, 2940 Westwood Blvd., #7, Los Angeles, CA 90064, ATTN: Irving Cramer, 213-470-7769.
McKinley, Celeste: see "Gleaners".
Metropolitan New York Council on Jewish Poverty, 9 Murray St., 4th Floor E. New York, NY 10007, 212-267-9500.
Misholim, 53 HaPalmach St., Jerusalem, ATTN: Noa Eran, 699-765.
Mitbach Yitzchak, 48 Montefiore St., Tel Aviv.
Morris, David, Shabtai HaNegbi St. 69, Apt. 8, Gilo Alef, Jerusalem, 767-894.
Mosniak, Alice: see "Toledo".

National Association for the Jewish Poor, 1163 Manor Ave., Bronx, NY 10472, 212-378-5865, ATTN: Gary Moskowitz.
National Organization on Disability, 2100 Pennsylvania Ave., NW, Washington, DC 20037, 202-293-5960.
National Yiddish Book Center, c/o Aaron Lansky, POB 969, Old East Street School, Amherst, MA 01004, 413-236-1241.
New Israel Fund, 111 W. 40th St., #2600, NY, NY 10173, 212-302-0066.

ORT (American ORT Foundation), 817 Broadway, NY, NY 10003, 212-667-4400/

Passover Food Packages, Washington, DC: B'nai B'rith Project Hope, c/o Len Elenowitz, 8801 Post Oak Rd., Potomac, MD 20854, 301-983-1345.
Pearlstein, Charles, 22522 N. Bellwood, Southfield, MI 48034, 313-352-0482.
PEF-Israel Endowment Funds, 342 Madison Ave., #1010, NY, NY 10173, ATTN: Sidney Musher, 212-599-1260.
Philabundance, 4320 Main St., 3rd Floor, Phila., PA 19127, 215-483-6444.
Primavera Foundation, Nancy Bissell, 602-623-5111, 735 S. Stone Ave., Tucson, AZ 85701
Project Ezra, 197 E. Broadway, NY, NY 10002, ATTN: Misha Avramoff, 212-982-3700.

Rabbanit Bracha Kapach, 12 Lod St., Jerusalem, 249-296.
Rachel's Table: 508-799-7600, or Judith Urbach at Fed's. 508-756-1543
    (To convince caterers to give leftovers to shelters: Robert Greenberg, 413-663-6087, 538-7798.)
Ranya Kelly: see "shoes".

Rape Crisis Center: Linda Feldman Rape Crisis Center POB 158, Jerusalem,
    ATTN: Maisoun Karaman, 245-554.
Rocky Mountain Hebrew Free Loan Trust, Harold Lande, 6560 E. Colorado Dr.,
    Denver, CO 80224, 303-756-8273.
ROFEH, 1710 Beacon St., Brookline, MA 02146, 617-728-0521.

SA-25, Ron Barshop, 512-366-1624.
Second Helping (Washington, DC), Anita Winsor, 202-331-7658
Sh'ma V'Ezer, 301-984-4455.
Shishim Plus, POB 71061, 1 Diskin St., Jerusalem, 690-747, ATTN: Ya'acov
    Kurtzman.
Shoes: Ranya Kelly, 7736 Hoyt Circle, Arvada, CO 80005, 303-431-0904.
Shorty Zarris, c/o Senior Support Services, 1420 Logan St., Denver, CO,
    313-832-1622.
Sova: see "food banks".
Special Education Specialists:
    Marci Fox, 408-358-1751 (synagogue).
    Sara Simon, 301-468-0220.
Steinbruck, Reverend John, Luther Place N St. Village, 1226 Vermont Ave., NW,
    Washington, DC 20005, 202-667-1377.
Synagogue Mitzvah Committees:
    The Marlboro Jewish Center, Marlboro, NJ: Anita Bogus,
        201-536-3358 (h), 201-431-1777 (o).
    Kehilath Jeshurun (KJ) in Manhattan (Rabbi Haskel Lookstein),
        Bob Leifert, 212-427-1000 (o).
    Temple Shalom, Succasunna, NJ: Rabbi Joel Soffin, 201-584-5666.
    Congregation Har Shalom, Potomac, MD, Robert Sunshine 301-340-2787.
    Beth El Tzedakah Collective, Sudbury, MA, Bob Lindenberg,
        508-443-5483, 329 Old Lancaster Rd., Sudbury, MA 01776.
    Ohr Kodesh, Chevy Chase, MD, Contact Zelda Segal, 9412 Linden Ave.,
        Bethesda, MD 20814, 301-530-9492.
Synagogue Shelters (i.e., synagogues with shelters for the homeless
    on the synagogue grounds):
    Shearith Israel, 1180 University Dr., NE, Atlanta, GA 30306,
        404-873-3147.
    Temple Israel, 1014 Dilworth Rd., Charlotte, NC 28203, 704-376-2796.
    The Temple, 1589 Peachtree Rd., NE, Atlanta, GA 30367, 404-873-1731.

TDD's: Potomac Telecom, 1010 Rockville Pike, Rockville, MD 20852,
    (TDD) 301-762-0851, (voice) 301-762-0851
TDD Directory: 814 Thayer Ave., Silver Spring, MD 20910,
    301- 589-3006; TDI-589-3786
Therapy Dogs International, Elaine Smith, 201-926-0308

Toledo Seagate Food Bank, 526 High St., Toledo, OH 43609, ATTN: Alice
        Mosiniak, 419-244-6996.
Torah Aura Productions, 1-800-BE-TORAH.
Tova's Kitchen, Yosef Karo St. 26, Jerusalem.
Travel/tours for people with disabilities: Irv Segal, The Guided Tour, 555
        Ashbourne Rd., Elkins Park, PA 19117, 215-782-1370
Trevor's Campaign for the Homeless, 137 E. Spring Ave.,
        Ardmore, PA 19003, 215-642-6452, ATTN: Frank Ferrell.
Tzedakah Boxes:
        Betsy Platkin Teutsch (David), 629 W.Cliveden St., Philadelphia, PA
                19119-3651, or Israel Giftware Designs, 215-627-6277.
        UAHC, 6300 Wilshire Blvd., #1475, Los Angeles, CA 90048.
        Congregation B'nai Jehudah, Rabbi Michael Zedek,712 E. 69th St.,
                Kansas City, MO 64131, 816-363-1050
                (Ask about boxes made by residents of Old Age Home).

Wedding Dresses: see "Rabbanit Bracha Kapach".
Western Pennsylvania Auxiliary for Exceptional People, 281 Sharon Dr.,
        Pittsburgh, PA, 15221, ATTN: Rabbi Moshe Goldblum, 412-271-1578.
Wigs for recovering cancer patients, Pearl Halikman, 407-783-7610, 632-2100 (h).
Wiesenthal, Dr. Simon, c/o Dokumentationszentrum, Salztorgasse 6/IV/5, Vienna,
        Austria

Yad Ezra (main office), 9-B HaRav Sorotzkin St., Jerusalem, ATTN: Shmuel
        Katz, 386-416.
        American Friends, Elihu Stone, 617-964-7000 (o), 617-784-2848 (h).
        Sewing Workshop: 4 Kineret St., Jerusalem.
Yad Sarah, c/o Uri Lupoliansky, 43 HaNevi'im St., Jerusalem, 244-047. Uri's
        home: 813-777.
        Tax-deductible contributions: American Friends of Yad Sarah, c/o Mr.
                Charles Bendheim, One Parker Plaza, Ft. Lee, NJ 07024,
                201-944-6020
Youngstown Community Food Center, Inc. and Gleaners Food Bank, Inc., 82
        Sugar Cane Dr., Youngstown, OH 44512, 216-726-9591.

ZAHAVI-Jerusalem, 1 Metudela St., Jerusalem, ATTN: Dr. Eliezer Jaffe. Jaffe's
        home: 37 Azza St., 637-450.
Ziv Tzedakah Fund, 263 Congressional Lane, #708, Rockville, MD 20852,
        301-468-0060.
        Treasurer: Bena Siegel, 11818 Trail Ridge Dr., Potomac, MD 20854,
                301-279-2605.
        Canadian Fund=Ziv Tzedakah Foundation, c/o Merle Gould,
                31 Glen Rush Blvd., Toronto, Ontario M5N 2T4, 416-486-7425.

Mitzvah Videos

(******=Highest Rating in History)

******Work of Trevor Ferrell (the boy who feeds homeless people in Philadelphia), 6 min., excellent, *the best.* It is the single most effective video I use in my lectures when teaching about the meaning of Tzedakah and Mitzvahs...for adults and kids. $25 contribution to "Trevor's Campaign", send to Frank Ferrell, c/o Trevor's Campaign, 137 E. Spring Ave., Ardmore, PA 19003, 201-642-6452.

******"Wonder Dogs Helping the Disabled" (an ABC 20/20 program, 15 minutes) — Dogs trained to work with physically disabled individuals (mostly people in wheelchairs, some deaf people, some with other special needs.) (*Wow!*) Kids of all ages are wowed by it. Contact Katheryn Horton, c/o CCI, 1215 Sebastopol Rd., Santa Rosa, CA 95407, 707-579-1985. ($10.00) They also have "Canine Companions, Dogs and the Disabled? You'd Be Surprised!", produced by Jean and Charles ("Snoopy") Schulz. (28 Minutes, also excellent, also $10.00)

"Breaking Through Denial", workshop and documentary footage on Jews and alcoholism. About 30 minutes. Contact Allan Secher, WJUF, One S. Franklin St., Chicago, IL 60606, 312-346-6700.

Sally Fox on Tzedakah — 6 scenes, role played incredibly well by the maestra of this art. Each scene, 3-5 minutes. Sally Fox, 377 Alden Ave., Columbus, OH 43201, 614-268-6225.

"Yad Sara", fabulous work of Israel's volunteers lending medical supplies free of charge to thousands of people. Real grassroots, front-line, life-saving Tzedakah. About 10 minutes. American Friends of Yad Sara, c/o Charles Bendheim, One Parker Plaza, Ft. Lee, NJ 07024, 201-944-6020.

Work of Celeste McKinley and Joseph Lordi (they run Gleaners Food Banks in Las Vegas and Youngstown, OH), filmclips from news coverage, varying lengths, 3 minutes on up. Awesome stuff. Contact Celeste McKinley, c/o Gleaners, 3120 S. Highland, Las Vegas, NV 89109, 702-731-4747 or 731-Food.

The work of Janet Marchese: amazing woman in White Plains, NY, who has helped place over 1,300 babies with Down's Syndrome and other disabilities in adoptive homes. CBS News coverage. Janet Marchese, 56 Midchester Ave., White Plains, NY 10606, 914-428-1236.

"A Smile in Their Eyes", ALYN Orthopaedic Hospital -- fine, fine place for kids in Israel...the non-institution institution; what things should really be like. American Friends of ALYN, 19 W. 44th St., #1418, NY, NY 10036, 212-869-0369.

"Best Boy", Oscar-award winner. Documentary story of an adult Jewish man's transition from living with his parents to a group home. Check film catalogues.

"A Test Of Love", incredible film of a young woman wrongfully placed as an infant in an institution -- they diagnosed her as retarded. Upon reaching majority, she sues to live on the outside, and wins! Beautifully done. Also called sometimes "Annie's Coming Out." (There's a book by the same name.) Consult video stores.

"Where I Want To Be" and "On Our Own" (2 videos about residents of Jewish group homes in Washington), each about 29 minutes. Contact Barry Fierst, Jewish Foundation for Group Homes, 11710 Hunters Lane, Rockville, MD 20852, 301-984-3839.

"A New Day Dawns — Jerusalem ELWYN", (13 1/2 minutes). A review of the activities of ELWYN's fine and wide-ranging work with adults with special needs who come to ELWYN's workshops for employment. Free. ELWYN, 111 ELWYN Rd., ELWYN, PA 19063, 215-891-2007.

"Whoopi Goldberg in Concert" (*very* strong language), striking material on human values, Menschlichkeit, decision making. Check video stores.

"The Shopping Bag Lady", well-known, wonderful, 21 minutes. Learning Corporation of America, 1350 Avenue of the Americas, NY, NY 10019.

"Here We Forget To Die", Life Line for the Old in Jerusalem: c/o Linda Kantor, American Friends of Life Line, 52 Wellington Dr., Orange, CT 06477, 203-795-4580.

"Someone Is Listening", 38 minutes on Jews who are deaf, with Rabbi Danny Grossman, free from: United Synagogue, Dept. of Education, 155 5th Ave., NY, NY, 10010, 212-533-7800.

And the old standby slide show of 4 Tzedakah projects in Israel, "Tzedakah: The Road to Dignity", Torah Aura Productions, 1-800-BE-TORAH.

Glossary

(H=Hebrew; Y=Yiddish)

Alef (H): the first letter of the Hebrew alphabet. Alef-Bet=the alphabet.

Aliya (H): literally "going up". "Making Aliya" = moving to Israel. (Israel was considered higher than all other countries.)

Anav (H): humble

Bet (H): The second letter of the Hebrew alphabet and the 1st letter of the Torah.

Beraysheet (H): "In the beginning...", the 1st word of the Torah.

Bikkur Cholim (H): The Mitzvah of Visiting the Sick.

Bima (H): The synagogue platform where the rabbi and cantor stand.

Birkat HaGomel (H): The traditional blessing recited after someone has escaped great personal danger.

Bubbe (Y): a grandmother.

Challah (H): The twisted loaves of white bread traditionally eaten on the Sabbath and holidays.

Charoset (H): One of the ritual foods for Passover, composed of wine, nuts, and other ingredients, commemorating the mortar the Children of Israel used in Egypt when they made the bricks for Pharaoh's cities.

Chassidic (H): referring to a Jewish religious movement founded in Eastern Europe in the 18th century by the Baal Shem Tov. Chassidism is known for its sense of joy and ecstasy, particularly manifested in prayer, song, and dance.

Chevra (H): any group; a group of friends.

Chevrah Kaddishah (H): the Jewish burial society.

Chumashim (H, sing.-Chumash): printed copies of the Torah.

Dreidel (Y): A toy top used for playing Chanukkah games.

Edel (Y): noble, said of a personal who has extraordinarily fine human qualities.

Etrog (H): a citrus fruit, used as a ritual object along with a Lulav for various ceremonies on the holiday of Sukkoy.

Gezunterhayt (Y): To your health! Go right ahead!

Goyyim (H-Y, sing.-Goy): non-Jews.

Hachnassat Kallah (H): the Mitzvah of providing for poor brides and couples about to be married.

Haftarah (H): the prophetic portion read in synagogue after the weekly Torah reading.

Halbashat HaKallah (H): Literally "dressing the bride". The Yemenite ceremony of dressing the bride in the traditional outfit.

Hamentaschen (Y): 3-cornered, hat-shaped, prune-or-poppyseed pastries baked for the holiday of Purim.

HaShem (H): God.

Havdalah (H): the ceremony at the end of the Sabbath and holidays that makes a separation between the holy days and the secular days.

Haymisch (Y): "homey", friendly, warm.

Hiddur Mitzvah (H): making Jewish tirual objects beautiful.

Kallah (H): a bride.

Kal V'Chomer (H): a form of Talmudic logical reasoning.

Kavod (H): dignity, respect.

Kiddush (H): the blessing over wine, also the food served in synagogue after Sabbath services.

Kind (Y, pl.-kinder, diminutive-kinderlach): a child.

Knesset (H): The Israeli Parliament.

Kol Nidray (Aramaic): a prayer recited the evening of Yom Kippur as the Holy Day begins.

Kvetch (Y): complain. Also, a complainer.

Lamed Vavnikit (H): One of the 36 Righteous People in the world.

Lehavdil (H): "We ought to differentiate", used when comparing 2 items which are remote, but still have some vague similarity.

Lulav (H): ritual object composed of a palm branch, willows, and myrtles, used in the synagogue and home for the holiday of Sukkot.

Maror (H): "bitter herbs", usually horseradish, eaten as a ritual food at the Passover Seder as a reminder of the slavery the Children of Israel experienced in Egypt.

Matzah (H): unleavened bread eaten on Passover.

Mazon (H): food, also a Jewish organization that raises funds to feed people. (MAZON — A Jewish Response to Hunger.)

Menorot (H-pl.; sing.-Menorah): a 9-branched candle holder for the holiday of Hanukkah.

Mensch (Y; adj.-Menschlich; abs.-Menschlichkeit): an upright, responsible, decent, caring, compassionate person.

Mezuzot (H-pl.; sing.-Mezuzah): a small container holding an inscription from the Torah that is hung on the doorposts of Jewish houses, according to instructions in Deuteronomy Chapter 6.

Midrash (H):Jewish literature from the first 7 or 8 centuries of the Common Era containing stories, aphorisms, and narratives. Also, any non-legal portion of the Talmud. Also used to refer to a specific story or tale.

Minyan (H): a quorum of 10 people, needed for the recitation of public prayers and certain other Jewish ceremonies.

Mishnah (H): the earlier portion of the Talmud, edited around the year 200 C.E.

Mishnah Torah (H): Maimonides' 12th Century Jewish Law Code.

Mishpat (h): Justice.

Mitzvah (H): literally "commandment" or "instruction" — good deeds done by people according to the prescriptions of traditional Jewish texts, such as visiting the sick, comforting mourners, and giving Tzedakah. In this book, Mitzvah is usually synonymous with Tzedakah. (See chapter called "Terminology" at beginning of book.)

Nachas (Y): satisfaction.
Narrischkeit (Y): foolishness.
Neshama (H): soul.
Nosherei (Y): munchies.

Oif mir Gezogt (Y): It should only happen to me!
Ongeshtupped (Y): stuffed, loaded with money.

Pirkay Avot (H): a section of the Mishnah containing ethical aphorisms.

Purim (H): Jewish holiday celebrating the victory of the Jews of Persia over the wicked Haman. The holiday is celebrated with great joy, dancing, parades, masks, and merrymaking.

Rabbanit (H): a Rabbi's wife.
Rashi (H): Medieval Biblical and Talmudic commentator.
Rebbetzin (Y): a Rabbi's wife.
Rebbi (H-Y): teacher *par excellence*, not necessarily a rabbi. Also, a leader of a Chassidic sect.
Reich (Y): wealthy.

Savtah (H): grandmother.
Schvitz (Y): a sauna.
Shabbat (H, Y=Shabbas): the Sabbath.
Shalach Manot (H): the Mitzvah of sending little packets of goodies around to friends on the holiday of Purim.
Shayn (Y): beautiful. Shayna Yiddishe Kinder=Beautiful Jewish children.
Shaytelach (Y, s.=Shaytl): wigs worn by some traditional Jewish women as a sign of modesty.

Shemirat HaMet (H): the Metizvah of watching over the dead body between the time of death and burial.

Shiva (H): literally "seven". The 7 days of moruning when the mourners remain in their home. Religious services are held, and comforters come to express their words of consolation.

Shoah (H): the Holocaust.

Shofar (H): ram's horn, sounded on the High Holidays as a call to repentance.

Shpatzier (Y): a stroll.

Shtickelach (Y): idiosyncrasies, noodgy human traits.

Shulchan Aruch (H): major code of Jewish Law.

Siddur (H): a prayerbook.

Simcha (H): joy, a joyous occasion.

Simcha Shel Mitzvah (H): the joy of doing Mitzvahs.

Sippuk Nefesh (H): satisfaction, usually spiritual satisfaction.

Sofer (H): a scribe.

Sukkah (H): a flimsy boothlike structure where traditional Jews live during the days of the Sukkot Festival.

Sukkot (H): the Fall festival celebrating a good harvest and commemorating God's kindness to the Children of Israel during their wanderings in the wilderness.

Talitot (H-pl.; sing.-Talit): a shawl-like garment with ritual fringes (Tzitzit) on the four corners, worn by Jews during morning prayers.

Talmid Chacham (H): a sage.

Talmud (H): an immense compendium of discussions, tales, aphorisms, legal give-and-take, and insights about Judaism, developed in Jewish academies (Yeshivas) during the first five centuries of the Common Era.

Tam, Tamim (H; abstract-Temimut): innocent, pure, straightforward, simple, naive the last two — in the positive sense of the term).

Tchatchka (Y): a toy.

Temimut (H): see "Tam".

Tikkun (H): fixing up, repairing. Tikkun Olam=repairing the world.

Torah (H): literally "teaching". Originally meaning the Five Books of Moses, expanded to include the entirety of Jewish study and learning. "To talk Torah" is to discuss these texts.

Tov (H): good.

Tzaddik (H): a Righteous Person.

Tzadeket (H): a Righteous Woman.

Tzedakah (H): the distinctly Jewish method of performing charitable acts. From the word "Tzedek", Justice.

Tzedek (H): Justice.

Tzitzit (H): ritual fringes on the corners of a Tallit (prayer-shawl).

Tzuriss (Y): troubles.

Vez's mir (Y, pl.-Vey iz unz): Woe is me!

Yarmulka (Y): a small, round head covering worn by religious Jews.
Yid (Y, pl.-Yiddn): A Jew.
Yiddishkeit: Judaism.

Zaken (H): an old person, an Elder.
Zeyde (Y): a grandfather.
Ziess (Y): sweet.
Ziv (H): radiance.

DANNY SIEGEL Is a free-lance author, poet, and lecturer who resides in Rockville, Maryland, when not on his speaking tours or in Israel distributing Tzedakah monies. He is the author of five books of poetry, four of which are now out of print, as well as three anthologies of his selected writings.

His current work, *Mitzvahs,* is Danny's latest work in attempting to focus the public's attention of the deeds of loving-kindness by good and caring people. His previous works on Tzedakah: *Munbaz II and Other Mitzvah Heroes, Gym Shoes and Irises, Books One and Two,* have become the standard guideline texts for personalized tzedakah.

His 1989 publication of *Family Reunion: Making Peace in the Jewish Community,* addressed the painful subject of disunity and polarization, making an attempt to sows the seeds of harmony.

Siegel is a popular lecturer at synagogues, Jewish federations, community centers, conventions, and retreats, where he teaches Tzedakah and Jewish values and recites from his works. His books and talks have received considerable acclaim throughout the entire North American Jewish community.

Shir Hadash
3000 Dundee
Suite 205
Northbrook, IL 60062